Real Queer?

Real Queer?

Sexual Orientation and Gender Identity Refugees in the Canadian Refugee Apparatus

David A. B. Murray

ROWMAN &
LITTLEFIELD
INTERNATIONAL

London • New York

Published by Rowman & Littlefield International, Ltd.
Unit A, Whitacre Mews, 26–34 Stannary Street, London SE11 4AB
www.rowmaninternational.com

Rowman & Littlefield International, Ltd. is an affiliate of Rowman & Littlefield
4501 Forbes Boulevard, Suite 200, Lanham, Maryland 20706, USA
With additional offices in Boulder, New York, Toronto (Canada), and Plymouth (UK)
www.rowman.com

British Library Cataloguing in Publication Data
A catalogue record for this book is available from the British Library

ISBN: HB 978-1-78348-439-3
       PB 978-1-78348-440-9

Library of Congress Cataloging-in-Publication Data
Murray, David A. B., 1962– author.
Real queer? : sexual orientation and gender identity refugees in the Canadian refugee
apparatus / David A.B. Murray.
   pages cm
Includes bibliographical references and index.
ISBN 978-1-78348-439-3 (cloth : alk. paper) — ISBN 978-1-78348-440-9
(pbk. : alk. paper) — ISBN 978-1-78348-441-6 (electronic) 1. Gay immigrants—
Canada. 2. Refugees—Government policy—Canada. 3. Sexual orientation. 4. Gender
identity. 5. Canada—Emigration and immigration—Government policy. I. Title.
HQ76.3.C2M87 2015
305.30971—dc23   2015028262

∞ ™ The paper used in this publication meets the minimum requirements of American
National Standard for Information Sciences—Permanence of Paper for Printed Library
Materials, ANSI/NISO Z39.48-1992.

Printed in the United States of America

Contents

Acknowledgments

As with all ethnographic endeavours, this book would not exist without the great gifts of time, patience and knowledge from research participants – current and former sexual orientation and gender identity refugees now residing in Toronto, Canada; LGBT refugee support group staff and volunteers; refugee lawyers, researchers and scholars; immigration consultants; and staff at the Immigration and Refugee Board (IRB) of Canada. To all of them, my deepest thanks and appreciation. I have done my best to accurately represent conversations and interviews with research participants and to protect the identities of those who generously gave their time to talk with me and/or allowed me to participate in various events and meetings. The opinions and arguments about refugees, the IRB and the refugee apparatus expressed in the following pages are my own and I take full responsibility for them.

My ideas and arguments have benefitted enormously from numerous conversations with scholars, students and friends. In particular, I would like to thank Wenona Giles, Jennifer Hyndman and Susan McGrath for providing important commentary on the genesis of the project and its objectives. I was lucky to have had the opportunity to share my findings and the benefits of feedback with audiences at the Centre for Refugee Studies at York University, The Department of Anthropology at York University, Adelaide University (Australia), Flinders University (Australia), LaTrobe University (Australia), The University of Sydney (Australia) and The University of the West Indies Cave Hill Campus (Barbados). A visiting professorship at Flinders University provided me with time and support to further develop this manuscript. I also benefitted from conversations arising from invited papers presented at the following conferences: The Canadian Association for Refugee and Forced Migration Studies (2012), The Caribbean Studies Association (2012 and 2014), The American Anthropological Association (2011 and 2014), the

National Women's Studies Association (2013), The International Association for the Study of Sexuality, Culture and Society (2013), International Strangers in New Homelands Conference (2012), the Association for Cultural Studies (2014) and the Canadian Anthropology Society (2015). In particular, I would like to thank fellow members of a panel focusing on queer migration organized for the 2012 Annual Meeting of the American Anthropological Association – Nathalie Ricard, Hinda Seif, Ahmed Afzal, Maria Amelia Viteri, Susan Terrio, Ruti Talmor, Susan Frohlick, Stacey Vanderhurst and Cymene Howe – out of which developed a special issue of *The Journal of Language and Sexuality* (and an earlier version of Chapter 5). Thanks also to William Leap for seeing the potential of the panel and shepherding me through the guest editorship duties of the *JLS* special issue. Earlier versions of some other chapters in this book have been published in the following journals: *Sexualities* (Chapter 1), *Anthropologica, Refuge* (Chapter 2) and *The Journal of Canadian Studies* (Chapter 7).

As this manuscript has gone through various iterations, I have also benefitted greatly from conversations with colleagues and peers including Daphne Winland, Kamala Kempadoo, Ena Dua, Alison Crosby, Naomi Adelson, Zulfikar Hirji, Shubhra Gururani, Melissa Autumn White, Lynda Mannik, Charmaine Crawford, Aaron Kamugisha, Halimah DeShong, Fatimah Jackson, Beverly Hinds, Andy Taitt, Akim Ade Larcher, Barbara Baird, Megan Warin, Steven Angelides, Gaynor Macdonald, Ryan Schram, Joan Atlin, Ashleigh Currier, Erin Durban, Nadia Ellis, Anita Fabos, Cynthia Wright, Nancy Nichol and George Paul Mieu. A number of former and current students provided significant assistance and/or feedback at various stages of development of this manuscript. Thank you to Michael Connors Jackman, Jillian Ollivierre, Danielle Cooper, Tamara de Szegheo Lang, Weronika Rogula, Joseph Wickenhauser, Eda Farsakoglu and Sahithi Tirumareddy.

I would like to thank the Social Sciences and Humanities Research Council of Canada for funding this research project through a Standard Grant from 2011 to 2014. The grant was administered through the Centre for Refugee Studies at York University, where I received an enormous amount of support from the coordinator, Michele Millard, former director Susan McGrath and current director Jennifer Hyndman. Thanks also to my home faculty, the Faculty of Liberal Arts and Professional Studies at York University, for providing additional funding in support of this project's completion, and to Colleen Robinson in the Department of Anthropology for administrative support.

The staff at Rowman and Littlefield International have been a joy to work with throughout the manuscript's development. I would like to thank Martina O'Sullivan, senior commissioning editor, for taking an interest in this project and shepherding it through the approval process. Thanks also to Sinead

Murphy for her helpful and prompt assistance throughout the publishing process.

Last and certainly not least, I say thank you to my circle of friends and family who have supported me through life's ups and downs before, during and (hopefully) after this project: Much love to Mum and Dad, Alison, Tammy, Leslie, Joan, Lynne, Jen, Sher, Alison C, Naomi, Dan, Heather, Dave, Felipe and Eddie Hassan Murlin (the cat).

Introduction

On a wintry evening in December 2006, while volunteering at a Toronto lesbian, gay, bisexual and transgender (LGBT) helpline (a free phone service providing referrals, information, and counselling), Edward, another volunteer, and I started to chat. Edward had recently joined the phone line and was still in training, and I was supposed to be mentoring him as I had been working there a few years. It was a slow night with very few calls, so our conversation veered away from training topics to more personal questions, like why we had joined the phone line. I told Edward that I had always wished there was a phone service like this when I was younger and I liked talking on the phone, so that's why I had joined. Edward's answer took me by surprise: He said he had been told by his lawyer to join an LGBT organization to 'get some experience' in the LGBT community. Seeing my look of confusion, Edward went on to say that he had arrived in Toronto a few months ago from Uganda, and had lodged a claim with the Immigration and Refugee Board of Canada (IRB) for refugee status based on sexual orientation persecution.

Edward was a member of a Ugandan group campaigning against LGBT discrimination in Kampala, but over the past year, harassment and death threats from various sectors, including the police, had increased. He had recently bought a plane ticket for The International Conference on LGBT Human Rights in Montreal, and he had heard through his organization that Canada was a place he could seek protection, so he decided he would look into this – although he didn't know how or where to start, he planned to ask around at the conference. However, upon exiting Trudeau airport in Montreal, Edward had a confusing conversation with a taxi driver who didn't speak much English: When he asked the driver for directions to the LGBT conference location, the driver told him that the conference was in Toronto (this was partially true: there was an international HIV/AIDS conference taking place in Toronto in a few weeks). Edward didn't know Canadian geography and thought Toronto might be close to Montreal, so he asked the taxi driver to take him there. The taxi driver took him to the train station at Dorval, pointed to the tracks, and said 'Toronto'. Confused, Edward bought a train ticket and five hours later arrived at Toronto's Union Station. He started to ask people for the location of the LGBT rights conference, but everyone ignored him. Finally, he encountered a friendly black man who told him he must be talking about the upcoming HIV/AIDS conference. Edward wasn't sure of anything at this point, so he said yes, and asked the man if he could help him find protection and accommodation. The man said he knew a place that allowed 'people like me' to stay. He took Edward to a men's shelter, where they gave him a room and the next day told him to go to an office, where he met a lawyer and told him he needed protection. The lawyer informed Edward that he would need to file for refugee status, and that he would help Edward prepare his claim and provide counsel at a hearing, where he would be asked questions and his case would be assessed by a member of the IRB. Edward's lawyer also told him that he would fare better at the hearing if he joined some LGBT organizations in Toronto, which would strengthen his claim by showing the Board member that he was an active member of the LGBT community.[1] I started to ask Edward more questions, as I didn't fully understand the connection between his claim for refugee status and demonstrating active participation in Toronto's LGBT community, but the phones started to ring, and after that night I never saw Edward again – the phone line shut down a few months later because of lack of funding.

Many months after this conversation, a friend and I were exiting a movie theatre on a chilly fall evening in downtown Toronto, and as we walked to our bikes, a man in sandals wearing a thin sweater and carrying a small backpack came up to us and asked in accented English (which my friend and I later believed to be Nigerian or Kenyan, although we weren't sure) if we knew any cheap hotels nearby. We were distracted (the movie we had seen was disturbing), and we only spent a few seconds answering his question, as we could only think of a Holiday Inn just around the corner. We pointed him in the direction of the hotel, got on our bikes and went back to discussing the film. About twenty minutes later, Edward's story suddenly popped into my head and I realized that this man could easily have been in the same situation as Edward. Feeling guilty, I made my friend turn around and we biked back towards the street where we had met, but he, too, was not to be seen again.

My fleeting encounters with 'real' and 'possible' gay refugees in the early 2000s occurred at a time when Canadian mainstream and LGBT media had begun to pay more attention to this particular category of migrants. A 2004 article in the national newspaper 'The Globe and Mail' reported that, 'Canada is seeing a surge in the number of refugee claimants who say they are homosexuals and will be persecuted if they are returned to their homelands. In the past three years, nearly 2,500 people from 75 different countries have sought asylum on the basis of sexual orientation' (Jiminez 2004). The article repeated the 'surge' metaphor as it provided a background context to this fact: 'Although claims on the basis of sexual orientation have been permitted since 1994 when the Supreme Court of Canada broadened the definition of (a) social group (who face persecution) to include homosexuals, immigration lawyers say they have seen a surge of cases of this nature in the past three years' (Jiminez 2004). While it is difficult to quantify the numbers of sexual orientation and gender identity (SOGI) refugee applicants in Canada over time because of challenges in accessing IRB statistics and changing standards of measurement,[2] what cannot be doubted is the 'surge' in media coverage of this category of migrants, occurring not so coincidentally at a time of heightened attention to global LGBT rights discussions and debates in Canada and numerous other locations around the world, in which Canada was regularly being identified as the apex of 'progress', a 'leader' in LGBT rights and a 'haven' for LGBT individuals from around the world seeking protection from violence, persecution and discrimination. (Allick 2011; Chase 2013; Glenwright 2011; *Globe and Mail* 2011; Graham 2010; Keung 2010; Ling 2013; Tepper 2014; but see Hasselriis 2013; Houston 2010; Larcher 2012; Ling 2012; Quan 2012; Wilton 2011 for more critical media coverage of SOGI refugees in Canada). By 2012, ministers from the Conservative majority-led federal government of Canada were making public statements endorsing the 'freedom nation' position, including the then Citizenship and Immigration Minister Jason Kenney sending an email to thousands of LGBT Canadians touting the government's plan to protect the rights of gay and lesbian refugees, and then Foreign Affairs Minister John Baird stating that he had an 'aggressive agenda' to stand up to countries where homosexuality is still criminal (Houston 2012; Glenwright 2012).

In most of this media coverage, a common storyline emerges with similar characters and narrative arcs: LGBT refugees' countries of origin are depicted as deeply homophobic and the refugee has no choice but to flee and seek refuge in Canada, where they are thankful to find freedom and protection. I call this the '*queer migration to liberation nation*' narrative, operating as a hegemonic discourse across numerous media platforms in which sexual, gendered, and national identities and cultures are related, conflated and organized into a nationalist morality tale in which a particular formation of sexual citizenship now operates as a cornerstone of what it is to be Canadian. However, there are numerous omissions, silences and gaps in the popular queer migration to liberation nation narrative that raise a number of questions: How do some people migrating across national borders come to be identified as 'SOGI refugees'? How do they learn about and experience the Canadian refugee determination process? What surprises or challenges them as they learn about this process? Do their experiences and opinions of the refugee determination system and life in their new 'homeland' of Canada challenge or reinforce the hegemonic queer migration to liberation nation narrative? How do SOGI-identified refugees talk about their past, present and future, their desires, identifications, movements and homes? What happens after the refugee claim has been decided?

Also omitted from the queer migration to liberation narrative are the voices of other participants in the refugee determination process: What are the experiences of the SOGI refugee support group volunteer, the lawyer representing a SOGI refugee claimant, or a staff member of IRB in the negotiation, performance and assessment of sexual and gender identity and 'refugeeness'? How might their experiences and positions in this process reflect different investments, opinions and perspectives?

Finally, we might also want to think more carefully about how sexual and gender identities in the refugee determination process are related to broader questions of immigration, nationalism and citizenship in the queer migration to liberation nation narrative: Is the refugee apparatus (part of a larger migration apparatus[3]) shaping or shaped by hegemonic discourses of sexual and gendered identity? Are SOGI refugee narratives challenging or changing hegemonic discourses of sexual and/or gender identities in Canada? How does this relatively new category of migrants (in terms of recognition by the nation-state) illustrate both the centrality and instability of sexuality and gender in the bureaucratic gate-keeping machinery of the contemporary nation-state? What are the effects of interactions between the refugee determination process, diverse sexual and gender subjectivities of transnational migrants, and local queer communities?

HOMONATIONALISM AND REFUGEES IN QUEER MIGRATION STUDIES

Through ethnographic explorations of differentially positioned participants, locations and objects in the Canadian refugee determination process, this book aims to illuminate the simultaneous centrality and instability of sexual orientation and gender identity as key components of citizenship, nation and (un)belonging. The arguments in this book begin with Lisa Malkki's crucial observation that the refugee should not be taken as a naturally self-delimiting domain of knowledge, and that the category of refugee is an epistemic object in construction (Malkki 1995). In developing the concept of 'refugeeness', Malkki challenges the taken-for-granted status of the refugee found in official definitions, that is, 'someone who, owing to a well-founded fear of being persecuted for reasons of race, religion, nationality, membership of a particular social group or political opinion, is outside the country of his nationality, and is unable to, or, owing to such fear, is unwilling to avail himself of the protection of that country'. [4]

However, rather than analysing the inequalities inherent in the structure of the episteme and the bureaucratic and legal system created around it, in this book I focus on how the refugee claimants, (and, to a lesser extent, some other participants in the refugee determination process) come to understand the meaning of the episteme and operations of the apparatus, how they obtain the knowledge to navigate this complex apparatus, and in so doing learn to become credible SOGI refugees. This process of becoming a credible SOGI refugee also invokes particular incarnations of nationalism and citizenship, which are themselves freighted with moral valences of proper assemblages of sexuality, gender, race and class. I will therefore also unpack some of these embedded racialized, classed and gendered moral valences contained in the refugee claimants' learning experiences.

The SOGI refugee is a new 'wrinkle' in the fabric of Canadian immigration and citizenship policies and broader narratives of Canadian identity, and illustrates both transformations to this fabric and ongoing attempts to iron out the wrinkles as quickly as possible. I argue that the impact of this newish migrant identity category and narrative (once again in terms of recognition by the state) is contributing to a reconfiguration of hegemonic national Canadian identity myths, such that a narrowly defined sexual and gender identity category, the authentic and grateful gay, lesbian, bisexual or transgendered refugee, is now being folded into hegemonic narratives of Canadian national identity and good citizenship. Put slightly differently, I am arguing that the refugee apparatus is contributing to the production of a new permutation of homonationalism, a highly delimited and normative narrative of same-sex sexual citizenship and national belonging, which now includes some migrant bodies, but excludes many others who do not fit the narrative's acceptable performances, characteristics, and/or aesthetics. This book's focus on how one sector of queer migrants confirms, contests and reconfigures nation-states' hegemonic narratives of belonging or regimes of citizenship employs Lisa Duggan's concept of homonormativity as 'a politics that does not contest dominant heteronormative assumptions and institutions, but upholds and sustains them, while promising the possibility of a demobilized gay constituency and a privatized, depoliticized gay culture anchored in domesticity and consumption' (2003: 50), and extends this through Jasbir Puar's concept of 'homonationalism', which invokes a privileged relationship between post 9/11 American nationalism and a particular raced, classed and gendered formation of gay identity in opposition to the threat of racialized foreign 'others' (2007). Puar outlines how homonationalism is used to justify heightened security and militarization of US borders in order to protect 'tolerant' America from the homophobic, intolerant, monstrous, racialized immigrant other. Lionel Cantú makes a similar argument in his research on sexuality and Mexican immigrant men, when he observes that 'the repeated narratives' in sexual asylum cases operate as discursive practices that have transformed the concept of the homosexual from a figure that was completely outside nationalist imaginaries to one of immutable essence, which has come to delimit and define US-Mexican national borders (2009: 56, 62).

Throughout much of the twentieth century, the homosexual was the deviant, criminal or 'bad' citizen in North American discourses of nationalism and citizenship (Canaday 2009; Kinsman and Gentile 2010), however, over the last 40–45 years, 'he'[5] has been gradually replaced, through pervasive activism and legislative change, by the figure of the out, proud and productive LGBT citizen who claims equality with his fellow heterosexual citizens and equal rights in all domains of social, economic and political life. In this book, I am arguing that more recently (over the last 20–25 years) we are witnessing another permutation in discourses of acceptable sexual citizenship, the authentic grateful lesbian, gay, bisexual or transgender refugee. Victim of a foreign nation-state with repressive, homo- or transphobic laws, practices and attitudes, the authentic grateful LGBT refugee is rescued and given the 'gift' of a socially legitimate and politically endorsed life (citizenship) based on his or her sexual orientation or gender identity by an 'enlightened' democratic nation-state like Canada or the United States, where such identities and orientations are ostensibly acceptable and protected. State institutions such as immigration and citizenship departments (including their personnel, archives, and affiliated professions and organizations) contribute to this newish version of homonationalism, that is, the production of a 'normative' homosexual, bisexual or transgender refugee, but in so doing they induce profound effects for those who do not fit the norm, that is, for those whose sexual orientation or gender identity is evaluated to be not credible, and is thus often labelled 'bogus' or 'fake'. In so doing, we see how the refugee apparatus contributes towards what Puar describes as a queer necropolitics, in which the expansion of liberal politics into diverse forms of governance, surveillance and military intervention folds certain queer subjects into life while simultaneously naming and rejecting other, often racialized queer bodies (2007: 35–36; see Haritowarn, Kuntsman and Posocco 2014 for an expanded discussion of queer necropolitics). Thus we can describe the refugee apparatus as malleable and adaptable as it transforms to include sexual orientation and gender identity as possible pathways to becoming acceptable citizens, but for those who do not perform or conform to the apparatus' definitions and perceptions of what authentic or credible SOGI refugees and their stories should look and sound like (and the evaluative processes based on those definitions and perceptions) or who cannot produce adequate documentation demonstrating their identity and/or persecution based on their membership in this particular social group, the risk of rejection, deportation and/or incarceration – in other words, the loss of socially legitimized life through citizenship – increases dramatically.

In applying the term homonationalism to a particular category of refugees, I am aligning my arguments with the burgeoning field of queer migration studies, which explores how overlapping regimes of power and knowledge generate and transform identity categories, particularly as they relate to gender and sexuality (Cantú 2009; Decena 2011; Epps, Valens and Johnson-Gonzalez 2005; Espin 1999; Hart 2002; Luibhéid 2002, 2008; Luibhéid and Cantú 2005; Manalansan 2003, 2006; Patton and Sanchez-Eppler 2000; Weston 2008; White 2013, 2014). This body of scholarship has been enabled by an understanding of sexuality as constructed within multiple intersecting relations of power including race, ethnicity, gender, class, citizenship status and geopolitical location. It also foregrounds ongoing transnational ties between migrants and their homelands and how migration affects others in both the old and new homelands, as well as those who migrate. Furthermore, queer migration studies not only reveal the fundamental ways in which sexuality undergirds the organization and boundaries of nation-state, citizenship and national identity projects but also connect migration and sexuality to transnational capitalism and neo-imperialism. At the same time, while queer migration scholars no longer take for granted the boundaries of the nation-state, nationalism and nation-based citizenship, they now theorize these concepts as critical loci for upholding and contesting regional transnational and neo-imperial hierarchies and for producing forms of exclusion, marginalization and struggle for transformation (Luibhéid 2008; see also Agathangelou 2004; Carillo 2004; Gopinath 2005; Kuntsman 2008; Puar 2007; Yue 2008; White 2013, 2014).

Queer migration studies are generally critical of the various distinctions made between 'legal immigrants, refugees, asylum seekers or undocumented immigrants' (Luibhéid and Cantú 2005: xi), as these terms are less reflections of empirically verifiable differences among queer migrants (who often shift from one category to another) than techniques of the nation-state's power, which classifies migrants in order to delimit the rights they may have or be denied, and the forms of surveillance, discipline, normalization and exploitation to which they will be subjected (ibid; see also Glick-Schiller et al. 1992; Povinelli and Chauncey 1999). However, we must take into account how these terms invoke different limitations and possibilities as they intersect with other forms of inequality and discrimination. For example, according to Miller, a person seeking asylum because of persecution on account of sexual orientation, gender identity or HIV status faces a particularly complex set of challenges. This is in part because asylum involves 'a moment of transnational judgment when the decision makers of one nation decide not only on the credibility of the individual asylum claimant, but on the errors or strengths of the protection of rights in the country from which the claimant flees' (2005: 143). Miller outlines numerous challenges to and problems with these moments of 'transnational judgment' in relation to sexual orientation refugee claimants, which resonate deeply with my fieldwork with SOGI refugees in Toronto.

Much of the queer migration scholarship has been generated by American scholars and focuses on issues pertaining to immigration in the United States (Canaday 2009; Cantú 2009; Epps, Valens and Johnson-Gonzalez 2005; Luibhéid 2002, 2008; Luibhéid and Cantú 2005). While there are broad conceptual and thematic similarities between Canada and the United States in terms of their settler-state histories and political and economic power as members of the Global North, there are also significant historical and contemporary differences between these countries in terms of constitutional law, social policy and attitudes towards homosexuality, immigration and refugees. In the Canadian context, there is a large and diverse body of research examining issues of immigration as it intersects with racism, gender, class, multiculturalism, nationalism and citizenship (see for example, Dua 2007; Iacovetta 2000; Macklin 2003; Thobani 2007; Valverde 2008) but, until recently, less attention has been focused on the role and significance of sexual and gender minorities in migration processes and attendant nation-state structures, hegemonies and policies, although this is rapidly changing (see Jenicek, Wong and Ou Jin Lee 2009; Jordan 2010; Kinsman and Gentile 2010; Ou Jin Lee and Brotman 2011; Ricard 2014; White 2013, 2014).

Canadian sexual and gender minority refugee policies and decision-making processes are now receiving sustained critique from socio-legal scholars who are analysing adjudicators' decisions on SOGI refugee claims and producing valuable insights into the challenges SOGI refugees face in producing credible documentary evidence about origin country conditions at their hearings and proving their 'credibility' to adjudicators, revealing the latter's problematic assumptions about homosexual, bisexual or transgendered identities (Berg and Millbank 2009; LaViolette 2004, 2009, 2010; Millbank 2009a, b; Rehaag 2008). However, there has been less sustained investigation of the Canadian refugee determination process from the perspectives of the claimants themselves. While much research on queer migration in Canada acknowledges the importance of studying the intersectionality of sexuality with the nation-state, gender, class and race, the unique and particular circumstances, negotiations and challenges facing SOGI refugees as they move through the claim process, their experiences of migration and the refugee apparatus, adaptation to a new homeland and the impact of their narratives on the citizenship-making institutions of the Canadian nation-state (and vice-versa), are only now beginning to receive in-depth critical analysis.

My overall objective is thus in line with recent anthropological, queer and feminist studies that demonstrate how discourses of gender and sexuality are critical to the maintenance of liberal and illiberal forms of power and domination and are at the core of capitalism, secularism and civil society. However, throughout the following chapters, I also employ an analytical framework that foregrounds refugee claimants' adaptive agency (and the limits imposed on that agency) when navigating the refugee apparatus, along with observations on some other participants and objects in the refugee determination process (lawyers, SOGI support group workers, IRB members, expert witness reports, and letters confirming membership in a community organization) in order to produce a text that begins to unpack and connect the diverse objects and persons that constitute the dense and fluid networks of the SOGI refugee apparatus.

A NOTE ON TERMINOLOGIES

The Refugee Apparatus: Throughout the preceding paragraphs and much of the book, I refer to the 'refugee apparatus', a phrase that I have adapted from Gregory Feldman's concept, 'the migration apparatus', which he in turn adapted from Rabinow and Foucault: Rabinow defines the apparatus as 'a device of population control and economic management composed of otherwise scattered elements ... (that) embodies a kind of strategic bricolage. ... It functions to define and regulate targets constituted through a mixed economy of power and knowledge' (Feldman 2012: 15). In essence, the apparatus is 'the network that holds these elements together' (2012: 16). Feldman focuses on key 'devices' of the migration apparatus, such as rationales of governance deployed by various actors, which enable the network connections of a 'global mobility machine built on a paradigm of suspicion' to operate across vast scales and adapt to particular political and economic contexts. (2012: 16–17). The refugee apparatus can be considered to be a particular assemblage of networks within the larger migration apparatus focusing on the surveillance, naming, management, evaluation and removal of a specific category of migrants. An important feature of both apparatuses is their inherent instability and adaptability: Despite the image of bureaucratic stability and the rhetoric of policy development through rational governance, migration and refugee apparatuses act and react to changes in national and transnational migration patterns and laws developed in relation to these changing patterns. However, these apparatuses and their attendant laws and policies are equally, if not more, active and reactive to changing public moralities or perceptions of immigration and/or particular classes of immigrants, resulting in a process of constant adaptation, or what Foucault calls 'normalization' (Feldman 2012: 14). The SOGI refugee is a good example of the adaptive/reactive abilities of the apparatus, in that this category of refugee identity has only come to exist in official policy documents and procedures over the last 20–25 years. However, while Feldman focuses on the devices that allow the migration apparatus to adapt to rapidly changing contexts in contemporary Europe, my focus shifts the attention to how differentially located participants – mostly those identified as SOGI refugee claimants, but also local support group workers, lawyers representing the claimants and some members of the IRB – learn and feel about, negotiate, re-inscribe or possibly subvert the 'logic' of the refugee apparatus.

SOGI vs LGBT refugees: 'Sexual Orientation and Gendered Identity' (SOGI) is a term that has come to be utilized in some academic, human rights and UNHCR policy documents and discourses to refer to a particular category of refugee/asylum claimants. However, at certain points in this book, I will also refer to 'LGBT' refugees as this acronym is popular among refugee support groups in Toronto where I conducted the major part of my fieldwork. In general, I utilize sexuality and gender terminologies as they are articulated by organizations and individuals and/or as they appear in texts; I do not privilege any one specific term, and I urge caution in the unexamined application of any of them. As anthropological, feminist, and queer researchers have demonstrated, all sexual and gender identity terminologies (including queer) are fraught with historical, political, linguistic and cultural baggage, which is heightened and intensified when inserted into the refugee apparatus. While many of the refugee claimants I worked with self-identified as 'homosexual', 'L,G,B or T' in interviews, I would once again stress that these are privileged terms inscribed through the bureaucratic and legal machinery of the refugee apparatus, and may be strategically employed rather than reflecting an individual's chosen self-ascription.

EXPLORING THE REFUGEE APPARATUS

There are many paths to becoming a refugee: This book explores one of those paths, in one location, focusing on just one subset of refugees: I worked only with 'inland' refugees, persons who had lodged a claim for refugee protection based on sexual orientation or gender identity persecution from inside Canada and were residing in Toronto for the duration of their claim; that is, they had lodged their claim for refugee status at a port of entry such as Pearson airport in Toronto or at a Citizenship and Immigration office located in Toronto after arriving in Canada. I did not work with any SOGI refugees who were resettled from outside Canada or privately sponsored, and/or were settled in different Canadian locations. Their experiences of other 'categories' of refugees or SOGI refugees settled in other locations could be quite different from 'inland' claimants in Toronto because of their movements through and engagements with different components of local national and transnational networks in the migration apparatus.

The findings in this book are based on ethnographic research conducted primarily from July 2011 to December 2012 (some additional interviews took place in 2013) with 'inland' SOGI refugee claimants residing in Toronto, which is recognized as the primary Canadian destination for this particular category of refugees.[6] I met the majority of participants through two LGBT refugee support groups managed by well-established Toronto LGBT organizations. The vast majority of participants (over 90 per cent) were from Caribbean or African nations and within these two broad regions, the majority were from Nigeria or Jamaica; however, there were also participants from Latin America, the Middle East and Eastern Europe. I conducted intake interviews with fifty-four individuals and did follow-up interviews with eight of these individuals for fifteen to twenty-four months, although the number and timing of interviews varied depending on the individual (see Conclusion). I also visited some members of this smaller group in their homes, spent time with them in other locations during leisure activities (such as meeting friends at a bar or coffee shop) and attended their hearings at the IRB offices in downtown Toronto.

During the fieldwork period, I also regularly attended LGBT refugee support group meetings at the two LGBT Toronto organizations. One of the groups met weekly in a venue located in the area popularly known as 'the gay village' in downtown Toronto, and the other group met monthly at a venue in the east end of the city. During my fieldwork period, attendance in both groups grew substantially; at the weekly group meeting, the numbers increased from approximately forty members in early 2010 (the first meeting I attended) to just under 200 by December 2012. While I attended the first group primarily as a 'guest', I was invited to volunteer in the second group and ended up facilitating the monthly group meetings, which mostly involved finding and inviting guest speakers. Both groups regularly invited guest speakers who would speak on topics that were thought to be relevant to the members' interests: Speakers included lawyers who work on SOGI refugee claims discussing how to prepare for the hearing, social workers with immigration/settlement organizations discussing a range of topics including where and how to apply for jobs (qualifying refugee claimants could receive a temporary work permit after filing their claim) and where to find accommodation and members of LGBT organizations in the Greater Toronto Area (GTA) discussing how they could provide support for members of this group. Through participation in the meetings as a guest or volunteer and listening to the presentations of various other individuals and groups affiliated with the refugee apparatus, I became increasingly interested in how differentially located actors in the apparatus both contributed to and challenged its normative status and helped to both construct and challenge the figure of the homonational SOGI refugee. I therefore pursued further interviews with support group organizers/directors, lawyers and IRB staff in order to better understand their perspectives, responsibilities and opinions about their roles and their relationships to SOGI refugee claimants.[7]

During fieldwork, conversations and participant observation with SOGI refugee claimants, their lawyers, support workers and IRB staff, I could not help but notice the central role of documents in all aspects of the refugee claim process.[8] The refugee claim process begins with filling out a form, and documents continue to play a central role in the life of refugee claimants throughout the entire process: They must obtain a wide range of documents such as eyewitness, psychological, medical, police and organization membership letters, official certificates (birth, national identity, educational and professional documents) and personal letters from family, lovers/partners (past and present) and friends. Documents thus occupied a great deal of time and emotional energy for the refugee claimants I worked with, and hence my attention became increasingly focused on their production, circulation and significance in relation to differentially positioned actors in the refugee apparatus.

CHAPTER ORGANIZATION

The following chapters are organized in roughly chronological order following the SOGI refugee claimant's entry into, movements through and exit from the refugee determination process. In some chapters, I shift focus from the refugee claimant's perspective to that of other participants who interact with the claimant (such as their lawyer, the support group worker, the IRB member and the expert witness) and their material effects (letters of support, expert witness reports and national documentation packages) in order to provide different lenses through which we may better understand how SOGI refugee identities and narratives are produced and evaluated throughout the refugee apparatus and are related to broader narratives of national belonging and citizenship.

In Chapter 1, I examine and challenge the architecture of the queer migration to liberation nation narrative. I note how this narrative supports Ahmed's observations on how migrants to the UK are subject to 'the happiness duty', a kind of moral training in which the migrant is supposed to gratefully learn the ways of the civilized empire (2010: 130). Through the migration stories of four SOGI refugees, I explore how we might challenge, complicate or mess up hegemonically straight sexual and gendered refugee narratives utilizing queer theorizations of migration, which emphasize the complex and diverse ways in which sexual and gendered desires, identities and relationships intersect with other desires. I also explore how multiple desires impact movements, relocations and regroundings within and across various national borders. However, I will also argue that SOGI refugees, like any other category of refugees, are highly vulnerable participants in the refugee apparatus, and that in order to successfully navigate the apparatus they must quickly learn the hegemonic narratives of refugeeness and the powerful structures within which they are located, resulting in migration stories that are compelled to contain statements that hue closely to homonational narratives while simultaneously complicating them.

In Chapter 2, I examine the category of the (in)authentic SOGI refugee in different domains of refugee support networks and in conversations among refugee claimants. Individuals who are claiming protection as refugees on the basis of sexual orientation and/or gendered identity persecution face the daunting double challenge of proving that their sexual orientation or gendered identity is 'credible' (that is, they are who they say they are) and that they have been persecuted based on their membership in this particular social category. This challenge led more than one claimant to ask at peer support group meetings, 'How do I prove that I'm gay/lesbian/bisexual and that I have been persecuted?' It also produced a number of comments by claimants, lawyers and support group workers about people they thought weren't 'real' LGBT refugees and were therefore making their own 'authentic' claims less likely to be viewed as credible by IRB adjudicators. I examine refugees' struggles to learn how to answer the question of proving one's LGBT identity and the attendant nervousness produced by pervasive state surveillance and talk about real vs. fake SOGI refugees. As I examine this struggle, deeply embedded in the gate-keeping mechanisms of the nation-state, I once more note the presence of homonationalism as hegemonic or normative in the conversations of refugee claimants, lawyers and support workers, producing a template of the 'real' or 'authentic' SOGI refugee. However, I also include some refugee participants' experiences with homophobic taxi-cab drivers and racist, transphobic police officers in Toronto that disrupt their 'inaugural homonationalism' and may cause some to question the 'truthiness' of this narrative.

Chapter 3 continues to examine the ways in which a particular formation of sexual orientation and gender identity comes to exist as normative or authentic in the refugee determination process through the analysis of a short fictional play about the SOGI refugee experience written and performed by former SOGI refugee claimants. However, in this chapter, I move beyond specific events or discussions associated with the refugee determination process in order to examine how creative aesthetic practices of transnational refugees are intertwined with the discursive terrains of North American queer culture and the refugee apparatus. I argue that the evolution of the play's narrative and characters' aesthetics, observed through rehearsals for the play, were impacted by, and struggled with, the politics of being SOGI refugees in the Canadian refugee apparatus, and that the SOGI refugee characters in the final performance of this play re-inscribed a normative sexual identity now valorized in Canadian nationalist discourses. However, I will also argue that the former refugees involved in the play challenged aspects of normative SOGI refugee identity through their debates and critiques of the play's characters' oral and aesthetic performances. Thus, this chapter extends and complicates the previous chapter's discussion of authenticity in the refugee apparatus by demonstrating that while the authentic SOGI refugee is highly relevant throughout the refugee apparatus, it is an unstable, mobile identity category that requires constant practice and much work whose artifice may be exposed in certain contexts by those who are required to invest in it.

In Chapter 4 I investigate another moment/space along the continuum of learning to be an authentic SOGI refugee, but rather than focusing on the experiences of the refugee claimants, I turn to another set of participants in the refugee apparatus, SOGI refugee support group workers and volunteers, and I focus on one of their activities, producing documents for SOGI refugee claimants' files. Through exploration of some sites and personnel involved in producing documents for SOGI refugee claimants and tracking changes to the processes involved in creating these documents, I argue that the concern for managing quality and reputation among low-level 'document brokers' (Hull 2012: 258) who want to produce documents attached to 'credible' or 'authentic' SOGI refugees reflects the regulatory modes of the Canadian refugee apparatus and its increased levels of suspicion and surveillance of human traffic crossing its borders. I observe how volunteers' concerns about writing 'quality' letters attached to 'real' SOGI refugees produce practices that rely on 'gut-feelings' or 'the gaydar', resulting in what Cabot calls a social aesthetics of eligibility (Cabot 2013: 111), which end up endorsing the ways in which 'regimes of care' (humanitarian groups, activists and certain movements for human rights) may reproduce inequalities and racial, gendered, and geopolitical hierarchies (Ticktin 2011).

Chapter 5 turns to the 'centrepiece' of the refugee determination process, the hearing. The objective of the IRB hearing is to determine if the claimant is who s/he says s/he is and meets the definition of a refugee outlined in the Canadian Immigration and Refugee Protection Act. In this chapter I focus on the words and performance of the key player who evaluates the SOGI refugee claimant's documents and performance – the IRB member. The member is the individual at the hearing who decides if the claim for refugee protection is accepted or rejected. I argue that it is important to find out what we can about the training and decision-making process of these bureaucrats and their perspectives on their duties and responsibilities. In sifting through various sites, events, interviews and documents pertaining to this process, my goal in this chapter is twofold: first, to identify the discursive contours through which SOGI refugee cases are assessed, that is, to examine the discourse and terminology utilized in the hearing by the member to assess the credibility of the claimant, and second, to identify adjudicators' non-linguistic, affective or emotional registers, which may influence the decision-making process, and to consider the relationship between these non-linguistic registers and the hegemonic linguistic evidence-based process of adducing the truth of a refugee claimant's story. In line with the previous chapter, I argue that affective labour in assessing SOGI refugee credibility invokes particular incarnations of nationalism and citizenship, which are themselves freighted with moral valences of proper assemblages of sexuality, gender, race and class, thus contributing to the hegemonic affective economy of the nation-state.

In Chapter 6, I return to issues of documentation, but focus on a different set of documents related to the hearing, National Documentation Packages (collections of articles and reports written or assembled by IRB staff about other nation-states' human rights records, social and political conditions and criminal codes) and expert witness reports (statements requested by a lawyer or adjudicator assessing a refugee claimant's home nation's social and political conditions and/or assessments of claims made by the refugee claimant). I explore sections of the IRB's National Documentation Package (NDP) for Barbados, which contains excerpts from my research on Barbadian sexual minorities and homophobia in that country, and I discuss the impact of NDPs on the decision-making process of adjudicators at the hearings of some SOGI refugee claimants in Toronto. I also explore issues that have arisen when I have been asked to write expert reports about social conditions for sexual and gender minorities in Caribbean nation-states. I argue that the effects of my voluntary and involuntary contributions to archives of documents about sexual and gender laws, practices and behaviours in other nation-states constitute another node of the production of homonationalism in the refugee apparatus.

Chapter 7 turns to the layered, complex and sometimes contradictory narratives of home in refugee research and their complex connections to discourses of national belonging in 'home' and destination nations. I begin this chapter with a brief discussion of the ways in which home operates as a central, yet troubling, concept in both refugee and queer studies. I then focus on the role and significance of home in SOGI refugee narratives presented to the IRB in documents and at the hearing, demonstrating how representations of home in these 'official' narratives re-inscribe the homonationalist narrative undergirding the refugee apparatus. The final section of the chapter

focuses on more informal discussions about home with SOGI refugee claimants in different social contexts. I observe that the queer migration to liberation nation narrative is articulated by many participants; however, many of
them continue to communicate with friends and family in their countries of
origin and have diverse, intense and complex feelings about their former
homeland(s), resulting in 'ambivalent homonationalisms' (White 2013). In
this exploration of the diverse experiences and meanings of home for SOGI
refugees, I argue for a conceptualization of home that recognizes simultaneous, complex attachments to multiple homes constituted across transnational
fields while simultaneously co-opting and undermining homonational discourses in the refugee determination apparatus.

In the Conclusion, I observe a contradiction produced through the previous
chapters: by spending the majority of the book on a particular moment
where a set of transnational queer migrants are placed into a bureaucratic
and legislative process designed to evaluate the credibility of their claim to
being 'authentic' SOGI refugees, we end up viewing them primarily or only
as 'SOGI refugees', without much attention to the rest of their lives before
or after the refugee determination process. In order to counterbalance this
overly determined moment/identity, I briefly follow up on some of the people
whose queer migration stories I presented in the Introduction in order to
illustrate diverse and unevenly unfolding lives of a small group of migrants.
We see how some individuals 'live on' in Toronto, while others disappear
abruptly, demonstrating the harsh reality of the refugee apparatus and its
necropolitical powers. I also return to the crucial point that the refugee apparatus continually reviews and revises itself, acting and reacting to changes
in national and transnational migration patterns and laws, and to changing
public moralities pertaining to immigration and/or particular classes of
immigrants – the never-ending process of normalization. I briefly outline
some of the effects of the 'new normalization' of the apparatus resulting
from changes enacted through the federal government's Bill C-31, which
came into effect in December 2012. There is mounting evidence from the
'front lines' – reports from lawyers, SOGI support workers, refugee advocate organizations and refugee applicants themselves – that the apparatus
has tightened even further, shrinking timelines and increasing the number of
categories of inadmissibility.

NOTES

1. Edward's story is presented in more detail in Murray 2009: 185–86.
2. While reports of most refugee decisions in Canada are unpublished (Rehaag
2008) and it is difficult to obtain the exact numbers of sexual minority refugees

because of changes in the organization of refugee claims statistics, according to the IRB Director of Access to Information and Privacy, between 2002 and 2006, six per cent of all principal claim cases were related to sexual orientation and, from 2009 to 2011, the overall percentage grew slightly to six and a half per cent (personal correspondence).

3. More on this term below.

4. http://www.unhcr.org/pages/49c3646c125.html (accessed 1 May 2015).

5. As Canaday, and Kinsman and Gentile point out, American and Canadian governments tended to be concerned mostly with male homosexuals in public life throughout much of the twentieth century, reflecting the heteropatriarchal power structures of their era.

6. Vancouver and Montreal are also major destinations. See Cooney (2007), Newbold and DeLuca (2007) and Ricard (2014).

7. Names and other identifying features of lawyers, refugee claimants, support workers and other participants in the refugee apparatus have been changed in order to protect confidentiality.

8. Melissa Autumn White's research on documentation (what she calls the 'intimate archives') of queer migrants and sponsors who have secured 'same-sex' family class migration privileges as a technique of affective governance also contributed towards my attentiveness to documentation in the refugee determination process (White 2010, 2013, 2014).

Chapter 1

Queering the Queer Migration to Liberation Nation Narrative

The 2005 documentary film 'Gloriously Free'[1] was summarized on the Canadian Broadcasting Corporation website as follows:

> 'Gloriously Free' is the first documentary to explore the world of gay immigration, and the desperate search of five young men to find welcoming arms outside their countries of birth – where persecution and hatred of alternative lifestyles may lead to torture or death. What they find is Canada, leading the world as the safest haven for persecuted gays and lesbians.[2]

A more recent documentary film, 'Last Chance' (2012), focuses on the similar topic of lesbian, gay, bisexual and transgendered (LGBT) refugees in Canada, but offers a more nuanced perspective on the migration stories of five LGBT refugee claimants, including some footage of the challenges they encounter with the Canadian Immigration and Refugee Board (IRB), particularly in relation to problematic IRB members (adjudicators) who do not believe their claims of LGBT identity and/or of persecution in their country of origin.

'LGBT refugees' appeared in another media format in September 2012, when thousands of 'lesbian and gay Canadians'[3] were surprised to find an email in their inbox from Jason Kenney, Canada's then minister of citizenship, immigration, and multiculturalism, which contained a similar message to that of the documentary films.[4] In this mass emailing, Minister Kenney informed us that, 'Canada is a place of refuge for those who truly need our protection. ... We welcome those fleeing persecution on the basis of sexual orientation ... (and) we have taken the lead in helping gay refugees begin new, safe lives in Canada.'

As noted in the Introduction, despite differences in opinion over the Canadian government's treatment of LGBT refugees, in these films, news articles and emails we see a similar story with similar characters, which I call the queer migration to liberation nation narrative: LGBT refugees' countries of origin are depicted as nations of 'hatred of alternative lifestyles' or 'rabidly anti-gay'[5]; the refugee has 'no choice' but to 'flee', 'escape' or 'leave', and decides to seek refuge in Canada because it is the 'safest haven for persecuted gays and lesbians' and 'Canada considers gays and lesbians to be ordinary people. ... This is where you go for freedom.'[6]

While I do not wish to dispute the facticity of certain claims in these media reports, in this chapter I want to examine the discursive effects of the architecture of the queer migration to liberation nation narrative, which operates as a hegemonic discourse across numerous media platforms in which nations, cultures, sexual identities and values associated with those identities are described, connected and evaluated in similar ways (Grewal 2005: 181). As these hegemonic narratives of liberation are repeatedly circulated through pages, screens and Sexual Orientation and Gender Identity (SOGI) refugee adjudication hearings,[7] I wonder about their effects on different groups of listeners, readers, decision makers and the story-tellers themselves. As with all storytelling, choices are made about what to include or exclude, what to speak about and what to be silent about. What don't we hear in hegemonic or popular narratives of sexual and gendered refugee persecution, flight and freedom? Why do some features and characteristics of refugees, their countries of origin and destination nations appear again and again, while others do not? Are there other ways to tell the story, and does it matter if we tell another version? These are some of the questions I wish to investigate in this chapter.

In thinking about the effects of hegemonic narratives, Sara Ahmed's discussion of migrants, happiness and empire provides a number of key insights that help to frame my argument. In her analysis of claims that multiculturalism is a failed project in the UK, she identifies the presence, or more accurately, the absence of the 'happy migrant', that is, someone who espouses national ideals, which are couched in terms of empire. Migrants to the United Kingdom are subject to 'the happiness duty', a kind of moral training in which the migrant is supposed to gratefully learn the ways of the civilized empire (2010: 130). As Ahmed reminds us, this is not a new discourse. Through the writings of classic nineteenth-century liberal philosophers John Stewart Mill and Jeremy Bentham, Ahmed demonstrates how the project of justifying empire as liberation from abjection has been around for a long time (2010: 122–25). However, the SOGI refugee queer migration to liberation nation narrative adds a new twist to Ahmed's 'happy migrant' in that some configurations of sexual orientation and gendered identity have recently become an additional feature of 'empire', that is, it is assumed that the SOGI refugee is a happy migrant because he or she has arrived in a nation where sexual diversity is held aloft as a feature of a 'civilized' society, opposed to 'uncivilized' societies characterized by their rampant homophobia. This is a similar argument to Jasbir Puar's analysis of the operation of homonational sexual identity politics in post 9–11 America, where a highly delimited definition of sexual identity—in other words, one that is gendered, raced and classed—is employed (in a deeply contradictory way) to justify the heightened security and militarization of US borders in order to protect 'tolerant' America from the homophobic, intolerant, monstrous, racialized immigrant other (2007).[8]

To put it in slightly different terms, these hegemonic SOGI refugee narratives are rendered literally and figuratively straight in their temporal, spatial and sexual orientation and gendered identity in that they follow an essentialist, linear path of sexual identity development (Ahmed 2006), from closeted, repressed and/or persecuted in their country of origin to 'out' and 'free' in Canada. These are narratives of unidirectional migration towards the nation of refuge, culminating in the liberatory moment of the refugee hearings where the claimants can officially 'come out' to the state who will protect them and allow them the freedom to be openly 'gay' 'lesbian' 'bisexual' or 'transgendered', with the expectation of grateful, docile citizenship in return. The result, as Jenicek et al. note, is reinforcement of a culturally racist paradigm, which reproduces simplistic imperialist tropes of the civilized West/uncivilized rest, but also silences ongoing experiences of homophobia, racism, sexism and classicism in Canada (Jenicek et al. 2009).

In this chapter, I explore how we might challenge, complicate or mess up these hegemonically straight sexual and gendered refugee narratives. Rather than reproducing a teleological narrative that is straight and forward in its temporal and spatial movements and sexual and gendered orientations, I ask how we might render it queer, and what difference, if any, that might make (Ahmed 2006). In rendering SOGI refugee stories 'queer', this chapter reflects arguments found in recent queer migration scholarship, introduced in the previous chapter, which reconfigures temporalities and geographies by decentring nationalist frameworks premised on space-time binaries, developmental narratives and static, homologous models of culture, nation, race, sexuality, gender, class, identity and settlement (Luibhéid 2008: 173). In challenging homonational components and characters in the queer migration to liberation nation narrative, I apply some of Ahmed, Castañeda, Fortier and Sheller's arguments about home and migration (2003), which challenge reductionist theories and assumptions about the meaning of migration and home[9] by 'blurring the distinctions between here and there' and considering how processes of homing and migration take shape through 'experience in broader social processes and institutions where unequal differences of race, class, gender and sexuality are generated' (2003: 5). 'Home' is a central and troubling concept in refugee research, and I will return to examine it in further detail in Chapter 7.

Through an analysis of conversations and interviews with four LGBT/
SOGI refugee claimants, I will apply these queer theorizations of migration, which emphasize the complex and diverse ways in which sexual and
gendered desires, identities and relationships intersect with other desires, and
explore how multiple desires impact movements, relocations and regroundings within and across various national borders (Cantú 2009; Decena 2011;
Luibhéid and Cantú 2005; White 2013, 2014). That is, I will illustrate how the
multiple, circuitous paths to becoming a SOGI refugee demonstrate that this
migrant terminology tells us very little about the individuals who are labeled
in this way other than how to think about them in relation to their mode of
entry into the gate-keeping mechanisms of the nation-state (Grewal 2005:
175). However, I will also argue that SOGI refugees, like any other category
of refugees, are highly vulnerable participants in the refugee determination
apparatus and its constitutive policies, laws and narratives, and that in order
to successfully navigate the apparatus they must quickly learn these narratives and the powerful structures within which they are located, resulting in
migration stories that are compelled to contain statements which hue closely
to homonational narratives while simultaneously complicating them (Lewis
2005; Luibhéid and Cantú 2005; O'Leary 2008; White 2013).[10]

It should be noted that my attempt to 'queer' the straight narrative of
SOGI refugees is based mostly on individual interviews, which often (but
not always) followed a structure that replicated the very framework I am
critiquing. That is, my questions were usually organized in a chronological
fashion, such that I would begin by asking the interviewees to provide some
background details about their family, childhood and the community they
grew up in, followed by questions about desires and relationships as they
moved into adolescence and adulthood, which would lead to questions about
their migration to Canada. Thus, at one level I am guilty of the very thing
I am trying to critique, in that the order and structure of questions asked in
the interview risks reproducing a Western chronotope of sexual and gendered
identity development and 'refugeeness' (the movements, actions and qualities
of becoming a refugee, Malkki 1995). However, while I am cognizant of the
limits of the informal interview as a research technique,[11] by paying attention to certain details in the answers, and the sometimes long and detailed
tangential discussions of adventures, events and actions that emerged out of
these questions, I hope to be able to reveal more of the rich complexity of
movements, desires, relationships and identifications in these participants'
lives. In addition, I include some comments and anecdotes that occurred
outside the 'official' interview context, such as conversations held before and
after the recording microphone was turned on, and from informal meetings
on the street, at a café or in a community centre lobby.[12] While I focus on
the narratives of four individuals from varied gendered, sexual, ethno-racial

and national backgrounds in order to illustrate the diversity and complexity of movement, identification and desire, I will note where certain experiences, feelings and opinions overlap with narratives of refugees from similar backgrounds or identifications. In other words, while I am trying to elaborate the variability of individual lives, experiences and desires that are too often reduced to stock characters in the queer migration to liberation nation narrative, I also try to be attentive to the ways in which certain components of these stories are repeated by different interviewees, and sometimes collude with this hegemonic narrative, which helps us to see how pleasure, fear, anxiety and desire organize, orient and relate bodies, and the ways in which these feelings may be reorganized and regulated through the moral economy of the state and its attendant surveillance in order to avoid rejection and/or deportation.

LIVING, LOVING, LEAVING

The following four narratives are condensed versions of discussions from formal interviews and informal conversations with participants. While it might seem rather obvious, it is nonetheless important to preface these narratives by pointing out that none of the interviewees began their lives thinking of themselves as refugees, and in fact for quite a few, 'refugee' was a relatively new identity term imposed upon them by the process through which they migrated across national borders and into the Canadian government's immigration apparatus. While I will elaborate the ways in which these narratives converge and diverge with a number of elements in the homonational queer migration to liberation nation narrative following this section, this obvious point – that most refugees only recently came to recognize or acknowledge this imposed identity – already begins to challenge any singular representation of the category 'LGBT/SOGI refugee'.

Joe

Joe, who is in his thirties, and self-identifies as a 'classic transsexual male', was born and raised in 'the Middle East'[13] in a 'middle class liberal Muslim' family who were financially 'comfortable'. Joe knew he was a boy from an early age and didn't 'feel' right as his body began to develop female features in adolescence. Joe remembered that as a child, he couldn't find any information anywhere about people like him, but around age of 9 or 10,

> I saw Boy George on the TV, and I said to my mother ... how can she be called Boy George when she's a woman, is she a man? ... And there was an awkward

response from my mother, so I was like, why is this person a boy. ... Later on ...
I was told by my sister, who was older and wiser, that he was a man but he looks
like a girl, so something was going on there.

Joe had huge fights with his mother when he told her he was a boy. She said
he was going against God and that he would be cursed if he kept talking this
way. However, Joe also had a nanny 'from a Caribbean island' who was
Catholic and conveyed a very different message about God: 'My nanny used
to say things like God is Love and God loves you just the way you are. ...
She would tell my mother to "just let me be".' Joe was so deeply affected
by his nanny's perspective that he converted to Catholicism after arriving in
Canada.

Joe remembered most of his childhood and adolescence in terms of strife
and difficulty, particularly in his relationship to his mother. He was sent to a
girls' boarding school in the United Kingdom where he was a difficult student
because he was angry and unhappy. By the time he entered university (in his
country of birth), he was starting to think of ways to get out of the country,
as it was clear there was no place for people like him there. He studied psychology as an undergraduate in order to find out more about himself but there
was no reference to his 'condition' in any of his classes or texts. After graduating and working in banking in his home town for a few years, Joe heard
about a local graduate program in cellular biology from his friend who told
him there were lots of opportunities to get postdoctoral fellowships and work
in other countries with this kind of degree, so Joe applied and was accepted.
He did well in the program, and was then accepted into a postdoctoral job in
a country in Northern Europe, which he thought would be more accepting of
transsexual refugees based on what he had read on the Internet. After arriving
in Northern Europe, Joe began to take hormones to initiate his transition, but
he soon discovered he wouldn't be eligible for asylum there. Increasingly
desperate, he emailed a Canadian friend of a cousin whom he had met a few
years ago back in his country of birth who had spoken to him about some
of her lesbian friends in Canada. He decided to tell her everything one night
while 'MSM'ing' (text-chatting), and she was very supportive. They began to
search the web together for information on immigrating to Canada, and after
emailing an immigration 'specialist' in Toronto, Joe was told he could apply
for refugee status once he had arrived in Canada. Joe had started to receive
threatening phone calls from his mother, who said she was going to send
someone to Northern Europe to bring him back, so he was starting to panic
that he might not get out in time. After a long and difficult wait, he finally
obtained a visitor visa to Canada, bought his plane ticket and boarded a flight
to Toronto. After a difficult first encounter with a Canadian customs officer
who aggressively accused Joe of having fake documents (which was not true)

when he announced he was seeking asylum, Joe found the other immigration officers at Pearson airport friendly and supportive. Joe felt that coming to Canada was his best chance to start living life on his own terms. He estimated that he had spent over a year doing research on immigration, transgender rights and related medical issues in Canada before arriving at Pearson airport and claiming asylum at customs.

Janine

Janine, who is in her early thirties and comes from Jamaica, had quite a different experience in migrating to Canada. Janine was born into a single-parent working class family in Kingston. She moved at least four times while she was young because her single mother didn't have money to pay rent, although she eventually found permanent employment as a phone company operator. Even though they didn't have much money, her mother thought it was important for the children to travel and experience the world outside Jamaica, so Janine was sent to stay with relatives in Canada for a few months when she was thirteen. She didn't remember much about her visit to Toronto with the exception of 'the lovely willow trees and the lake … but I never thought I would end up in Canada'. Janine remembered having crushes on girls when she was very young, and by the time she had finished high school, Janine knew she was 'bisexual' (this is the term she used in our discussions). She got along best with 'gay guys' (her term), which also helped her to see how poorly some of them were treated in Jamaica. Janine said she could never come out to her family, as they are very religious and wouldn't accept it, 'it would be World War III'. However, by the end of high school, she told some of her gay friends, and that was all she needed as 'they were becoming my family'.

After graduating from high school, Janine found work in the tourism industry doing different jobs in hotels, and she gradually moved up the chain to be head concierge at an upscale resort. Janine loved working in tourism, as she got to meet people from all over the world and found that most of the Jamaicans she worked with were more open-minded and 'accepting'. With a relatively good salary, Janine was able to travel more, and her favourite destination became Belgium, where she met a Belgian woman and began to have a relationship with her. She began to think about moving to Belgium because she met many 'people like me, so I didn't feel like such a freak'. She also travelled to the United States, where, one time, she 'did something really stupid' and got caught for shoplifting a pair of pants from a department store. She was taken to court, and accused of grand larceny, but when the judge found out she was returning to Jamaica in a few weeks, he told Janine to report to the US embassy there. However, when she went to the embassy in Kingston, they weren't able to locate any record of arrest, so she assumed it had been dropped.

It was around this time that Janine started to receive anonymous threats. The first one was posted on her Facebook page from someone she didn't know, saying 'Jesus hates gays', and then she started to receive threatening phone calls, including one where someone said, 'battygal mus die' (battygal is Jamaican patois for lesbian). Her initial reaction was 'fuck you', but her gay friends told her that now that she had been targeted she needed to leave. A couple of her gay male friends had been beaten, and one killed, so she knew these were not idle threats. She decided to go to Australia for a vacation, because she had met some really nice Australians in Jamaica and she heard it was an easy-going place. Once she was there she would decide what to do next. She bought a plane ticket that required her to change planes in Toronto, and thought everything was in order. However, when she arrived at Pearson airport, she had to go through customs to transfer planes, and they said her documents were 'questionable' (she did not have a visa to enter Canada, and the letter of permission that she had received from a police officer was not acceptable), so they did a background check and found an outstanding warrant for arrest for the shoplifting incident in the United States, which was now over six years old. Janine ended up in the detention centre at Milton (also known as 'The Milton Hilton', she said), a Toronto suburb located west of the airport, for thirty-five days. No one knew she was there until her mother in Jamaica became worried after not hearing from her, and contacted family members in Toronto, who then contacted the police and found out where she was. While in the Milton Hilton, Janine met a Polish woman whom she liked and trusted, and who eventually told Janine that she could get legal support and apply for refugee status in Canada: 'She was the smartest person at the Milton Hilton and was my guardian angel,' Janine said. Looking back on it, Janine had a somewhat fatalistic perspective:

> Whether or not that (immigration transit) document was real or not, I'm alive and God's divine intervention ... (is what's) bringing me here ... you know, I'm here and I know that God didn't want me in Australia and I know that God wanted to save my life. And I'm here.

Odu

I met Odu, who is in his early forties, at one of the refugee support group meetings. Odu was born in Lagos, Nigeria. His family is Yoruba (an ethnic group) and he was 'brought up to believe in Christ' by his parents who were very religious. Odu's parents were middle class (father a bureaucrat and mother a nurse), and he went to a private Christian school where he was popular and did relatively well. He remembered looking at boys in high school, and 'I liked what I saw', but he wasn't sure if this was normal, although he did 'do some things' with a friend. He went to university to study economics, and this was where he started to meet other men like him (Odu never used the words 'gay' or 'homosexual' in our conversations). There was a restaurant near the university where they used to hang out, he said, and when he went there he saw that the younger men would often meet up with older married men and go off in their cars for a while. 'The married men had places they could take you, and they would give you gifts ... nothing ever happened to them, I felt protected around them [because] they were rich.' However, Odu went on to say that they were not nice men, and then asked me to change the subject. When I asked him if he knew of any organizations or support groups for LGBT people at the university or anywhere else in the country, he shook his head saying, 'No, because I was so scared. I didn't want anyone to know. I was like, really in denial. No one (knew) what I was doing. ... I kept this a secret from [every]one'.

After university and a year in the national youth service (obligatory for all Nigerian university graduates), Odu opened a hairstyling shop for men and women in a city in northern Nigeria (away from his family), which did well and allowed him to have his own apartment. However, a few years later he married a woman:

> When I was about thirty-five my parents became so worried, they said I have to get married to a woman. ... I didn't know what to do. So, there was this man I was seeing. He was an older man. And he was a guy who said, 'you have to do it'. He's married as well. He's got wives. And [he said], 'that's what you have to do'.

Odu continued to see a man while he was married to his wife and thought everything was going well until one day, after his wife had told him that she was going to Lagos for a few days to visit her family, he invited his friend over to his house, but suddenly his wife walked in the front door, 'and blew our cover'. She yelled at him and then left to tell his family. 'Everything went haywire,' said Odu, and he left his apartment to stay at another friend's place who told him he couldn't stay there for long. Odu's friend knew that 'there are places you can go away to', and through some connections put Odu in touch with a 'travel agent' who said he could 'arrange everything' for a fee. Odu withdrew all his savings, and delivered the money, along with his passport and some photos, to this individual. A few days later, he called to say everything was ready, and told Odu to meet him at the airport. Odu had no idea where he was going until he got to the airport and saw his plane tickets. The 'travel agent' accompanied him on the flight from Lagos to Frankfurt and on to Toronto. When they arrived in Toronto, the agent told Odu to say to the customs officer that he wanted to claim asylum in Canada. Odu was petrified that he would not get through customs and would be sent back to Nigeria. When he told the officer he wanted to claim asylum, the officer asked why, and Odu wasn't sure what to say – he didn't know he could claim asylum based on his sexual practices, and didn't want to tell a security person about this as he knew what would happen to him back in Nigeria if he admitted this to anyone in a similar position. Odu told the officer that he would be killed, and when the officer asked why, Odu replied, 'because of who I am'. The officer guessed, 'because you are gay?', and Odu said 'yes'. Odu was then placed in the detention centre at Rexdale for two weeks because he had entered Canada with a fake passport and visa, and had to wait for his 'real' documents to be sent to Toronto by his friend back in Nigeria, whom Odu had been permitted to call. While he was at the detention centre, he met some 'nice refugee support workers' (he couldn't remember what organization they were with) who helped him fill out forms, and arranged for him to move to a men's shelter in the city after he was released from the detention centre. At the shelter, Odu heard another man speaking English with a similar accent who turned out to be Yoruba from the same area that he had grown up in. When Odu told the other Nigerian he was claiming asylum (but not on what basis), the Nigerian put him in touch with his lawyer, who was also Nigerian, 'and then things started to move from there'.

During our conversations, Odu told me twice that he had never thought of leaving Nigeria, 'because I was doing pretty well, I had my business ... if I could (have kept) it to myself, I could do it for the rest of my life', but the marriage had changed everything.

Latoya

I first met Latoya in 2004 when I was conducting research on homophobia and sexual diversity in Barbados (Murray 2012). She attended a support group for LGBT youth organized by United Gays and Lesbians Against Aids in Barbados (UGLAAB), the only support group in Barbados at that time. Latoya was in her mid-teens and self-identified as a 'queen', a fluid term with a variety of meanings, but generally referring to someone identified as cis-male who has sex with other males, and performs, dresses, or displays various degrees of femininity.[14] At that time, Latoya told me that he wanted to spend more time 'as a woman', although he was still dressing in men's clothing and presenting as a man when he went to school or walked the streets during the day. Most of Latoya's social life was spent with other younger and older queens and self-identified gays who attended the support group meetings, went to local bars and partied together, and generally helped each other out.

Most of this group of queens came from poor to working class neighbour-hoods around Bridgetown, the capital city of Barbados, and gravitated to UGLAAB because its founder and president was a well-known queen who was one of the few public voices of 'Barbadian gays and lesbians' when there was any media coverage on the topic, and also had a reputation for helping younger queens who were having problems with their families. In 2004, Latoya was still living with his mother and father, who she said were ok with who she was: 'My mother accepts me as her daughter (and) my father buys me girl's clothes.' Latoya wanted to leave school and look for work at that time, but said jobs were difficult to find; one of her friends told me that they occasionally 'worked the streets' (engaged in sex work), although Latoya did not acknowledge this to me. Despite the hardships and challenges she faced, I nevertheless thought that Latoya was relatively content in Barbados. She had friends, a support group and supportive parents. While some UGLAAB members asked me about 'gay life' in Canada and indicated they were think-ing about migrating because they'd heard life was easier there, others like Latoya did not seem interested in leaving and/or told me that they had heard life there could be difficult for other reasons (racism, homophobia, weather, jobs).

Seven years later, I was surprised to see Latoya and another queen from Barbados walk into a Toronto LGBT refugee support group meeting, although I think they were as surprised to see me. Latoya was more perfor-matively feminine than I remembered her in Barbados – she was wearing a tight black mini-skirt, a purple faux angora sweater, high heels and bright blue contact lenses. When we met afterwards to talk, Latoya told me how, over the past few years, she had entered some (gay/queen) beauty pageants in Barbados and Trinidad and was really enjoying the whole experience, but everyday life in Barbados was getting worse, particularly as she was now try-ing to live as a woman 'full-time'. She also had a relationship with a man who had eventually become violent with her, so she broke up with him, but one night, when she was leaving a party, he came up to her on the street, held a knife to her throat and forced her to go back to his home, where he raped her. She escaped when he went out to buy food later that morning, and called the police, who arrested him and charged him with assault. He was jailed for only about six months, and Latoya was fearful he would try to find her when he got out. Meanwhile, she knew five other queens who had gone to Canada to claim asylum and 'made it through', so she called one of them in Toronto who told her what to do. Latoya's mother and aunt paid for her ticket to Toronto, and after she arrived, she went straight to Gigi's (another Barbadian queen) apart-ment (Barbadians do not require visas to visit Canada, which generally results in easier movement through airport customs). A couple of days after arriving, Gigi gave Latoya the address of the Citizenship and Immigration Canada

office on Kipling Avenue, and told her what to say. Gigi also put Latoya in
touch with the lawyer she had used, and told her to start attending the refugee
support group meetings at the LGBT community centre downtown.

CONVERGENCES AND DIVERGENCES

These four narratives move through multiple life experiences: childhood,
adolescence, work, family, sexual experiences, romantic relationships,
dreams and aspirations, discrimination, violence, loss, multiple migrations
and settlements. We might begin to compare them by making a self-evident
point that we have four different individuals of different ethno-national backgrounds and gendered and sexual orientations, a point that challenges any
attempt to singularly define the meaning and content of the category of sexual
orientation and gendered identity refugee. Unlike other categories of refugees
who make a claim based on religious, political or ethnic persecution, and
are therefore connected to socially recognized cultural, religious or political
collective identities and/or organizations (well-known examples in Canada
include the Rwandans, the Roma or the Tamil Tigers from Sri Lanka),
SOGI refugee claimants often do not have easily verifiable public markers
such as documented histories, publicly known collective associations and/
or geographic homelands. However, even this generalization is problematic
in that while many nations (or at least many large cities in these nations) do
have LGBT organizations with varying levels of public visibility, there was
great variability in interviewees' familiarity with and/or connections to these
organizations. For example, Latoya had been participating in an LGBT youth
group in Barbados since her mid-teens, and Janine socialized mostly with
'gay men' during her adult life in Jamaica and knew of LGBT organizations
like JFLAG (Jamaican Forum of Lesbians, All-Sexuals and Gays). While
Odu knew of no official organization in Nigeria, he gradually found a space
where men 'like him' could meet other men relatively covertly. Joe grew
up in his country of origin thinking there was no one like him until he saw
a Boy George video and later started to search for 'trans' topics online. He
had not connected with any LGBT network or organization until he arrived
in Toronto.

Differing degrees of knowledge about and relationships with LGBT organizations and networks exist even within national or regional contexts, that
is, individuals from the same country or region may have different levels of
awareness of LGBT organizations, communities or networks for a variety of
reasons, or they may choose to have significantly different degrees of association with these networks and groups for multiple reasons. While Janine
and Latoya sought out and socialized in networks of similarly oriented or

identified people, some people from other Caribbean societies I interviewed, especially those from places like St. Lucia or St. Vincent and the Grenadines, were not aware of or connected to any kind of LGBT group.[15] Age, gender, sexual activities, class, education, location, religion, access to the Internet, and/or feelings of fear or disidentification are just some of the reasons that might explain the differing degrees of knowledge about and relationships to local, regional or national LGBT organizations or social networks.

It is important to stress the significance of feelings of identification or disidentification with local and/or transnational sexual orientation or gendered identity terminologies, as these feelings may significantly impact an individual's transition into the Canadian refugee apparatus, which recognizes SOGI refugee claimants as eligible for refugee status because of persecution based on their membership in a 'particular social group' (LaViolette 2009: 440; Munoz 1999). However, in most Canadian Immigration and Refugee Board and socio-legal discourses, sexual and gender minorities tend to be identified or described as 'homosexual, lesbian, gay, bisexual and/or transgender', such that individuals who make a claim based on persecution as a member of this 'particular social group' do so through the utilization of 'LGBT' terminology (LaViolette 2009: 440–41).[16] As numerous scholars of transnational sexualities have pointed out, these are identity terms located in and produced through particular social, cultural, racial, class and political histories, which also have transnational mobility, but this does not necessarily equate to identical definitions and meanings in local contexts (Berg and Millbank 2009; Lewin and Leap 2002, 2009; Murray 2009; Miller 2005; Manalansan 2006; Ou-Jin Lee and Brotman 2011).[17]

The participants demonstrated differing degrees of knowledge about and comfort with sexual and gender identity terms. In our conversations, Odu did not once refer to himself as gay, homosexual or bisexual. He would sometimes talk about meeting 'men like me' in Nigeria or how he was treated because of 'who he was' but it was not until he was telling me about his encounter with immigration at Pearson airport that he attached himself to the term 'gay' and even then it was done through the voice of the immigration officer. On the other hand, Joe was quite sure of his gendered identity from an early age, and was seeking out information on 'transsexuals' (his term) by the time he was in high school. Latoya, whom I had known for a longer period than the other participants, identified as a 'queen' in Barbados, but was now claiming refugee protection on the basis of persecution as a transgender individual. Elsewhere, I have discussed how these two terms may not be synonymous in meaning, in that queen operates as a more fluid category that melds a gendered sexual orientation (in popular North American discourse, 'gay') with a sexualized gendered identity (in popular North American discourse 'male to female transgender' with a preference for cis-male sexual partners) (Murray

2012). Janine self-identified as 'bisexual' in our conversations, but also told me that she wasn't comfortable with this term: 'We're born the way we are, why can't people just accept this and not impose labels?' Thus, as Ou-Jin Lee and Brotman have observed, the sexual orientation and gendered identities of refugee claimants, like those of any human, are fluid and contextual, shifting and changing over time in relationship to social location and context, which are themselves in constant flux and influenced by complex social, political and economic forces at local, regional and transnational levels (2011: 254). This results in different levels of familiarity and comfort with the sexual and gendered terminologies utilized by the IRB and other Canadian refugee support groups and organizations, and potentially results in different outcomes in the claim for refugee status (more on this in Chapter 5). While this may seem like a very obvious point from an anthropological perspective, it deserves to be highlighted in the context of the homonational LGBT refugee narrative, which enforces a specific script built on racialized, classed and politically contextualized definitions of sexual orientation and gendered identity.

Another area of significant difference in these individual narratives relates to movement and migration within and across borders. That is, in contrast to the queer migration to liberation nation narrative in which the SOGI refugees appear to have lived their entire life in an oppressive homophobic nation, then migrate directly across national borders to the liberation nation of Canada, some of these participants' narratives reveal lives of continuous movement and migration either within or across national borders. Joe spent most of his adolescence at a boarding school in the United Kingdom, and then pursued postgraduate fellowships in Europe. Janine visited relatives in Canada when she was a child and travelled frequently to Europe and the United States when she was an adult. Odu had never left Nigeria, but he had moved around the country attending a university in another city, participating in the cadet youth service, and then establishing a business in a town far away from his family. Latoya had spent her entire life in Barbados, but had moved to different neighbourhoods in and around Bridgetown with her family when she was a child and with other queens as a young adult as they looked for safe and affordable accommodation. Once again, there are diverse reasons and explanations for these varying degrees of mobility, ranging from the socio-economic positions of birth-families, local or regional migrational norms or practices, educational or job opportunities, and/or the desire to move to spaces in which one could feel free and live safely. The intersection of desire with other migrational motives resulting in multiple movements within and across borders exemplifies a queer migration perspective (Luibhéid 2008) and challenges normative migration models, which often presuppose heteronormative push/pull factors like 'family security' (see, for example, Cohen and Sirkeci 2011).

Another key characteristic in the queer migration to liberation nation narrative is the intentionality of the LGBT refugee claimant seeking out Canada as the chosen safe haven, which often serves as the climax to this narrative, 'proving' the Canadian nation-state's progressive, tolerant national identity. Individual claimants are often quoted as saying that they came to Canada so they could be free to be themselves and that Canada is a place that protects the rights of sexual minorities, implying that they had prior knowledge of Canadian laws, policies and attitudes pertaining to sexuality, gender and refugees and that they had made the choice to migrate there. While it is true that these kinds of statements could be found in some interviews (Joe and Latoya), when reviewing the transcripts of most interviewees what emerges is the complex and arbitrary nature of many decisions, actions and movements that results in the individual lodging a refugee claim in Canada. Joe's first choice to claim refugee status was a country in Northern Europe because he was more familiar with the region, having attended high school in the United Kingdom. He only decided to come to Canada after discovering how difficult it would be to immigrate to Northern Europe and initiating communications with his cousin's friend in Toronto. Latoya's decision to seek refuge in Canada was based on her being part of a social network of fellow Barbadian queens, a number of whom had already successfully travelled to Toronto and claimed refugee status. Other Caribbean refugee claimants, particularly those from Jamaica, also migrated through similar diasporic Caribbean queer networks.[18] On the other hand, Canada was not a predetermined destination for either Odu or Janine. Both of them were forced to leave their homes relatively quickly because of threats of violence; Odu paid dearly for the services of a 'travel agent' who clearly knew something about Canadian refugee laws, and prepared forged travel documents for Odu to get there, but Odu knew nothing about Canada until he saw his plane ticket at the airport in Lagos. Many of the Nigerians I interviewed had a similar story, in that most had arrived in Toronto through similar means (accompanied by 'travel agents' with forged documents) with no knowledge of their destination prior to their departure. Janine was intending to travel to Australia for a holiday, where she was going to investigate the possibility of immigration, but was stopped at Pearson airport in Toronto because of problematic travel documents, which triggered the outstanding warrant for her arrest from the United States. Thus, for refugee claimants like Janine, Canada was an accidental destination, while others learned about Canadian immigration and refugee policies and practices from friends and acquaintances who had already made the journey and gone through the process.

A final area of comparison in the narratives is in relation to feelings about and relationships to Canada and countries of origin. The queer migration to liberation nation narrative usually ends with the SOGI refugee claimants making an emotional statement relating to their feelings of freedom, relief, happiness and desire to make Canada their new home (this is especially the case in media coverage of refugee claimants who are facing deportation because of negative decisions). The narrative thus ends with an emotional turn that reinscribes Ahmed's trope of 'the happy migrant', in which the viewer or reader witnesses the migrant other's desire to be given the 'gift' of Canadian citizenship via the granting of refugee protection. In the final moments of this narrative, there is rarely any reference to the SOGI refugee claimants' feelings about their country of origin and/or family or friends there. The implication is that they are starting anew, being reborn into the liberatory democratic nation-state where they will be model citizens, thus reinscribing a colonial, homonational script in which a particular configuration of a grateful 'out' and 'proud' sexual or gendered identity is now held aloft as an example of the exemplary immigrant accepted into the Canadian nation-state. I will return to these depictions of sexual and gendered identities in relation to old and new 'home' nations in more detail in Chapter 7, but suffice to say at this point that these depictions of home/lands and their attitudes towards sexual and gender minorities in the queer migration to liberation nation narrative contain assumptions about sexual or gendered identity development that reflect beliefs and values of mainstream Euro-American sexuality and gender discourses.[19]

In our conversations, some participants would make statements about their feelings for Canada and their country of origin that resonated strongly with the queer migration to liberation nation narrative, which may have been due in part to my presence as a white North American gay identified cis-male academic asking questions that the interviewees might imagine to be similar to those that are asked by the IRB adjudicator at their hearings, and in part to their knowledge that replicating the homonational narrative is an important component of the model refugee identity circulated in media and stories about successful refugee claim hearings. Odu and Janine were quite explicit in articulating feelings of gratefulness and relief to be in Canada where they felt safe and free when I asked them what they thought about life in Toronto. However, different perspectives emerged at other moments of the conversation or in relation to different topics. For example, as Janine talked about her one-month incarceration at the Milton detention centre, she mentioned how she had met other women who were in the process of being deported who gave her good advice when she became frustrated at how slowly her case was being handled.[20] Through her own experience and through listening to her fellow inmates' stories, Janine said, 'I learned a lot about how the system works, and how unfair it is'. Thus while participants might articulate genuinely sentimental feelings towards the nation of Canada in some contexts (noting that these feelings may be articulated in relation to the interview context), they were also learning that xenophobia, homophobia and racism were components of life in Canada, but were topics to be elided when speaking as a refugee to someone who may be associated with the refugee apparatus.

CONCLUSION

In this chapter I have analysed four migrant narratives that complicate the homonational 'queer migration to liberation nation' narrative found in most mainstream media representations of LGBT/SOGI refugees and in the refugee determination process itself. Through these individual narratives, I have tried to challenge reductionist, essentialized definitions and descriptions of migrant sexual and gendered desires, identities and communities and relationships to Canada and 'countries of origin' found in the SOGI refugee queer migration to liberation nation narrative. The diverse movements, motivations and (dis)identifications found in these individual narratives queer any singular essentialist definition or representation of the LGBT/SOGI refugee, and, more generally, challenge attempts to theorize cultures of migration in terms of singular push/pull factors, and straightforward chronologies of movement, processes of adaptation or integration. They support Ahmed et al.'s important point that processes of homing and migration cannot be adequately theorized outside spatialized relations of power in which unequal differences of race, class, gender and sexuality (amongst other factors) are generated (2003: 5–6).

However, I have also drawn attention to certain comments and opinions found in these conversations that reinscribe certain features of the homonational LGBT/SOGI refugee narrative, which may be due to a number of factors, one being the identity of the interviewer and the power dynamics inherent in the interview and/or ethnographic encounter. Keeping in mind the effects of power dynamics within the interview and ethnographic encounter reminds us that all narratives are stories told and received in highly mediated ways, which in turn reminds us of the limits of the narrative as a research method and form of knowledge. Anthropologist Cheryl Mattingly argues that narrative is a 'practice of reading minds', meaning that we must think of narratives as interpretive strategies, paying special attention to the motives, beliefs, and motions of actors and interlocutors. Narrative mind reading is 'part and parcel of the most ordinary sense making, and it is both culturally shaped and critical to the production of cultural knowledge' (2008: 136–39). Researchers engaged in cross-cultural analysis in highly charged border-zones like the refugee apparatus, where multiple forms of difference are encountered and negotiated, must recognise the limits of and potential misreadings inherent in the work of translating and interpreting any narrative, a point that feminist and queer scholars have also emphasized in their reflexive engagement with personal narratives.

Narratives are situated at the intersection of human agency and social structure, simultaneously revealing agency or subjectivity and the ways in which larger socio-political forces such as patriarchy, heteronormativity, racism, and political and economic systems constrain individual lives (Annes and Redlin 2012; Personal Narratives Group 1989). For sexual minority and gendered identity refugees who are immersed in the Canadian refugee apparatus and its complex legal, bureaucratic and socio-political processes, learning how to speak and behave in ways that fit the character of the LGBT refugee in the queer migration to liberation nation narrative may be perceived as a key strategy to a successful refugee claim and to moving out of a position of extreme vulnerability vis-à-vis precarious citizenship status through gaining permanent residency (Decena et al. 2006).

Diverse personal, social and political forces operating at different scales are part and parcel of the narrative process itself, yet they should not prevent researchers from working with queer narrators to develop and circulate their own narratives that challenge the silences, simplifications and symbolic legal and political violence rendered through the dissemination of powerful hetero- and homo-normative discourses that reduce the socio-political vitality of queer lives into passive subjects upholding the gate-keeping regimes of twenty-first century late-liberal democratic nation-states.

NOTES

1. The title of the film is a slight tweaking of a line from the Canadian national anthem, 'God keep our land, glorious and free.'

2. http://www.cbc.ca/documentaries/glorious.html (accessed 3 March 2013); when this chapter was being reviewed in January 2015, the web-page was no longer accessible. For a similar summary see http://www2.omnitv.ca/programming/lang_docs_details.php?id=42 (accessed 20 April 2015).

3. http://www.cbc.ca/news/politics/jason-kenney-s-mass-email-to-gay-and-lesbian-canadians-1.1207144 'Jason Kenney's mass email to gay and lesbian Canadians', 25 September 2012 (accessed 5 March 2013).

4. A big part of being surprised had to do with the question of how the minister's office obtained the email addresses of thousands of 'lesbian and gay' Canadians.

5. http://www.cbc.ca/documentaries/glorious.html (accessed 3 March 2013).

6 Excerpts from 'Last Chance' (Entrecote 2012). For a more detailed analysis of Canadian media coverage of sexual minority refugees, see Jenicek, Wong and Ou Jin Lee (2009).

7. The effects of this narrative in SOGI refugee hearings will be examined in greater detail in Chapters 5 and 6.

8. See Decena (2011) for a similar argument about Dominican immigrant men.

9. See, for example, Cohen and Sirkeci (2011).

10. See Grewal (2005) and Razack (1998) for similar arguments on gender persecution as deployed in refugee discourse.

11. See Cvetkovich (2003: 210) for a detailed discussion on the limitations of interviewing as a research method.

12. Interviewees were provided with transcripts of formal interviews and informal conversations for review and approval. Many identifying details have been changed in order to ensure anonymity of participants. Odu is a composite character built out of interviews with two participants with similar backgrounds and experiences.

13. Joe requested that I should not identify his country of origin.

14. For more information on this topic, see Murray (2012).

15. This was the case for a young man from St. Lucia, and an older self-identified bisexual man from Grenada.

16. For a more detailed overview of Canadian refugee law and SOGI/LGBT refugee cases, see Berg and Millbank (2009), LaViolette (2009), Rehaag (2008) and Millbank (2009a, b).

17. I will examine in more detail the challenges and problems arising from the non-reflective use of this terminology in Chapter 5.

18. Once again, there were exceptions to this general pattern.

19. See Grewal (2005) and White (2013) for similar discussions of gendered and/ or sexual conformity, victimhood and gratitude in the narratives of gender persecution refugee claimants and same-sex family class migrants, respectively.

20. It took three hearings before a judge before she was declared 'trustworthy' and released from the detention centre on bail (provided by family members who live in Toronto).

Chapter 2

Becoming an 'Authentic' SOGI Refugee

At a support group meeting in a Toronto LGBT community centre for SOGI refugees who had received a positive decision from the IRB and were in the process of applying for permanent residency (the next step to obtaining Canadian citizenship), the conversation focused on what the members had liked and disliked about the weekly SOGI refugee *claimant* support group (i.e., another support group for persons who were in the process of applying for refugee status, and waiting for their hearing) they had previously belonged to. Most of the conversation focused on positive aspects of the group – how it was a 'home away from home' providing emotional support and important information for SOGI people going through the refugee claim process and adapting to a new life in Canada. However, towards the end, one member, Terry, started to talk about how things had changed since she first started attending the meetings about ten months before. She noted that the weekly meetings used to have only forty to fifty people attending but recently the number had grown to almost 200. Terry now felt unsafe at the meetings because she had been 'hit on' by some of the men there and she saw some people from her own country who she didn't think were gay or lesbian. For example, a few weeks before, she had seen a woman in the meeting and then later outside, she saw a guy feeling the woman up. 'I know she's claiming refugee status as a lesbian and it pisses me off.' Terry wished there was some way to find out who the 'fakers' were and get them out: 'They're using our tactics and they're making it harder for people like us.' She was worried about her friends who were suffering back in her country of origin and planning to come to Canada, but in her opinion the system was getting so 'corrupt' that it would be increasingly difficult for them, as the fakers were making adjudicators more suspicious of claims based on sexual orientation and gendered identity persecution. Others in the group murmured their agreement and one person added how the refugee claimant support group was now 'alienating and unfriendly ... [with] 99 per cent new faces, it feels totally straight'. The facilitator responded that their concerns were duly noted and would be addressed by the group's administrators.

Perhaps not so coincidentally, this conversation about fake refugees in an SOGI refugee claimant support group contained themes similar to the comments made by the Canadian government in its introduction to Bill C-31 in 2011, the aim of which was to 'reform' and fundamentally change certain components of the refugee apparatus in Canada by speeding up the claim process, introducing mandatory detention and denying appeal procedures for certain categories of refugees (The Bill passed in the House of Parliament in June 2012 and was implemented in December 2012; see Conclusion for further discussion.) Jason Kenney, then Minister of citizenship and immigration, and his Conservative Party majority government claimed that the reforms were in part motivated by the fact that the 'system is clogged with false applications' (Smith 2012) and the refugee backlog is due in part to 'fraudulent claims' (Ling 2012).

In this chapter, I argue that the talk of 'false, fake and fraudulent' versus 'true, authentic and genuine' SOGI refugees is another hegemonic narrative that pervades different levels of popular discourse and networks of the Canadian refugee apparatus (Mountz 2010). The 'true vs false' refugee dichotomy is premised in part on the fact that the refugee determination process is a quasi-legal juridical structure in which most cases are predicated upon the credibility of the claimant, along with documentary evidence of the claimant's country (Showler 2006).[1] In other words, a process focused on the determination of the 'credibility' of a refugee claim is premised upon the assumption that truth can be deduced through analysis of factual evidence, which consists of, in most refugee cases, primarily oral narratives and written documents. The objective of evaluating credible evidence is to determine if the claimant fits the definition of a refugee outlined in the Canadian Immigration and Refugee Protection Act (IRPA), much of which is based on the United Nations Convention and Protocol Relating to the Status of Refugees. However, individuals who are claiming protection as a refugee on the basis of sexual orientation and/or gendered identity persecution face the daunting double challenge of proving that their sexual orientation or gendered identity is 'credible' (that is, they are who they say they are) and that they have been persecuted based on their membership in this particular social category. This challenge led more than one claimant to ask at the peer support group meetings, 'How do I prove that I'm gay/lesbian/bisexual[2] and that I have been persecuted?'

If we examine refugees' struggle to learn how to answer this question and the attendant pervasive state surveillance around real versus fake SOGI refugees, then we can better understand the struggle between diverse historical and socio-cultural sexual and gendered practices, desires and identities and homonational narratives in the refugee determination process. As we examine this struggle, deeply embedded in the gate-keeping mechanisms of the nation-state, we see once again how a particular narrative of sexual and gender identity and experience premised upon a particular arrangement of sexual, gendered, raced and classed experiences and histories emerges as hegemonic or normative, thus producing a template of the 'real' or 'authentic' SOGI refugee. As I argue throughout this book, a highly delimited SOGI identity has become an additional feature of hegemonic Canadian national identity discourse that is already raced, gendered and classed, and serves to undergird and enforce the privileged position of the neo-liberal Canadian nation-state's political, moral and economic power on the transnational stage. That is, the 'authentic' SOGI refugee is now valorized in Canadian nationalist discourses as a key figure upholding its civil, democratic and progressive values. She is the 'victim' who has arrived in a nation where sexual diversity is (selectively) held aloft as a feature of a 'civilized' society, opposed to her country of origin's 'uncivilized' nature, characterized by its rampant homophobia. Examining the category of the (in)authentic SOGI refugee in different domains of refugee support networks and in conversations among refugee claimants reveals the discursive power of homonationalist formations and the ways in which they work to include few and exclude many, thus further enforcing a neo-liberal multicultural national agenda that masks the centrality of race, gender, class and other intersecting structures of inequality (Eng 2010: 9). The folding in of a specific formation of an 'authentic' SOGI identity into the asylum and immigration system reinforces 'the invidious distinctions made between migrants in migration policies, which are based on North-South relations, their class position, race/ethnicity, gender or other marker of differences including disability and sexual orientation' (Bakan and Stasiulis 2003: 12). This results in the granting of citizenship to preferred subjects bearing particular valorized documented, performed and/or aesthetic combinations of race, gender, class and sexuality.

More generally, I argue that learning about the relationship between one's own sexual and gendered desires and more widely circulating socio-sexual and gender identity terminologies and discourses is a never-ending process for everyone because of the multiple changing political, cultural and economic forces that continuously impact, undergird and transform those terminologies and their meanings. However, for the SOGI refugee, this process of learning is intensified through migration into a hyper-visible moment of state scrutiny. The process of becoming an authentic LGBT refugee reminds me of Povinelli's observations on multicultural domination of indigenous subjects in Australia, which forces subaltern/minority subjects to identify with the impossible object of an authentic self-identity (2002).

In the following sections, I provide examples of how SOGI refugee claimants learn to tell their stories and of 'real vs. fake' refugee talk among refugee claimants and their support workers in various contexts – support group meetings, interviews and informal conversations – that together elucidate the centrality of homonationalism as an underlying precept of the Canadian refugee apparatus and Canadian neo-liberal multiculturalist discourses, which privilege particular intersections of sexual, raced, classed and gendered belonging while simultaneously occluding ongoing practices of racism, sexism, class exploitation and border securitization (Eng 2010; Mountz 2010; Thobani 2007).

LEARNING TO BE LGBT

There are multiple moments or spaces in the life of SOGI refugees in which they may voluntarily or involuntarily learn about, confront, reflect on, and/ or claim a particular socio-sexual and gender identity: First, in their country of origin, as children and young adults, they may learn about 'queerness' in a local context, that is, how sexual and gender diversity is viewed, evaluated, rewarded or penalized by their family, community, city and/or country. For those who grow up in urban areas, or who have access to communication technologies that provide access to 'foreign content' (such as international films, videos and the Internet), or for those who live in areas where people from 'outside' nations/cultures come to visit, work or live, there is often a second space or moment of learning, in which they read about, encounter or see images of 'others' who engage in similar sexual and gender activities or performances, but who look, sound and behave differently and/or utilize terminologies that make different associations between gender and sexual practices and identity formations. A third moment/space of learning for SOGI refugees may begin just after they arrive at Pearson airport or enter the offices of Citizenship and Immigration Canada in suburban Toronto and submit their application for refugee status. From this moment on, the individual must learn about becoming an authentic LGBT refugee as noted above. This is perhaps the most hyper-visible, self-conscious and deliberative period because of the refugee's tenuous position in an apparatus in which the state now scrutinises their past sexual and gendered behaviour in order to assess whether that behaviour fits a particular definition of sexual orientation and/or gender identity, and if so, whether that sexual orientation and/or gender identity is subject to persecution in the individual's country of origin. A fourth moment/ space of learning often occurs simultaneously alongside the third; this is the process of learning about how sexual diversity and gender identities are organized, named and located in the refugee claimant's new surroundings (in this case, metropolitan Toronto). This learning occurs in refugee support group meetings, and in interactions with lawyers and other groups associated with the refugee settlement process, but it also occurs through everyday experiences on public transit, while shopping, in jobs, in accommodations and in surrounding neighbourhoods. A fifth and final moment/space of learning may occur after a successful hearing,[3] in which the now 'official' convention refugees can begin to apply for permanent resident status in Canada, and make plans for the future, envisioning themselves as Canadian citizens without fear of deportation. The state's hyper-scrutinisation of the convention refugee's sexual orientation and/or gender identity retreats (but never completely disappears), and the individual may readjust their sexual and gender desires and practices to what they are comfortable with; for some, this may entail very little change from their pre-hearing life; for others, there may be adjustments that align with personal comfort and safety determined through past experiences, and/or which are made in relation to other factors like jobs, family, romantic relationships and community support networks.

Each of these five space/moments merits further inquiry, given the complex locations and differential intensities for anyone who goes through the refugee process; in the remainder of this chapter, I focus on the third space/ moment, which begins after the refugee claim has been submitted and ends at the hearing, in which learning to become an authentic SOGI refugee is most intense, and becoming is, in a sense, doubled or possibly trebled, as the individuals are not only learning about the organization and relationships of sexual, gendered and other identity terminologies and formations in a new society, but they are also learning how IRB members think about and assess their refugee claim, that is the credibility of their membership in a particular social group (their sexual orientation or gendered identity), and the credibility of their claims to persecution.

Almost all the participants I met in the SOGI refugee support groups were in the pre-hearing stage of the process; that is, they had arrived in Canada, submitted their refugee claim upon arrival at a border crossing or airport, or after arrival at a CIC office, and were now waiting for their hearing, where they would be cross-examined by a Board member based on the evidence contained in the refugee claim application.[4] Up until December 2012, this could be a long wait, taking anywhere from eight to twenty-four months.[5] During this initial waiting period, refugee claimants were often quite busy, dealing with various levels of local, provincial and federal bureaucracies: this included obtaining documentation pertaining to the refugee claim (see Chapters 4 and 5), applying for legal aid, visiting law offices, taking medical exams, applying for a work permit, applying for a temporary Social Insurance Number (from the federal government, which was required by employers in order to be able to hire a worker) and then trying to find a job, while also

applying for social assistance (Ontario Works). Furthermore, many interviewees were highly mobile, searching for permanent and/or safe accommodation – some were staying with family, some were in shelters and some
were sharing apartments with room-mates who they were not 'out' to and/or
did not feel safe with.

Most interviewees were told by lawyers, support group facilitators and/or
fellow refugee claimants that while they were waiting for their hearing and
applying for work permits and social insurance numbers, they should also
start attending SOGI refugee claimant support groups and volunteering with
local LGBT, HIV/AIDS and other community organizations as these organizations would then be able to write letters confirming their membership and/
or volunteer contributions, which could then be submitted to the IRB as part
of the documentation that would help demonstrate their credibility as participating and engaged members of the LGBT community.[6]

Most of the interviewees spoke about the vital importance of attending
meetings of the SOGI refugee support groups – for many, this was the first
time they had been in a safe space with 'people like me' (Odu), where they
could talk with each other, find out information about what was expected at
hearings, learn how other lawyers were treating their clients and find out what
jobs other refugees were obtaining, along with other issues pertaining to the
refugee determination process and settlement.

LEARNING THE LETTERS

At one of the weekly meetings of the support group, two members of a
Toronto HIV/AIDS organization were making a presentation on stigma,
discrimination and oppression. The presentation began with a PowerPoint
slide displaying the acronym 'LGBTTIQQ2SA', and one of the presenters
asked the group to name, and then define each of the words derived from this
acronym. The first few letters were easily answered, with people in the group
calling out 'Lesbian', 'Gay' and 'Bisexual', but then things got a bit murkier.
Fewer people were able to name both 'T's (transgender and transsexual), and
only one person from among the approximately 140 group members identified what 'I' stood for (Intersex). 'Queer' was named by a few, but 'Questioning' was unknown to all (including me). '2S' (two spirits) was recognized by
a few, but 'A' (Allies) appeared to be another new label for most people in
this group. Following this exercise, one of the presenters handed out sheets
of paper with the question, 'When I hear (blank space) I know I am being
discriminated as a LGBTTIQQ2SA' and asked them to fill in the blank space.
He then asked people to say what they had written so that he could create a list
on a whiteboard at the front of the room, and the group quickly came up with

a long list of mostly derogatory terms for homosexuals in different societies: chichiman, battyman, fish (Jamaica), pede (Cameroon), makoume, zame, and sewer rat (St. Lucia), koni (Afghanistan), shoga and moffee (Kenya and Nigeria), kuchu (Uganda), sodomite (Nigeria). The group was more animated during this portion of the meeting, and as some words were named, there was laughter and giggling from other group members who were presumably from the same country or language area. The list got longer and longer, and the group became increasingly animated until the presenter had to ask some people to stop laughing as these terms could be hurtful to others in this group.

These two adjoining moments at the meeting, one of relative silence and another of boisterous noise, encapsulated, for me, some of the complexities of the process of becoming an authentic SOGI refugee in Canada. As I noted in the previous chapter, few SOGI refugee claimants arrive in Canada thinking of themselves as 'refugees', and some do not think of themselves as members of a particular sexual minority or gender identity group or may not recognize or identify with sexual minority and gender identity terms as they are defined and organized in Canada. However, in the period leading up to their IRB hearing, the SOGI refugee claimants must learn relatively quickly how to 'be' or at least 'occupy' one of these LGBT identity categories authentically, as their hearings are dedicated to assessing the credibility of their claims to be members of a particular social group, who have faced persecution in their country of origin. They are reminded repeatedly by their lawyers, peer support group leaders and one another that there are a number of components, characteristics and assumptions utilised by IRB members to determine the credibility of an SOGI refugee claim, and that if they learn and understand these assumptions and characteristics associated with 'LGBT' identities, and integrate them into an appropriate narrative of identity formation and persecution based on that identity, then they stand a better chance of a successful hearing. Thus we might think of all refugee claimants as incommensurate or potentialities until their hearing, a test of actualization, commensurability (Povinelli 2001) and authenticity, in which some do well, and some do not.

LEARNING THE PROCESS

At the refugee support group meetings, immigration and refugee lawyers were sometimes invited by the facilitator to speak to the group about the refugee process in Canada, preparing for the hearing, and obtaining and working with legal counsel. The visiting lawyers often received undivided attention from everyone in the group, as opposed to other presentations that focused on how Canadian banks operate or finding accommodation, where I could see quite a few people texting on their cell-phones, or quietly whispering to each other.

Of the four lawyers that I heard speaking to the group over a twelve-month period, each had a significantly different presentation style, with some using anecdotes from hearings they had attended to get across their point, and others using PowerPoint presentations that contained United Nations Convention and Protocol Relating to the Status of Refugees definitions and concise lists of what to do and not to do in preparation for a hearing. One lawyer who spoke to the group combined PowerPoint slides and a presentation style that a couple of group members noted afterwards was similar to that of a drill sergeant addressing his troops. The lawyer began by providing the group with a timeline of the refugee claim process, and spent a fair amount of time focusing on the Personal Information Form (PIF), which all claimants must fill out and submit to the IRB within twenty-eight days of making their claim.[7] The most important part of the PIF, she said, is the narrative, 'which is where you tell your story', but she then recommended getting a lawyer, 'to help make sure it's your own voice'. She then provided some insight on the purpose of the PIF and some strategies on how to write it: 'When the Board Member gets the story, they want to relate the story to the person; the PIF must be in your own voice, it doesn't matter if there are grammatical errors. ... If the story sounds too much like a PhD and you only have a grade 5 education, that creates doubt.' Furthermore, she went on, the PIF must be synchronized with all the other documents that are submitted – letters from family, lovers and friends; hospital and police records; school transcripts, etc. She then advised, 'to take out things that will negatively impact you; if someone who doesn't really know you writes a letter or says something that's not right, take it out'. She continued,

> From the day you put in your PIF, your PIF is your bible, like a book you keep close to you; you read it every day; your life depends on it. If you ignore it you could lose your life. ... Read read read read read your narrative. Put yourself in the mind of the judge: How would you make him believe you? What do I need to show that I have a same sex partner or friend? If I was punched and kicked and then ran to a friend's house, what is my friend's name? What time of day did this happen? What's the distance between the houses? You have to pre-empt the judge.

The lawyer also commented on the importance of refugee claimants knowing legal definitions:

> You should know the legal definition of a 'Convention Refugee': You must demonstrate that you cannot return to your country of origin; that there is serious risk to your life, based on membership of a particular social group – sexual orientation, race, religion, nationality, political opinion, all qualify as membership categories. ... Canada can't save everybody, you can't come claiming that everyone is poor back in Burundi and it's hard to get a job.

The personal narrative component of the PIF generated a lot of discussion among refugee claimants. Whether they learned about its importance from their lawyers, from one another, or from reading guidelines on the IRB website, the personal narrative was recognized as the central item around which their claim would be built and assessed by the Board member. Even though claimants were told by the lawyer that the PIF 'is where you tell your story', the lawyer immediately followed this statement by recommending that they get a lawyer *'to help* them tell their story', but didn't elaborate at that moment as to why they would need help in telling their own story or what kind of 'help' would be needed. However, through encounters like this, claimants learned that the personal narrative was not simply a matter of telling their 'life story' as they saw fit – there was a particular structure or framework for this narrative, and it had to include important features or components that addressed the jurisprudential objective of determining credibility of a refugee claim. In other words, the personal narrative becomes an 'evidentiary' document: evidence is given by the claimant about his or her claim through this narrative, and that evidence is evaluated in relation to other documents and the testimony of the claimant at the hearing (see Chapter 5). So even though the lawyer told the group that the PIF must be 'in your own voice', she went on to provide some specific examples of what that voice should comment on or include, i.e. a friend's name, the distance between the house you were punched in and your friend's house that you ran to, the time of the day at which the violent event took place etc. These are elements of a very particular kind of storytelling, one that fits the parameters of a courtroom in which facts are elicited and tested in order to determine the truth or falseness of a defendant's claim. In other words, the personal narrative is located within and structured by the formulism and formalism of Western juridical concepts and processes (Johnson 2011: 62).

Not surprisingly, listening to presentations such as that of the lawyer could stir up anxiety among refugee claimants. Ruth, who is in her 50s, from St. Lucia, and self-identifies as lesbian, said that the whole PIF process was nerve-wracking, because after she wrote and submitted it to her lawyer, she remembered things that had happened to her that she thought were significant. She said, 'There were things you try to forget, or your mind blocked because it didn't want to remember them, but they come back suddenly, maybe when you're being asked the (same) question again.' For example, after she submitted her PIF to her lawyer, she remembered an incident where she'd been driving her car, and as she passed a man, he yelled 'sodomite' and threw a rock at her. She remembered hearing the window glass break, and felt a bit of the glass hit her, but thought she was ok and drove on, until at a stop sign a woman in another car looked over and told her there was blood coming down the side of her face. She ended up needing two stitches for this.

But since it wasn't in her PIF, she wasn't supposed to talk about it. 'It's this kind of business that can lead to confusion,' she added.

Shawn, who is in his 20s and from Grenada, had met with his lawyer a couple of times to discuss his PIF and how he would be questioned at the hearing. In one of our interviews, he discussed these conversations with his lawyer:

> *David:* Did (your lawyer) say that the Board Member probably will ask questions like, which day were you attacked?
>
> *Shawn:* Well, the way he said, it's like, 'What happened on June the 22nd, 2010' and I'm supposed to describe what happened. So, you don't want to confuse June 2010 with June 2009.
>
> *David:* Right ... I have heard some people say that they know what happened to them, but when they're in the hearing they're nervous because everybody is looking at you, so it's sometimes hard to remember the dates. ... Do you feel like you have to rehearse it to yourself?
>
> *Shawn:* Yes, I think it reduces the anxiety of it, because I'm used to studying for exams. So, it is an exam that I have to study for.

Shawn had learned from his lawyer that his PIF would become a piece of evidence from which he would be asked questions about 'the facts' in his hearing in order to corroborate his written testimony. Shawn realized that the PIF was a particular kind of storytelling in which certain events, dates, locations and names would form the central line of questioning at the hearing, so he was now approaching it like an exam that he needed to study for. For Shawn, this was not too scary as he was a university student and said he was used to studying for tests. Shawn had also discussed the PIF and other aspects of preparing for the hearing with other refugee claimants. From these discussions, he had learned of the importance of submitting other documents to help strengthen his case, such as media coverage of homophobic events in Grenada.

> *David:* Do you get, do you share with other refugees when you find good articles or good information, about things back in Grenada, do you share that?
>
> *Shawn:* Well, Marvin (another refugee who had recently had a successful hearing) would do that, because he went through it. And he loves to do that. So, he would say, 'Shawn here's an article related to your case'. I would read it and I would say, okay this is related or no it's not related. And there are times when I would say to a friend who is going through the refugee claim, 'Here's an article on gay (issues) ... you might want to take a look at it. I'm not sure if it's related to your case, but you can take a look at it to see if it's related, yes or no.'

In this conversation, Shawn demonstrates his knowledge of the definition of a 'convention refugee' and the organization of the IRB hearing in that he knows what documentary evidence must be presented to the Board member to demonstrate that 'members of the particular social group' that he belongs to face persecution in their country of origin. Through his conversations with other refugees like Marvin who have gone through the process, he was now scanning Grenadian newspapers online and printing out any articles that dealt with 'gay issues'. Shawn felt that the more articles he could find and submit to his lawyer (who would forward them to the IRB as part of his application file), the more he would strengthen his chances of a successful hearing. In this case, Shawn knew that his personal narrative was not enough, and that additional documentary evidence was required in order to meet the criteria of being not just an LGBT-identified person but an authentic SOGI refugee.

FEAR OF FAKES

While the SOGI refugee claimant support groups were spaces in which people learned about the refugee determination process and how to present their personal narratives, they were also social spaces in which people made new friendships, flirted and sometimes started up new romantic relationships. However, a few participants made comments similar to the one at the beginning of this chapter: they were somewhat wary of these groups, as they felt there were individuals from their home nations in attendance who they 'knew' were not lesbian, gay, bisexual or transgendered and, in fact, had been homophobic towards them back home. Rumours about who is or is not a 'real' or 'genuine' SOGI refugee and ongoing anxiety over being able to demonstrate the authenticity of one's own sexual orientation were a common topic of conversation at support group meetings, discussed by both group members and facilitators. One refugee support group volunteer, who wrote letters for refugee claimants confirming their membership, attendance and participation in the support group, told me that he sometimes felt uncomfortable writing a letter for particular individuals who he didn't think were really gay. When I asked how he knew this, he said, 'Well, there was one guy from Nigeria who shook my hand so hard I thought it would fall off – plus, he said he had a wife and child back home.' The firmness of the handshake and the reference to a wife and child made him suspicious of the refugee claimant's 'true' sexual orientation. Another group leader told me there were some people attending the support group meetings who she suspected weren't gay but were coming 'just so they can get the letter confirming (their) membership (in the group)', because they had heard the organization's letter had become the gold standard among IRB members when determining sexual orientation credibility. Another group facilitator told me that Board members were becoming more suspicious of the Nigerian gay and bisexual claimants because so many of them had exactly the same story: a family member threatened to beat/kill/ ostracize the claimant when the former found out that the latter had had sexual relationships with men, forcing the claimant to leave immediately without any plan, funds or identification documents. The facilitator claimed that some Board members believed these Nigerian claimants were being trained, either by an 'agent' back in Nigeria, a lawyer in Toronto and/or by communicating with one another about 'what works', in order to get a successful decision.

It should not be all that surprising to find this genuine/authentic vs. fake/ bogus refugee discourse in various nodes of the refugee apparatus, which is built upon a series of legal and legislative policies that presuppose clear-cut definitions and processes to determine who does and who does not qualify as a refugee. As Hall notes, legislative developments within asylum and immigration systems are underpinned by moral distinctions between the 'undeserving' asylum seeker and the 'deserving', genuine refugee (2012: 104). If refugee claimants do not present their story in the right order with the necessary components, if they present a story that contains too many components that are similar to the narratives of other SOGI claimants, or if they don't comport themselves in a way that conforms with a support group volunteer's (or another refugee's or adjudicator's) preconceptions of 'authentic SOGI' narratives, bodily comportment or talk, then they run the risk of being labelled inauthentic or fake.[8] The persistent surveillance of authenticity at all levels of the refugee apparatus illustrates its centrality as a gate-keeping mechanism for the nation-state. Thus, while the Canadian government claims to enact policies and procedures ensuring protection of persecuted individuals and groups, 'authenticity' operates as a selective value throughout the determination process, ensuring the exclusion of those who do not fit the particular, highly delimited categories of 'deserving' convention refugees.

As I argue throughout this book, demonstrating 'authentic' sexual orientation or gender identity in the refugee determination process becomes deeply entangled with socio-sexual terms that carry particular socio-cultural meanings and histories (which are, themselves, in constant flux); yet, particular interpretations of these terms circulate in privileged positions within refugee discourses, policies and events. Thus, for example, an Afro-Caribbean woman from a rural, impoverished community in St. Lucia who has had sexual relations with women and men may not identify or feel comfortable with socio-sexual identity terms like 'lesbian' or 'bisexual' used by lawyers, support group workers and IRB members, as these terms are freighted with particular Euro-American racial, gendered and class qualities and/or circulate with different meanings in St. Lucia. However, if she does not produce adequate documentation to support her personal narrative, answer questions or perform in ways that reproduce the Board member's understanding of particular sexual orientation identities such as 'lesbian' or 'bisexual', then she risks failing to be 'credibly' bisexual or lesbian. Thus, in addition to Cantú's observation that the asylum process requires queer applicants to attribute their persecution to a reified version of their country of origin's national culture that is cast in racialized, colonialist terms (2009: 55–73), I am arguing that the credibility of SOGI refugee claimants is also evaluated through processes and questions that impose a prism of assumed understandings of 'real' or authentic gay, lesbian, bisexual or transgendered identities that reflect primarily white, middle-class experiences and beliefs about those sexual and gendered identities; these experiences assume a universal sameness of LGBT identities, and produce predetermined assumptions about what a handshake should feel like, how one should act in SOGI support group settings or how a narrative of SOGI persecution should be constructed (or conversely, when such a narrative becomes suspiciously repetitious).

Berg and Millbank (2009) discuss how refugee adjudicators often apply these assumed universal understandings of sexual identity based on a staged model of sexual identity development that operates with particular assumptions about sexual identity as fixed, discoverable and moving from a position of closeted to 'coming out', in which the hearing serves as the apotheosis to this narrative (207–15).[9] While Berg and Millbank point out the numerous and profound problems inherent in applying a staged model of sexual development to adjudicate SOGI refugee narratives, I think it is important to note that many of the refugee claimants with whom I worked were not naïve about this model and other components of the adjudicating process. They spent a great deal of time and energy learning about the structure and process of the hearing and what was necessary to ensure that they would appear as credible and authentic, both in their file and at the hearing. In other words, the refugee claimants were actively engaged with the system in which they had been placed and exercised agency in their efforts to meet or fit into these racialized, gendered and classed standards of evaluation (albeit to greater or lesser degrees of success depending on the individual claimant) presupposed upon universal sexual and gender categories. As they learned about the refugee apparatus in Canada in support groups and in conversations with lawyers and one another, they also learned about the terminologies and criteria utilized to determine credibility, which would be used to critically evaluate refugee claims.

'Real vs. fake' refugee questions take on additional freight when they are applied to racialized bodies, which applies to most of the refugee claimants I interviewed, as they were from Caribbean or African nation-states and, upon arriving in Toronto, came to be identified as a 'visible minority' in addition to being a 'sexual minority'. As numerous scholars have noted, the 'black' body is always/already doubted or debated in North American mainstream, white, LGBT discourses based on assumptions about 'down low' (hidden

homosexual) practices and 'macho' black masculinities that are problem-
atically classified as homophobic (Ferguson 2004; Johnson and Henderson
2005; Manalansan 2009). Doubt or disbelief is augmented when racialized
queer bodies are also refugee bodies. These 'foreigners' are perceived to be
seeking state protection (and eventually citizenship) based on their claim to
being persecuted on the basis of (perceived) sexual orientation, practices and/
or gender identity and practices. However, their claims are judged, evaluated
and scrutinized according to normative white, middle class, LGBT identity
scripts in everyday settings as well as every step of the way through the
refugee process – from the Canadian Border Services Agency officers at the
airport, to support group volunteers, to some fellow refugee claimants and,
finally, to IRB members. Some of this suspicion may be generated through
cross-cultural *mis*translations (which are often linked to racialized stereotypes), but I would argue that suspicion is more profoundly generated through
the racialized, gendered and classed hierarchies and normativities that undergird the networks of the refugee apparatus itself.

All SOGI refugee claimants are negotiating proscribed identity narratives
before, during and after their hearings and struggle to make hidden, invisible and/or highly personal aspects of the self legible according to the terms
and rules of refugee apparatus (this includes interactions with adjudicators,
support workers, volunteers and other refugees). These terms and rules are
premised upon the exclusionary process of determining an authentic refugee,
resulting in the need to constantly search for and condemn the fake refugee
as much as save the authentic one. When differential understandings of self,
desire and identity come into contact with a refugee determination process
premised upon specific formations of socio-sexual identity reflecting Euro-
American white, middle-class cis-gender subjectivities, the potential for
misinterpretation and, in turn, accusations of 'false identity' are all the more
likely.

HOMONATIONALISM AND THE REAL SOGI REFUGEE

Homonationalism is a discourse that requires and augments authentic vs.
fake SOGI refugee formations, as witnessed in some refugee claimants' comments and support group conversations: Odu, whom we met in the previous
chapter, told me that walking around the streets during Toronto Pride festivities made him realize that 'Canada was the place for me, for here I can be
myself'. He said he could never go back to Nigeria and 'go back into hiding'
after experiencing this event. At a refugee support group meeting, held a few
months after the Pride festivities, the theme of the evening was 'learning
about Canada'. The facilitator presented a number of PowerPoint slides with

information or questions pertaining to Canadian political organizations, laws and social customs. One of the PowerPoint slides contained the following quote: 'Canada is known to have the best living conditions, the most money, the lowest poverty in the world and is considered the most civilized country in the world.' The facilitator asked the group what they thought about this statement. A number of people shouted out that they agreed, but others said it was not true. The facilitator responded with, 'How many countries can you go to apply for refugee status and get social assistance and legal aid? Not the USA for sure, you get nothing, not even legal aid. ... Holland's a little better but you have to wait five years to get status and you must learn their language and get a job.' One person then raised a hand to ask, 'If you don't believe this statement, then what are you doing here?'

Odu's sentiments and the opinions expressed at the support group meeting might be labelled 'inaugural homonationalism' based on the claimants' recent arrival into Canada and their initial experience of the stark contrasts between life in their country of origin and the celebratory atmosphere of Pride festivities, which could be interpreted to represent Canadian national attitudes towards diverse sexualities (a message that is often conveyed through Pride festival publicity and advertising). These comments about the freedom and opportunities in Canada resonate with homonationalist discourses found in Canadian mainstream media discussing SOGI refugees, rights and activism outlined in the previous chapter. As Jenicek, Wong and Ou-Jin Lee observe in their analysis of Canadian media coverage of sexual minority refugees, 'SOGI refugees now constitute another group of "mediating agents," deployed by the mainstream press to maintain numerous imperialist binaries, with the acceptance of sexual minorities offering a fresh example of the West's progressiveness and cultural superiority' (2009: 637).

Based on the above comments, it appears that, for some refugee claimants, their initial experiences in Toronto 'fit' the homonationalist narrative of Canada as a nation that embraces LGBT people, supports LGBT rights and is representative of a progressive liberal democratic nation-state. However, as noted in the previous chapter, it is important to keep in mind the social and political context in which these inaugural homonationalist claims were made. For example, in interviews, participants may have associated the interviewer (a gay-identified, middle-aged white male affiliated with a university) to be in a similar position of authority and power to that of an IRB adjudicator and/or that it was important for their story and opinions to be presented consistently in any pre-hearing context and to fit the authentic SOGI refugee character that is part of the queer liberation to migration nation narrative. Part of this narrative of authenticity includes a requisite statement of gratitude towards the host nation for 'rescuing' the refugees from persecution and 'allowing' them to be free as an 'out' LGBT-identified member of society.

A similar dynamic may have been operating in refugee support group meetings, where members attended not only to obtain information about the refugee process and life in Toronto but also to obtain a letter from the group facilitator confirming their membership in the group. This letter would then be submitted to the IRB as part of a package of documents attesting to the claimant's credibility as an SOGI-identified person. Supporting homonationalist statements like 'Canada … is considered the most civilized country in the world' might be a strategic move to ensure one is viewed as an authentic SOGI refugee deserving a strong letter of support (see Chapter 4), as it aligns the speaker with the 'progessive, open and liberated' sexual identity they are assumed to be seeking in their migration to Canada.

However, in subsequent conversations with some of the participants, inaugural homonationalist declarations were sometimes replaced with questions and critiques based on encounters that took some of the sheen off the 'promised land' veneer. For example, Odu told me how he was taking a taxi from Union Station (the central train station in Toronto) to the 519 Community Centre on Church Street and, as they drove up Church Street, the taxi driver, who was 'a Pakistani guy', according to Odu, said that he didn't like this area. When Odu asked him why not, he appeared uncomfortable and, when Odu asked him to stop in front of the 519 building, Odu said he became really uncomfortable. It was, for Odu, a moment when he realized that not everyone here likes 'gays' and that he might have to exercise caution about what he says to whom in Canada, although he was aware that here he could, in theory, go to the police if he was harassed or assaulted because of his sexual orientation and that was very different from back home.

Another interviewee, Rene, who was from a small Caribbean nation, spoke about how much he loved the fact that he could dress up as he liked in Canada, which meant going out in drag in public. However, after a few months, he reported that he had been stopped by the police three times, questioned aggressively as to what he was doing on the street and told not to think about doing 'business' around there. Rene was incensed, as he was not a sex worker and wasn't bothering anyone. He was quickly discovering that he was being racially and transphobically stereotyped by the police. Even though he had been told he could trust the police here more than back in his country, he said he was no longer sure if this was true.

Rene's and Odu's experiences with homophobic taxi-cab drivers and racist and transphobic police officers complicate the authentic SOGI refugee's inaugural homonationalist statements. Their increasingly complicated relationship with Canadian society is similar to the ways in which Canada was positioned in the queer migration narratives outlined in the previous chapter. These migrants' complex relationships to their new 'home' nation are similar to White's (2013) findings with LGBTQ migrants and sponsors who have secured same-sex family class migration privileges. Running through the narratives of her informants is 'a latent homonational affect – a hesitant cleaving to the nation, an ambivalent attachment at best, underpinned as it is by relative precariousness and a sense of vulnerability' (White 2013: 51). As Grewal notes in her analysis of Sikh women from the Punjab who claimed refugee status in the United States, the concept of 'transforming' is a key aspect of authentic refugee discourses that involve movement into and celebration of the West (2005: 184). In moving from one nation-state to another, SOGI refugees may indeed have to transform in their narratives of subjectivity and identity, learning that to espouse homonationalist sentiment is a key component of the authentic SOGI refugee identity in the West. However, what is actually experienced may not be a simple transformative movement from repression to freedom; rather, it may be an experience whereby one kind of discourse of sexual and gendered identity may be replaced by another one, and in which new or different forms of erasure, discrimination and inequality are imposed (Grewal 2005: 184).

CONCLUSION

SOGI refugee claimants face daunting challenges negotiating an apparatus in which questions of authenticity are constructed through bodily appearances, comportment and narratives that are consistently evaluated for their fit with Western homonationalist discourses. The scrutinization, surveillance and changing modes of evaluation of the authentic SOGI refugee body throughout all spaces and moments attached to the refugee determination process create substantial challenges and anxieties for anyone placed into this process. As Razack notes, IRB members, lawyers, legislators and journalists are the describers and the imaginers whose gazes construct asylum seekers either as unworthy claimants or as supplicants begging to be saved from the tyranny of their own cultures, communities and nations (1998: 97). Sexual orientation and gender identity persecution, like gender persecution, as deployed in refugee discourse, can function as a deeply racialized, culturally essentialist concept in that they require – mostly but not always[10] – that Global South SOGI refugee claimants speak of their realities of sexual and gender violence outside and at the expense of their realities as colonized, racialized peoples (Razack 1998: 99). The inaugural homonationalist sentiments about Canada as a free and liberated space for queer people articulated by some participants reinforce a similar dynamic of the 'sexually exceptional' West (Puar 2007), enshrining 'a narrow concept of diversity defined in terms of freedom and choice ... that not incidentally chime(s) with a neoliberal free market ideology whose inherent exclusions are harder to name' (Haritaworn 2012: 3).

Yet, these inaugural homonationalist sentiments may be questioned over time, as individuals encounter homophobia, racism and other forms of discrimination in their daily lives in Toronto, resulting in ambivalent homonationalisms (White 2013) that also challenge the conceptualization of a 'real' or 'authentic' universal LGBT identity.

As Luibhéid (2008: 179) has argued, successful refugee claims often require generating a racialized, colonialist discourse that impugns the nation-state from which the asylum seeker comes, while participating in an adjudication process that often depends on constructs of an immutable identity refracted through colonialist reified models of culture shorn of all material relations. Furthermore, queer refugee claims may be taken up by mainstream Global North LGBT groups and human rights organizations in ways that perpetuate homonationalist discourses, which in turn support neo-colonial transnational relationships even as they seek to support queer refugees and condemn the homophobic nations they come from (Luibhéid 2008: 179–80). The effects of authentic SOGI refugee narratives and their homonationalist features expose the exclusionary dynamics of asylum definitions and processes and their critical role in underpinning the securitization and privilege of the neo-liberal state (Goldberg 2009). More important, when the histories of imperialism, colonialism and racism are left out of authentic refugee narratives of sexual and gender identity formation, persecution and migration, we are not able to see how these systems of domination produce and maintain violence against racialized sexual and gender minorities both within and beyond national borders.

These snippets from presentations and conversations with differentially positioned individuals in the particular space/moment of becoming authentic SOGI refugees resonate with Povinelli's observations on the effects of multicultural domination of indigenous subjects in Australia, which works by inspiring subaltern/minority subjects to identify with the impossible object of an authentic self-identity. For indigenous peoples, this is a 'traditional' form of society and subjectivity associated with an imagined past, but because they are in the present, and part of the present, they can never fully achieve this fantasy, so the multicultural nationalist is always disappointed, and the indigenous can never be really real (Povinelli 2002: 6–7). The SOGI refugee faces a similar challenge of identifying with the impossible object of an authentic LGBT self-identity. For the refugee, this is a socio-sexual and gender identity that is deeply embedded in a normative Euro-American sexual and gender identity formation, that is, a staged model of sexual and gender identity development applied to one of four sexual and gender identity categories (lesbian, gay, bisexual or transgender). The onus is on the refugee claimants, who often come from a society that does not operate with this Euro-American normative model, to prove to the Board member that their story of who they are and what happened to them (and the documents supporting this story) match this model. Furthermore, socio-sexual and gender identity must be linked to a set of assumptions and beliefs attached to the object identity of the 'authentic refugee', that is, someone who has faced 'persecution' in his or her country of origin and has been forced to flee from that country because he or she cannot obtain protection from the state. Both of these 'impossible objects' – LGBT and refugee identity – are defined by past and present state legislation and policies, international legislation (such as the UNHCR Convention and Protocol Relating to the Status of Refugees), and local, national and international refugee and LGBT rights organizations.

While it may be theoretically plausible (if not imperative) to contend that 'LGBT' and 'refugee' identities are malleable, diverse and subject to transformation because of multiple intersecting social, political and economic forces, it is not in the interest of the refugee apparatus to define or think about them in this way (perhaps it is not even possible). Thus, implicit (in the case of LGBT identities) and explicit (in the case of refugee identity) definitions and assumptions are developed and applied by the IRB, whose responsibility is to determine the credibility and authenticity of the claims of the persons before them according to a model based on Western jurisprudential paradigms of determining the truth.

From the moment they submit their refugee claim to the moment of the decision at their hearing, refugees exist in a space/moment of 'incommensurability' (Povinelli 2001), a state of affective potential, in which the paradoxical yet unknown enters upon the world of norms, in this case the state's rules and regulations defining the 'authentic' refugee, which now includes the sub-category of the authentic LGBT refugee. This space/moment of emergence or becoming authentic is key to theorizing the pivot point between incommensurability and mandated commensuration. The emergent SOGI refugee is akin to the introduction of an incommensurability into social life, the latter defined through the regulation and operation of intersecting sets of norms (Dave 2011: 651). The SOGI refugee claimants quickly learn that they are an unknown entity in the eyes of the Board member, and that they will be judged according to a pre-existing set of criteria to determine whether or not they have the state's approval (and all the rights and privileges that go with it) to be identified as a 'convention refugee'. Massumi takes 'emergence' as a bifurcation point in which multiple and normally mutually exclusive potentials coexist, but from which only one can be chosen (2002: 32–33). However, the emergence of an authentic SOGI refugee is marked by a constitutive overdetermination: despite the deeply diverse social, sexual and gender experiences of these individuals, an already existing set of socio-sexual-gender political classifications in the refugee apparatus of the destination nation-state forces closure of potential through its commensuration with existing norms.

The presentations and conversations focusing on PIFS, LGBTTIQQ2SAs, and real vs. fake refugees among refugee claimants, lawyers and support workers illustrate how 'the asylum process rests not only on law but also on the limits of humanity, of how humans treat each other, and on the very grey, often painful space between creativity and vulnerability' (McGranahan 2012: 22). Learning to be an authentic SOGI refugee is a process that involves creativity, intense learning and rapid adaptation to a new set of terms, ideas and norms about the relationship of one's sexual and gender practices and desires to the socio-political world in which they are rendered sensible. The creative and adaptive potential of the refugee claimants, along with the knowledge and skills of their lawyer and their support group facilitators, are crucial components of a successful refugee hearing. However, the stakes are high and stacked against them, as the nervous state continuously works to manage and control migration, and in particular the movement of refugees who are increasingly viewed as illegal interlopers until proved otherwise (Feldman 2012).

NOTES

1. Peter Showler is former chairperson of the Immigration and Refugee Board of Canada. I analyse documentary evidence in more detail in Chapters 4 and 6.

2. For most transgender claimants that I worked with, 'proving' their identity was not a major concern as they had already transitioned or were in the process of transitioning, which could be witnessed in person by the adjudicator (and also seen in relation to their prior gender identity as recorded in various identity documents). However, many faced significant challenges in proving that they faced persecution (as defined and interpreted by the IRB) in their country of origin.

3. For those who 'fail' their hearing, the fourth moment/space intensifies as the claimants seek other legal/bureaucratic solutions to prevent deportation, all of which involve ongoing surveillance and evaluation by state authorities.

4. All refugee claimants with whom I worked had legal counsel present at the hearing.

5. Under the Bill C-31 legislation enacted in December 2012, this waiting period has been reduced substantially.

6. Additional recommended documentation to help demonstrate sexual orientation and gender identity credibility included personal photographs of the claimant and their partner(s) or of the claimant attending LGBT events like the Pride March in Toronto or LGBT gatherings/events in their country of origin, letters from current and past romantic partners and/or letters from friends and family members attesting to the claimant's sexual orientation or gender identity.

7. This form was changed to the 'Basis of Claim (BOC)' form after the passage of the refugee reform bill, implemented in December 2012.

8. The next chapter contains a more detailed discussion of bodily and oral affects in the determination of SOGI authenticity.

9. This will be discussed in further detail in Chapter 6.

10. While not forming a substantial part of my interview set, SOGI refugee claimants from Eastern European bloc countries like Russia, Ukraine and Croatia also attended support group meetings, which complicates an argument premised on a single factor such as race. At the same time, while these individuals may be classified as 'white' in mainstream Canadian ethno-racial discourses, their 'originary' location in non-Western European nation-states may place them lower in the transnational developmental hierarchy in which Western European and North American political regimes locate themselves and their 'cultures' at the apex.

Chapter 3

How to Be Gay (Refugee Version)

'When the going gets tough, the tough reinvent.'

—RuPaul, *Workin' It!: RuPaul's Guide to Life, Liberty,*
and the Pursuit of Style (2010)

'Tell the officer all your documents are in your handbag over there, and then walk with more of a swish when you go get them.' Andrea, the play's director, wasn't happy with the actor playing Mando Bullock, a gay male refugee claimant, in a scene where Mando lodges his refugee claim in a Citizen and Immigration Canada (CIC) office in Toronto. Andrea wanted there to be some 'fun and lightness' in the scene and the actor playing Mando to be less wooden in his performance. In addition to asking him to imagine he now had a handbag and to walk with a swish, Andrea told Mando to raise his voice higher when he told another man in the waiting room that he was gay.

During the five-week rehearsal period for this short (twenty-minute) play about gay refugee experiences written and acted by a group of former SOGI refugees and performed at a holiday party for SOGI refugee claimants and their friends at a LGBTQ community centre in Toronto, numerous changes to the script, scene blocking, props and characters created debates and tensions between the participants and director, and resulted in a final performance that was quite different from the play as it was first written and acted. A few months after the play was performed, I read queer theorist David Halperin's new book, *How To Be Gay* (2012), which explores 'gayness ... as a (cultural) practice' in America, and wondered how helpful (or not) it might have been if the theater troupe and other SOGI refugees who were in the process of submitting their claims had read it. However, upon further reflection, I came to realize that Halperin's (and some other queer theorists') musings about gay culture or queer life in America were already linked to these performances, and could provide some insight into how and why the final performance looked the way it did.

In the previous chapter, I argued for acknowledging the importance and impossibility of authenticity in the pre-hearing stage of the SOGI refugee determination process, and I examined how various participants in the refugee determination process – claimants, support group facilitators, and lawyers – discuss and learn about key terminologies, qualities and features necessary to substantiate a successful claim for persecution based on membership in this particular social group. In this chapter, I continue to examine the ways in which a particular formation of sexual and gender identity comes to exist as normative in the refugee determination process through the production of a short play written and performed by former SOGI refugee claimants. However, in this chapter, I move beyond a discussion of specific events associated with the official processes of the Canadian refugee apparatus in order to examine how creative aesthetic practices of transnational refugees are intertwined in the discursive terrains of North American queer culture and the refugee apparatus, which may help to explain why this play's rehearsals resulted in an actor playing a gay refugee claimant swishing through a CIC office with his handbag. That is, I will argue that the evolution of the play's narrative and characters' aesthetics was impacted by and struggled with the politics of sexual minority refugees[1] in the Canadian refugee determination system and invoke some re-theorizing about the production of queer identity and culture.

By focusing on the rehearsals of a non-professional play about SOGI refugee experiences written and performed by former SOGI refugees, I hope to demonstrate a theoretical perspective emphasizing what I call the 'performativity of performance', which will provide analytical insight into the ways in which the play's participants (and more generally, the play of participants) are embedded in and struggle with wider political and social processes and identity discourses. I ask how it is that a particular performance of 'the gay refugee' comes to exist as representative of what is believed to be an 'authentic' SOGI refugee identity and narrative as outlined in the previous chapter. How do choices about characters' words, speech stylings, kinesics, clothing and accessories reinscribe or trouble this normativity? How are these choices (dis)connected to popular or hegemonic assemblages of sexuality, gender, 'refugee' ness and nation that circulate through various discursive networks of refugees, migrants/immigrants and LGBTQ communities, academia and the state, such that certain assemblages come to represent the good or authentic gay refugee while others come to represent the bad or fake gay refugee?

I argue that a performativity of performance perspective helps to illuminate struggles between diverse historical and socio-sexual practices, border politics and nationalist queer identity formations. As we examine performative struggles, which in the case of transnational refugees, are deeply embedded in the gate-keeping mechanisms of the nation-state, a particular narrative of sexual identity and experience emerges as hegemonic or normative, reproducing a template of the 'real' or 'authentic' sexual minority refugee outlined in the previous chapter. However, at the same time I will argue that the refugees involved in the play challenged aspects of the queer migration to liberation narrative through their debates and critiques of Mando's oral and aesthetic practices. Thus, this chapter extends and complicates my previous discussion of authenticity by demonstrating that authenticity is highly relevant for specific institutions, the employees of those institutions and various other players voluntarily associated with or involuntarily placed into these institutional processes that seek to solidify and categorize sexuality as part of the gate-keeping mechanisms associated with immigration and citizenship.

The play's rehearsals and final performance provide another lens through which to examine SOGI authenticity in the refugee determination apparatus as a highly unstable value with a tenuous relationship to 'the truth' of one's being, as Foucault would say. The debates around the authentic 'gayness' (or straightness) of its characters also reveal the instability of homonationalism's normative underpinnings, normativities that are continuously reinforced through multiple sites and discourses, including queer cultural analysis and productions. For example, while much of queer theory has challenged 'identitarian' projects and their attendant essentialisms and hierarchies of gendered, classed and raced privilege, there continue to be theorizations of gay or queer cultures, communities, styles and/or aesthetics. Two relatively recent examples include David Halperin's *How to Be Gay* (2012), and Judith Halberstam's *The Queer Art of Failure* (2011). Despite these authors' substantially different theoretical and political locations, I will argue not only that both texts work in different ways to complicate essentialist concepts of queer identity or culture by emphasizing grounded analyses of queer practice, but also that they contribute (albeit indirectly) towards understanding the production of homonormativity in the refugee apparatus.

Thus, in highlighting the development and changes made to an amateur play about SOGI refugee experiences, and how the end result conveys essentialized representations of 'gay identity' or 'queer life' that can also be found in North American queer cultural productions and the refugee apparatus, I hope to demonstrate the powerful and discursive effects of homonormativities circulating through governmental, academic and everyday locations. At the same time, I hope to also demonstrate the instability of homornormativities and their always contingent positioning through debates and dissent over the speech and conduct of the play's characters by the performers, a group of transnational queer migrants who now live in Canada as officially recognized convention refugees.

In the following section, I explain the 'performativity of performance' perspective through critical engagement with two key theorists of performativity and performance, Judith Butler and Erving Goffman. While acknowledging the significant contributions of anthropological research on theatre and performance, I have found that the application of Goffman's analysis of 'everyday performance' and Butler's arguments about the 'performativity of gender' generates a productive framework through which behavioural rituals and practices, particularly those found in the performing arts, can be linked to wider social, cultural, political and economic discourses and hierarchies. I then turn to the rehearsals for the play, focusing primarily on script changes, character development and conversations before, during and after the rehearsals pertaining to these changes and developments. Finally, I return to the work of Halperin and Halberstam, in order to examine how their arguments help to illuminate the homonormative tropes found in the play and in the wider refugee apparatus.

THE PERFORMATIVITY OF PERFORMANCE

Performativity and performance are not one and the same thing, although these terms are often utilized interchangeably in anthropology of theatre analyses, which can cause conceptual blurring (see Loxley 2006: 139–66). As Edward Shieffelin observes, performance has been defined in at least two ways in social science research: 'The first refers to particular symbolic or aesthetic activities such as ritual or theatrical and folk artistic activities, which are enacted as intentional expressive productions in established local genres. Performance in this usage refers to bounded, intentionally produced enactments which are (usually) marked and set off from ordinary activities' (1998: 194). The second use of performance 'is associated with the work of Erving Goffman … and the symbolic interactionist school. The focus here is not on a type of event but rather on performativity itself: the expressive processes of strategic impression management and structured improvisation through which human beings normally articulate their purposes, situations and relationships in everyday life' (1998: 195).

Judith Butler's theorization of gender and sex incorporates elements of Goffman's use of performance, and weaves them together with Foucault's arguments about power and discourse. She claims that the subjective experience of gender (and, for that matter, all other identities) is performatively constituted by the very expressions that are said to be its results (1990: 25). Performativity is the reiterative and citational practice by which discourse produces the effects that it names. A performative works to the extent that it draws on and covers over the constitutive conventions by which it is mobilized. In this sense, no term or statement can function performatively without the accumulating and dissimulating historicity of force (1995: 205; see also Morris 1995). While both Goffman and Butler stress the importance of observing the utterance or act in the moment and the context of its articulation, Butler's 'performative' differs from Goffman's in her emphasis on the potential *ambiguity* of the utterance or act; that is, Butler focuses on how we are not always successful in the way our 'strategic impression management' (Goffman's term) is received and the ways in which that act embeds itself in discursively produced hegemonic discourses already in circulation. She recognizes the power of words and actions to enforce norms, but at the same time acknowledges how they may be interpreted in unspecified, unpredictable ways that may question and challenge normative givens (of gender, for instance [Butler 1993]).

The creation of subjects who belong to a discursive norm (of heterosexualized gender in this case) also creates its own 'abject', that which is outside the domain of the subject. What (or who) is abject both delimits and destabilizes regulatory regimes of truth while they are simultaneously a product of them. Thus, in the case of gender, it is wrong to assume that gender is always constituted coherently and consistently; indeed, we should never presume a stabilized subject category of 'woman' or 'man' (1990: 6). Butler's performative framework undermines gender's apparent systemic, contained and natural existence, exposing it to be an utterance that is only rendered legible through reference to the circulation of powerful historical, social and political antecedent discourses, but that can never be fully realized or stabilized – its totality can only remain an ideal. Butler readily admits that gender is deeply rooted in the popular imaginary but argues that it is, like any identification, an imagined ideal that is permanently deferred.

Since the publication of her key arguments about gender and performativity (1990 and 1993), a number of critiques have emerged that highlight some significant problems in these formulations. These include 'the persistent kernel of methodological individualism (in Butler's work, such that) ... an individualistic account of subject formation (is) framed in exclusively cultural terms' emphasizing particular performances (i.e., gender parody as an example of resistance), 'in abstraction from structural determinants such as material interests or crisis tendencies of the social system.' (Boucher 2006: 112–14). However, others remind us that Butler positions gender as a compulsory performance and she rejects the idea that gender performativity is based on 'radical free agency' such that we can 'get up and put on a new gender today' (Davis 2008: 102). A related critique of Butler is that she does not seriously consider how other modalities such as race, neo-colonialism or late liberal capitalism impact the performativities of gender (Salih 2002: 60, 64), nor does she reflect on how certain individuals and groups may be invested in stabilizing categories of gender and sexuality based on experiences of violence, silence and erasure. These latter critiques are particularly relevant to the ethnographic analysis of the refugee performances outlined below. An ethnographic approach will illustrate the importance of exploring everyday practice in relation to the power of discursive performativities of gender and sexuality, fleshing out (quite literally) the embodied ramifications of gender performativity in particular moments and locations by individuals and groups of diverse socio-cultural backgrounds.

The analysis presented below thus refers to both performance and performativity, accounting for both fluidity and stability; more specifically, I analyse rehearsal performances, discussions and debates about the performances, and changes to performances through a performative lens that acknowledges both the creative instability of everyday performances, different investments in these performances, and the political and social structural determinants that impose limits on the expressive possibilities of a set of particular identity formations. In other words, I will not only investigate a number of intentionally produced enactments set off from ordinary activity (a play about the refugee experiences), but also will focus on actions as they are uttered, performed and then repeated in rehearsals, keeping in mind how the possibility of expression is impinged by normativities created through governmental institutions like the refugee apparatus, queer cultural productions and everyday practices. Governmental institutions like immigration bureaucracies are particularly invested in the production of standardized, stable means of understanding sexuality, gender and citizenship; however, ethnographic analysis of creative play may reveal the instability and potential fluidity of those understandings, or at the very least the tensions that lie in attempts to reproduce stable formations.

PERFORMING THE REFUGEE

Research on refugee claimants' experiences of refugee assessment and support systems of various nation-states has demonstrated how various participants in these systems (ranging from claimants to lawyers, judges and support workers) perform 'refugeeness', a particular identity formation characterized by victimhood, passivity and gratitude in order to be identified as 'authentic' refugees (Hall 2012: 104; see also Grewal 2005: 183–84, Kea and Roberts-Holmes 2013; Malkki 1995; Ou-Jin Lee and Brotman 2011; Razack 1998: 119). As Hall notes, 'This iconic and imaginary figure ... has been shaped by international legal categories through which humanitarian protection is administered and allows the "correct" objects of compassion aid and pity to be recognized' (2012: 104). As we saw in the previous chapter, those who do not follow the homonational script of the authentic refugee are more likely to be labelled undeserving, fake or bogus and are thus subject to detention and/or deportation. As levels of restriction, suspicion and surveillance in refugee apparatus increase, and refugee applications and/or successful claims decrease (Mountz 2010: 130–31),[2] asylum seekers are forced to produce performances and narratives that cleave as closely as possible to the refugee-granting nation's image of the ideal refugee (Kea and Robert-Holmes 2013: 100–03). However, as Szczepanikova (2010) observes, while the disempowering effects of these performances should not be overstated, refugees themselves utilize them strategically in order to access resources and navigate systems that are unfamiliar and highly suspicious of the subjects they claim to be supporting.

Research focusing on SOGI refugees has consistently stressed how their personal narratives are told and received in highly mediated ways that meet judges' standards of credibility (Berg and Millbank 2009: 197). As I noted in the previous chapter, the narrative performances of SOGI refugees are perhaps even more circumscribed than those of other categories of refugees, as they must not only perform authentic refugeeness but also perform authentic sexual orientation or gender identity, or, more specifically, gay, lesbian, bisexual or transgendered identities as defined or interpreted by asylum adjudicators. Throughout this book I argue that the credibility of SOGI refugee claimants in the refugee determination process is evaluated through processes and questions that impose a prism of assumptions about sexual or gendered identity that reflect white, middle-class Canadian LGBTQ experiences and beliefs about 'our' and 'other' cultures. The development of the play by ex-refugee claimants and support staff at a Toronto LGBTQ community centre provides an interesting case study in which to examine the influence of the queer migration to liberation nation narrative as this support group consisted of members who now had 'convention refugee' status (i.e., their claim for refugee status had been accepted by the IRB, and they were now permanent residents or in the process of applying for this status), and thus they were no longer obligated to perform an 'authentic' SOGI refugee identity for the IRB, which hypothetically might result in performances and discussions that were more diverse and 'true to self'. However, it may be relevant to note that funding for this support group was partially provided through a grant from the federal Department of Citizenship and Immigration and that members of the group were informed by the group facilitator that the play would be presented to an audience that would include current refugee applicants (i.e., individuals who had lodged an application and were awaiting their hearing date), factors that could impact how the story of a gay refugee was presented.

MAKING MANDO BULLOCK

The support group consisted of about 10–15 former SOGI convention refugees who met weekly at a LGBTQ community centre in Toronto to discuss
topics ranging from writing CVs and preparing for Canadian job interviews to
discrimination in the LGBTQ community and relationships with family and
friends in members' countries of origin. The group had diverse membership,
although the majority were cis-gender-identified men from Caribbean nations
who desired other men (there were also cis-gender-identified women who
desired other women, trans-identified persons, and members from African,
Middle Eastern and Eastern European nation-states; the age range varied
from the mid-20s to the mid-50s). The group was facilitated by Teresa, a
full-time staff member of the community centre, who was responsible for
developing discussion topics and providing assistance to group members in
various capacities. Most members of this group had attended the community
centre's other support group for refugee claimants (those who had filed an
application and were still waiting for their hearing), which is where I first
met them. When they 'graduated' to the 'convention refugee' group (that is,
after their successful IRB hearing), I received permission from the facilitator
to follow them and join the group's meetings.

Most of the members were not surprised when, one evening, Teresa
announced that the group was going to develop a short play 'about the
LGBTQ refugee experience' for the upcoming holiday festival party at the
community centre. Over the previous few weeks, there had been presentations from a scriptwriter, an actor and a set designer, which had some members speculating that this was more than just about learning what types of
jobs could be found in the theatre profession. The facilitator then introduced a
middle-aged woman who had just walked into the room as Andrea, 'a professional theatre director' who would help us create and rehearse the scenes for
the play. We were told that Andrea was involved in amateur and professional
theatre productions around Toronto. She and Teresa were already acquaintances who had both migrated to Canada from Caribbean countries, and
when Teresa told Andrea about her idea to get the support group members to
develop a play, Andrea volunteered to help out.

We then began to collectively discuss what a play about 'the LGBTQ refugee experience' would look like. After a relatively short discussion generated
mostly by the group members (Andrea would occasionally provide some
advice, telling them, for instance, that 'that might be difficult to stage', but
otherwise would let the group develop ideas on their own), it was agreed that
the play would consist of three short scenes: the first scene would take place
in 'the country of origin' (unspecified) focusing on an individual's motiva-
tion for leaving his or her country, a second scene would focus on lodging the

application with the CIC, and a third scene would involve the IRB hearing and receiving the decision letter in the mail.

We were then broken up into three sub-groups by Teresa and asked to develop each scene by writing a script including dialogue and set instructions (i.e., brief descriptions of the location, props and blocking for the characters). I was placed in the subgroup for the third scene. There were four of us, and Alex, a cis-gender man, and one of the younger group members, said he had background experience in theatre and thus became the de-facto leader as he had a number of ideas about what we should do. Alex wanted us to create a pantomime scene (no words spoken) in which two people would stand facing the audience with envelopes containing their refugee hearing decision in their hands, and then open them simultaneously while he sang 'Amazing Grace' or a song with a similar theme about redemption. Upon reading their letters, one reader would break out into a big smile and the other would look very sad, indicating a positive and a negative outcome. I would then walk onstage as a Canadian Border Services Agent, handcuff the individual with the negative outcome and lead him offstage.

Each group then performed its scenes for Andrea. Scene one involved a mother who is at home cleaning her son's room and discovers a photo of her son kissing another man. Her son walks in and she begins to yell at him for this 'abomination' and 'shameful thing' and calls for the neighbours to come over. She tells her son to leave the home, as he falls to his knees crying and begging her to forgive him. A neighbour then walks in and upon hearing what the son has done, begins to beat him.[3] The scene ends with the son running away from the house. Scene two began with a woman sitting at a desk doing paperwork (she mimed opening folders, stamping pages and typing on a keyboard). Another woman enters the office, and says she would like to apply for refugee status (thus indicating this was a Citizenship and Immigration Canada office). The office-worker replies in a bored voice that she needs to see identification, which she then reviews with a blank facial expression, returns to the applicant and tells her to go to window 'x', and then window 'y' to obtain and fill out additional forms and documents. My group then performed the third scene as outlined above.

Andrea was not impressed with our performances, saying that much work was needed to improve dialogue, staging and continuity between the scenes. As she critiqued each of the scenes, she wrote her notes on a whiteboard, and encouraged the group to revise their scenes. One of the first major changes was to create a character, 'Mando Bullock' (a name invented by Emmanuel, the actor playing him, who said that 'Mando' was word play based on 'man do man', and 'Bullock' was a play on 'buller', an English Caribbean term for homosexual) who would now be the principal figure of the play and would be present in all three scenes, thus creating more narrative cohesion between them. Mando would now be the son who enters his mother's home after she discovers a photo of him kissing a man; he would be the applicant entering the CIC office in Toronto to lodge his refugee application; and he would also be one of the two men receiving the hearing decision letter in the final scene. Some group members were not happy with the decision to build the play around one character – they felt it should include additional voices that might reflect different experiences from that of 'a gay man' (as one member put it), but Andrea responded that in such a short play it wouldn't be possible to include multiple principal characters, and that it was preferable to try to collect all the stories and tell them through one character. Despite some grumbling and irritated looks, Andrea's opinion was backed up by Teresa, and thus prevailed.

Scene One: In the following weeks, Andrea had us perform and revise our scenes repeatedly, and spent a great deal of time focusing on each actor's performance, asking them to think about their relationships with other characters in the scene, their underlying feelings in the moment, and/or their gestures or postures in order to convey those relationships. Much attention was focused on Mando, as Andrea wanted to see more character development over the three scenes. For example, in the first scene, when the mother begins to yell at Mando, Andrea asked Emmanuel to be 'less hysterical' so that the audience could understand what he was saying, and to better convey his 'hidden' sexual identity. There was also some debate over whether Mando should be fearful or angry in response to his mother's discovery of the photo. Some of the group members thought it was important that he show how frightened and upset he was by his mother's words and the neighbour's actions – yelling, pleading and crying would be 'more honest', as Samuel, one of the other actors put it, and would help to explain why we would see him in a CIC office in Scene Two. However, Andrea decided that Mando should not 'over-react' in this scene – the fearfulness of the situation would be obvious to the audience, and too much hysteria might result in the audience finding the scene melodramatic and artificial.

Another section of Scene One that Andrea focused on in the rehearsals was when the neighbour enters the house and begins to beat up Mando. The group member playing the neighbour was a soft-spoken, thin young man who usually didn't say much during regular group meetings, and his first attempts to beat Mando were met with a great deal of laughter from the rest of the group, because, as one person put it, his actions looked like they were 'straight out of a drag queen wrestling match'. Andrea wanted the actor to try and be more intimidating when he walked in, and to push Mando around instead of mimicking a professional wrestler and jumping in the air to do a 'smackdown'. As the weeks went on, Andrea remained unimpressed with the 'beat up' scene, and in the end, the character was replaced with a female neighbour who entered the house and verbally shamed Mando instead of engaging in physical contact.

The final aspect of Scene One that changed over rehearsals was the dialogue between Mando and his mother. In the first draft of the script, when Mando's mother confronts him with the photo, he responds, 'Mummy, I told you I was that way.' Andrea decided this should be revised to read, 'Mummy, I told you I was gay.' Again, there was some disagreement among group members over this change, as they felt that 'gay' was not the term Mando would use in front of his mother,[4] but Andrea said it was important to establish Mando as someone who identified as gay in order for the following scene to work.

Scene Two: While this scene remained in the CIC offices, Andrea made a number of changes after Mando was inserted into it. The scene now began with Mando sitting in the waiting area of the CIC office alongside two other men. Mando would ask each of them where they were from and why they were there (Andrea said that including these two new characters would help address the concern about including other SOGI refugee stories). 'Sam' was a quiet, nervous man from 'the Middle East' and 'Patrick' was a masculine, unfriendly man from St. Vincent and the Grenadines (these were the actual regions/ countries of origin of the actors playing these characters). In the initial enactments of this scene, Mando was open about his sexual orientation, flirting with Patrick when he asked him, 'So where are you from, sweetie', and responding with a loud, exuberant, 'Me too, honey' when Sam explained that he was filing a refugee application because he was gay. Patrick responded to Mando's query by saying that he was also filing for refugee status as a gay man, but that 'I ain't into none of that gay stuff. I was told that if I play gay I can get in.' In a subsequent rehearsal of this scene, Mando upped the 'performative gay' quotient by standing up and sashaying around the office like a runway model after he heard that Sam was gay, eliciting whoops of laughter from some of his fellow cast members. However, other group members like Tom felt that Emmanuel was 'overdoing' it. Tom said that he thought Emmanuel/Mando was 'too much ... no-one would behave like that in an immigration office'. Andrea agreed, and eliminated Mando's 'sashay' around the office. She also felt that the actor playing Patrick wasn't masculine enough, and asked him to say his lines in 'patois' (a local Caribbean dialect) to make him sound rougher and to heighten the differences between him and Mando.

However, as we moved closer to the public performance at the holiday festival, Andrea changed her mind and decided that there should be more 'lightness and humour' in Scene Two to contrast the dramatic intensity of Scene One. She therefore encouraged Mando to speak and move in a way that conveyed his sexual orientation more clearly, that is, keeping terms of endearment like 'sweetie' and 'honey' in his conversations, flirting more overtly with Patrick and squealing with pleasure when he found out that Sam was gay. It was in one of these later rehearsals that Andrea encouraged Mando to imagine he was carrying a handbag when he was called up to the window in the CIC office. While Mando was increasingly 'gayified' in this scene, Andrea also spent more time 'straightening' Patrick – in addition to being told to speak in patois, the actor playing Patrick was also told to lower his voice, spread his legs apart when he was sitting and show more irritability and discomfort in response to Mando's words and actions. The actor playing Patrick said that playing straight shouldn't be all that difficult, "I've been doing it all my life,' but he nevertheless struggled to meet Andrea's directives.

Scene Three: Andrea thought that the pantomime approach to this scene partially worked, but that it needed some dialogue in order to help the audience understand what was happening. Therefore, the scene was revised to start with Mando calling Sam and Patrick on the phone to see if they had received their refugee hearing decision letter, and Mando recommending that they meet at Sam's place and open their letters together. When this scene was first performed for the group, Mando and Patrick (who 'faked' being gay) received a positive decision, while Sam (who was gay) received a negative decision, but Teresa (the group facilitator) wasn't happy about this, saying it would 'send the wrong message' to the audience (i.e., that even if you're 'really' gay like Sam you may not receive a positive decision, while a 'fake gay' applicant (like Patrick) might be successful). There would likely be people in the audience who hadn't attended their refugee hearing yet, and this message might make them become even more anxious about the outcome of their hearing. Therefore, the scene was changed so that Sam and Mando now opened their letters together and discovered they had received a positive decision, while Patrick's outcome was moved to another sequence later in the scene.

In the revised scene, Mando phones Sam and then heads over to his house; after opening their letters and rejoicing together, Sam and Mando then go to Patrick's apartment to find out what is happening, but when they arrive, Patrick's room-mate answers the door and tells them that Patrick is at his hearing at that very moment. The scene then switches to the IRB hearing room, where Patrick is standing facing a Board member (played by me) who shakes his head negatively, then points at a security guard to come and handcuff Patrick and lead him out of the room. This latter part of the scene (in the IRB hearing room) was done wordlessly, while the rest of the troupe sang an excerpt from the spiritual song, 'Nobody Knows the Trouble I've Seen.'

During rehearsals for Scene Three, Andrea also made a number of changes to the interactions between Sam and Mando. When Mando arrives at Sam's house and the two men greet each other, she felt Mando should do more than just say 'Hi' when Sam opened the door. She wanted him to be more demonstrative in his affection for Sam, to which Emmanuel said, 'you mean like a regular gay greeting, you know kiss, kiss, hug?' (he mimed kissing Sam on both cheeks and exaggeratedly hugging him as he said this). Andrea nodded her head affirmatively. She also wanted bigger emotional outbursts from both of them when they opened their decision letters, particularly from Mando. Andrea had the two actors do a number of takes of this moment, each time asking Emmanuel/Mando for 'more' of a reaction. Mando's reactions progressed from smiling and saying 'oh my god, I made it', to letting out a scream of joy and running around the room, to falling on his knees in front of Sam and knocking his head repeatedly against Sam's stomach, which happened to also resemble a mimed blow-job, and resulted in much laughter from fellow cast members. Andrea decided that it was a good idea to 'increase the humour/drama' in this scene and kept the 'blow job for joy' action, even though the actor playing Sam said he wasn't comfortable with this scene. Once again, a few of the other actors grumbled that this was 'over the top' and that no one would behave like this when they received their letter, but Andrea said it should be kept, based on the humorous reaction it elicited from the cast when it was first performed.

Andrea also provided further coaching tips to the actor playing Patrick and to me as the judge in our pantomimed scene. Patrick needed to stare 'harder' at me when I was conveying my negative decision, and to walk 'more dejectedly' as he was being led out of the hearing room by the security guard. I was told to wear glasses and pretend that I was shuffling papers prior to looking at Patrick to shake my head negatively.

Opening Night. The final rehearsal prior to 'opening night' (in actual fact, the one and only public performance of the play) was spent mostly on performing the scenes with sound effects (such as a phone ringing in Scene Three), props and set pieces (which were very minimal, mostly consisting of large sheets with drawings of a house window (Scene One), an office sign (Scene Two) and a Canadian flag (Scene Three)), as well as working on timing, entrances and blocking (where characters would be positioned in relation to each other and the props). Leading up to this rehearsal, there was ongoing grumbling among a few of the group members that the characters had become increasingly stereotyped, primarily Mando and Patrick as gay and straight; however, no one complained directly to Andrea once the final rehearsal was underway.

Unfortunately, I have very little memory of the performance at the holiday festival as I had been in a high state of anxiety about my one-minute role as the IRB member in Scene Three and couldn't find my 'prop' glasses, so I was running around the room looking for them during Scenes One and Two.

Afterwards, Andrea told us that we had done an excellent job, and that she could tell that the audience was 'moved' by the performance. At the support group meeting following the performance, Teresa asked how members felt about the whole process, and to my surprise, those who spoke were very positive about the entire experience. One of the members said, 'We touched a lot of chords, and people loved the play – you heard people gasp at the end when the judge said no to Patrick and he was arrested.' Another member said she was proud of what the group had achieved as 'it said something important to people'.

GUIDELINES FOR HOW TO BE GAY

While the rehearsal process presents us with a rich array of material to examine, for the purposes of this chapter I will focus primarily on the evolution of and changes to the character of Mando Bullock, the 'gay refugee', with a secondary focus on 'Patrick', the 'fake gay refugee claimant'. Over the course of the five-week rehearsal period, numerous discussions and debates about Mando's speech, dress, movements and relationships took place, with a general movement towards heightening or intensifying words and actions that would explicitly signify he was a gay man. So, for example, we saw Mando's dialogue with his mother changed from 'Mummy, I told you I was that way' to 'Mummy I told you I was gay' in Scene One. In Scene Two, Mando was directed to physically and orally respond more exuberantly and flamboyantly when he finds out that his fellow refugee claimant Sam is gay, to insert more terms of endearment like 'sweetie', when talking with Sam and Patrick, to carry a 'handbag', and to walk around the CIC office with more of a 'swish'. In Scene Three, Sam and Mando were told to change how they greet each other, such that Emmanuel asked Andrea if what she was looking for was 'a regular gay greeting', and Mando's response to his positive decision was revised to be more emotional and humorous by having Mando fall on his knees and move his head back and forth against Sam's stomach, feigning a blow-job. As some of these changes were implemented, various members of the theatre group complained that the 'revised' Mando character was 'too much', 'over the top' or 'overdoing it', and didn't represent how someone would behave or speak in those particular contexts, indicating that for them, Mando did not represent an authentic gay refugee identity. However, Andrea justified making these changes based on 'the dramatic arc' of the storyline, the need to differentiate the characters, and/or to add some levity to what was a 'heavy' message. Interestingly, when Andrea made changes to 'Patrick' in an attempt to make him more visibly/aurally 'straight' (asking the actor to speak in patois, spread his legs apart when sitting and show more physical discomfort when Mando was near him), there were no criticisms of this representation of heterosexual masculinity being 'too much', stereotyped or unrealistic.

Queer theorist David Halperin's book, *How to Be Gay* (2012), provides an interesting reflection on the performance of gay identity. Halperin wrote this book as a response to a very public debate that arose from an undergraduate course he taught at the University of Michigan with the same title as the book, for which he was attacked by both right-wing and LGBTQ media. Fully cognizant of the controversy inherent in such a title, Halperin argues:

> In order to be gay, a man has to learn to relate to the world around him in a distinctive way. Or rather, homosexuality itself, even as an erotic orientation, even as a specifically sexual subjectivity, consists in a dissident way of feeling and relating to the world. That dissident way of feeling and relating to the world is reflected in gay male cultural practices. ... Gayness, then is not a state or condition. It's a mode of perception, an attitude, an ethos: in short, it is a practice. (2012: 12)

Halperin believes that there is a set of relationships, 'between sexuality and cultural forms, styles of feeling and genres of discourse' (2012: 13) and he therefore desires 'the sexual politics of a cultural form' (2012: 15), which he argues can be located in the gendered subjectivity of gay men (gay male masculinity and gay male femininity). But what about the cultural politics of a sexual form? What about the form as norm? In arguing that there is 'a' set of relationships between sexuality and cultural forms, that is, a set of characteristics, or aesthetic practices that is premised primarily around gendered subjectivity in order to define what is 'gay', Halperin draws our attention to the cultural practices of a group of men invested in a notion of fixed sexual identity and rigid gender binaries. He argues that 'gay male effeminacy lies at the heart of gay culture' (2012: 304–05) for some gay-identified cis-males, which helps to codify a particular set of aesthetic practices and beliefs of a particular set of same-sex-desiring cis-gender-identified men who identify as 'gay', and provides important insights about gayness as a practice that is learned, socialized and strengthened through the imagined shared community of this particular group. Halperin notes that the cultural practices he's discussing are characteristic of 'gay male communities' in the United States and that his book does not 'address the dynamic complex nature of the relation between homosexuality and globalization' (2012: 16–18), alerting us to the fact that these cultural practices represent subjectivities that are raced, classed and gendered. However, this observation does not fully acknowledge their complexity or entrenched privileged and hegemonic status, that is, that these practices are generated through hierarchies and histories of race, ethnicity, migration, class, education, religious (dis)affiliation, age and ability. In other words, one of queer of colour and transnational feminism's key critiques – the centrality of intersectional analysis in the production of gendered and sexual subjectivities – is an aspect of 'how to be gay' that is underplayed throughout Halperin's book.

Halperin's quasi-ethnographic analysis of a set of hegemonic practices indicative of 'American gay male culture' bears some similarities to Puar's discussion of homonationalism in which 'a' particular instantiation of homosexual identity is defined primarily through racialized, classed and binary gender performances with the nation-state as culture container, implying that men who desire other men in the United States are not really 'gay' if they are not cognizant of, or do not participate in, these cultural practices and performances that constitute the 'gay (white, middle-class American) self'. If we suture Halperin's discussion of hegemonic gay cultural practices to Puar's conceptualization of homonationalism we see how the possibility of not performing an authentically gay self may emerge, or more specifically, how a performance of a gay male self that does *not* reflect the experiences and privileges of a hegemonic gay cultural identity (structured through race, class, education, gender-normativity) renders the performer suspect, that is, not 'really' gay.

It is through this suturing of Halperin to Puar that we can see connections between the production of a gay refugee character in a play about the SOGI refugee experiences, and debates about authentic or real 'gay' SOGI refugee claimants in various realms of the refugee apparatus. The ongoing 'work' on Mando's performance in the play's rehearsals, such that the actor playing Mando became more 'legibly' gay through transformations in language, speech, emotion, bodily comportment and accessories that aligned his performance more closely with Halperin's depictions of normative gay American male cultural practices, culminating in a final performance where Mando represents a successful SOGI refugee claimant,[5] demonstrates how a privileged interpretation of sexual orientation circulates through the refugee apparatus and its diverse interlocutors. Over the five weeks of rehearsals, Andrea, the play's director, shaped a performance that cleaved closely to Halperin's description of a privileged American gay male cultural subjectivity. I argue that this cleaving was not happenstance; rather, it reflected popular North American ideas and assumptions about how a 'gay male' sexual identity should look, feel and act. These ideas and assumptions circulate through diverse mainstream North American sites and discourses, including the refugee apparatus. In the previous chapter, I argued that the talk of 'false, fake and fraudulent' versus 'true, authentic and genuine' SOGI refugees pervades conversations and discussions of refugee claimants, lawyers and support workers, and reflects how the refugee determination process is a quasi-legal juridical apparatus predicated upon the credibility of the claimant. I also noted that in determining credibility, adjudicators often apply their own understandings of sexual and gender identity based on a staged model of sexual and gender identity development, which is itself based on specific cultural, gendered, raced and classed experiences and operates with particular assumptions about sexual identity as fixed, discoverable and moving from a position of closeted to coming out. However, as we saw in the previous chapter and now in the context of the play put on by former refugee claimants, adjudicators are not the only ones making judgements about who is or is not 'really' gay. This pervasive staged model of sexual identity development reflecting hegemonic white, middle-class gay cultural practices (as noted by Halperin) contains key indicators that adjudicating bodies, support workers, lawyers, refugees (past and present) and cultural producers use to 'decode' and decide what merits an authentic, 'credible' performance of gay identity.

Judith Halberstam's *The Queer Art of Failure* (2011) operates from a significantly different theoretical position than Halperin, focusing on the affective dimensions of being queer, in particular, 'failing (as) something queers do and have always done exceptionally well' (2011: 2–3), and arguing for a resignification of failure through a queer lens. Halberstam asks what kinds of rewards failure can offer, and how we might see failure as a way of resisting forms of legibility imposed by the modern state as a way of sorting, organizing and profiting from land and people (2011: 9). Thus, failure may be considered as a mode of un-being and unbecoming that can lead to a different relation to knowledge (2011: 23) that undermines or elides hegemonic discourses of success, accomplishment and satisfaction produced in and through late-liberal capitalism and neo-imperial nation-states. Yet, despite this important challenge to hetero- and homonormative discourses of 'pride' and 'success', Halberstam does not reflect on the possibility of differential effects of failing for differentially positioned queers: for many queer migrants, failure, at least in terms of navigating the immigration and citizenship apparatus of the destination state, is not an option they can afford to consider when the alternative is detention or deportation. Thus, in Halberstam's arguments, there is a glossing over of who is included in or belongs to 'queer' and the different investments in queerly passing or succeeding, particularly in relation to forms of legibility recognized by the state (Scott 1998).

'Authentic' gay identity and failure to achieve this imaginary subjectivity are deeply intertwined and clearly marked in the narrative arc of a play about the SOGI refugee experience. If one is an 'authentic' gay refugee claimant, demonstrated through performative stylings and utterances communicating male effeminacy that hue closely to homonationalist representations of (white, middle class, middle-aged, non-religious, able-bodied, urban) gay male identity circulating through the refugee apparatus, then one is more

likely to successfully obtain convention refugee status. A 'fake' SOGI refugee claimant, represented by a character whose performance communicates
a hyper-masculine, racialized, and classed heterosexual identity (opposite in
every way to 'authentic' gay male effeminacy) will likely fail to obtain convention refugee status.

However, it is important to remember that throughout the play's rehearsals, there were comments and complaints from some group members about
Mando's performance becoming caricatured and unrepresentative of how a
SOGI refugee would 'really' act in a given situation. These misgivings conveyed the mismatch some felt between a play that was supposed to represent
the experiences of sexually persecuted minorities applying for refugee status
in Canada and their own experiences and perceptions of 'normative' sexual
and gendered subjectivities, perceptions that were attentive to and critical of
the ways in which a particular hegemonic performative style of 'gay identity'
appeared to be a crucial component of what is necessary to obtain a successful SOGI refugee claim. Yet, despite the misgivings of some group members
about stereotyping and unrealistic character traits as the rehearsals progressed
and Mando became 'gayer', a particular representation prevailed, and the
audience at the holiday festival (some of whom were in the process of preparing for their hearing) received a clear message about what authentic 'gay
male' sexual orientation should look like and how it should be performed in
order to achieve a successful refugee claim.

CONCLUSION

In their examination of narratives of female asylum seekers in the United
Kingdom claiming asylum on the basis of forced female genital mutilation,
Kea and Roberts-Holmes argue that asylum seekers perform a victim identity in order to verify and strengthen their narratives in an environment of
heightened suspicion and surveillance generated by state discourses of 'bogus
asylum seekers' and refugee reform designed to decrease the numbers of
migrants and asylum seekers in Britain:

> One could interpret this as both a form of 'resistive performativity' because
> they work against the state system that is designed to turn down the majority
> of asylum claims, and a form of compliance or strategic essentialism as they
> comply, through interactions with asylum adjudicators, with the production of
> their own victim identities in attempting to have their claims recognized. ...
> The production of a victim identity ... needs to be located in the neo-colonial
> relations of subordination that have partly informed ... asylum and refuge
> policy. (Kea and Roberts-Holmes 2013: 99–100)

The performative narratives of sexual orientation and gendered identity refugee claimants, like women claiming asylum on the basis of forced female genital mutilation, are connected to and structured through the refugee determination apparatus, in which a performance of a hegemonic North American socio-sexual identity (an assemblage of aesthetic practices reflecting a set of privileged raced, classed and gendered histories and experiences) is assumed to be transnationally stable and must be performed in order to meet the bar of credibility, a bar which is increasingly raised because of the state's nervousness around migration and the need to prove its ability to guard its borders from the 'illegal migrant' in a global climate of mass migration, an expanding and malleable category that often ends up targeting racialized, poor, gendered and sexualized categories of individuals and groups.

However, I am not convinced that the performances in the play at the Toronto LGBTQ community centre conveyed a form of 'resistive performativity' similar to what Kea and Roberts-Holmes observed in their work with asylum seekers; rather, I have argued that the final performance of this play reflected hegemonic homonational discourses found throughout the Canadian refugee apparatus and identified in some iterations of queer theory. At the same time, I have argued for acknowledging the agency of refugee claimants in terms of how they actively learn about and attempt to successfully navigate the refugee apparatus into which they have been placed. In this chapter, I have tried to demonstrate how the play's *rehearsals* presented an opportunity to observe elements of 'resistive performativity' as characters and scenes were formed and reformed, and group members debated among themselves and with the director about the content and meaning of the narrative and characters. By focusing on these repetitions, revisions of and changes to speech, gesture, and movement throughout the rehearsal period, we witness the simultaneous instability of sexual orientation as an identity formation and the power of the nation-state's refugee apparatus to render certain imagined performances as legible, authentic and legitimate, rewarding a few and potentially punishing many more.

NOTES

1. As will be seen below, the play's main characters are either 'gay' or 'straight' men. No transgender, bisexual, or lesbian characters were developed for the play, which may have been due to the fact that the majority of the group involved in the play were same sex-desiring cis-gender males.

2. For example, the Canadian government implemented a substantially revised refugee determination system starting in 2013. See Conclusion for further discussion of these changes.

3. No one in the group queried the logic of a neighbour entering the house and beating up the son. This may have been due to the fact that the majority of the group were from Caribbean nations where communities were close-knit, relationships with neighbours were more intimate and/or different ideas of privacy circulate.

4. Both Mando and his mother were played by actors who were from Caribbean countries. In fact, the majority of the actors, as well as Andrea and Teresa, were from the Caribbean, which may have influenced ideas about language choice and social interactions.

5. And concomitantly, how Patrick, a straight male character masquerading as gay became increasingly masculinized in his speech patterns and bodily comportments, which were associated with a bogus refugee claimant.

Chapter 4

Producing Documentation for SOGI Refugee Claims

At a meeting for volunteers who helped to facilitate the monthly SOGI refugee support group in a downtown LGBT organization, the main topic was how to deal with the increasing numbers of group members and their needs. When I first joined the group as a volunteer in June 2011, there were approximately 35–40 people showing up for each meeting; by July 2012, there were almost 100 members in attendance. When one volunteer said that this increase was proof that 'we're doing something right', the group leader reminded us that many of the refugee claimants attending these meetings were doing so in order to get letters confirming their membership in the support group and/or their participation as volunteers in other activities run by this organization. These letters would then be submitted to the IRB as part of the refugee claimants' files. The group leader told us that the letters were viewed by IRB adjudicators as 'the gold standard' of evidence confirming a refugee's claim to be a member of a particular social group based on sexual orientation or gendered identity. The problem was that volunteers who wrote these letters on behalf of the organization were overwhelmed by many last minute requests for letters, or requests from members who had only recently joined the group and attended one or two meetings. Furthermore, some of the volunteers stated they felt uncomfortable writing letters for people who they didn't think were really gay, lesbian or bisexual. We debated for some time on how to revise the letter writing process in order to ensure better accountability, accuracy and timeliness; in the end, we decided to create a new form and revise two other forms that would help us better track membership and attendance and introduce more structure to the letter writing process: First, people attending the support group for the first time would fill out a revised membership form asking for more details about their refugee application status; second, we would circulate a revised attendance sheet at each meeting; and third, we would now ask members to fill out a new form when they wanted to set up a meeting with a volunteer for a letter to be written; furthermore, no letter would be written unless a group member had attended at least three meetings. It was also decided that if a volunteer didn't feel comfortable writing a statement about a refugee claimant's sexual orientation – 'if the gaydar doesn't go off' were the group leader's exact words – then they shouldn't feel obligated to make any statement about it in the letter.

This meeting and its outcomes – more documentation and more regulations in order to maintain the quality of a key document ('the letter') and the reputation of the organization, along with a heightened sensitivity to making claims authenticating the credibility of a refugee claimant's sexual orientation in the letter – raise a number of interesting questions about governmentality, 'credible' SOGI refugee claimants and the role of local support service workers in the production of refugee documentation and surveillance and control of this particular form of queer migration. In this chapter, I investigate another moment/space along the continuum of becoming an authentic SOGI refugee, but rather than focusing on the experiences of the refugee claimants as I have done in the previous two chapters, I now turn to another set of individuals, refugee support group workers and volunteers, and I focus on one of their activities, producing documents for SOGI refugee claimants' files.

In this chapter, I want to move away from the tendency in socio-legal refugee research to analyse the linguistic content of documents in order to illustrate processes of exclusion and inclusion by the state; rather, I will focus on the meanings and effects of the production and proliferation of documentation in the Canadian refugee apparatus. Through exploration of some sites and personnel involved in producing documents for SOGI refugee claimants and tracking changes to the processes involved in creating these documents, I will argue that the concern for managing quality and reputation among low-level 'document brokers' (Hull 2012: 258) who want to produce documents attached to 'credible' or 'authentic' SOGI refugees (as opposed to 'fake' or 'bogus' claimants) reflects the regulatory modes of the Canadian refugee apparatus and its increased levels of suspicion and surveillance of human traffic crossing its borders, which simultaneously reflects the instantiation of an increasingly foundational belief of the fake refugee or refugee as a 'potential fraud' (Fassin and Rechtman 2009: 273). As Cabot notes in her research on refugee support workers in an Athens non-governmental organization (NGO), these workers are part of a system predicated on defining and only supporting eligible and credible refugee claimants where 'eligibility practices are persistently haunted by epistemic anxiety: pervasive uncertainties that manifest in an endemic climate of mistrust and which, for workers, reflect the epistemological problem of how to know, really, about those whom they must judge' (2013: 454). These epistemic anxieties produce practices that rely on social aesthetics of eligibility (Cabot 2013) – affect, comportment, intuition, 'gut-feelings', 'the gaydar' – in addition to legal and bureaucratic definitions and protocols, and end up endorsing the ways in which 'regimes of care' (humanitarian groups, activists and certain movements for human rights, which operate as a set of regulated discourses and practices grounded on the moral imperative to relieve suffering) may, in fact, reproduce inequalities and racial, gendered and geopolitical hierarchies (Ticktin 2011).

Finally, I will return to one of the structuring arguments of this book by noting how these regimes of care and their documents contribute to the production of homonationalism, a privileged discourse containing a highly delimited definition of sexual identity and conduct that is folded into the nation-state's discourses of the good immigrant and proper citizen. By exploring these socio-technical bureaucratic processes of document production by support group workers and volunteers, we can therefore better understand how documents operate as ambiguous mechanisms of administrative control and how they construct, reconstruct and render in/visible certain subjects, objects and citizens (Hull 2012: 256).

I begin this chapter with a brief discussion of the anthropology of documents and research on documentation in queer migration and refugee studies. I will then return to some sites of SOGI refugee document production, in order to further explore the discussions, debates and concerns of document brokers, with an emphasis on the aesthetic and somatic dimensions of document production. I conclude by addressing how this interrogation into the production and circulation of documents reveals their malleable, duplicitous power (Hetherington 2011): that is, inasmuch as documents may be viewed as a mode that authenticates the identity of and relationship between the writer and recipient, they may also be viewed with disbelief, suspicion or doubt, often by members of the very institution that created or demanded them.

DOCUMENTS AND MIGRATION

In Matthew Hull's review of anthropological research on documents and bureaucracy, he notes that until recently documents had not received much attention from anthropologists for a number of reasons, including their traditional association with other social science disciplines, anthropology's interest in exploring 'everyday activities' within organizations (in which documents are associated with 'formal' structures) and a tendency to overlook them as a problem in their own right because anthropologists produce and use documents in much the same way as their subjects of study use them (Hull 2012: 252). However, in recent times, there has been increased attention to the mediating role of documents, that is, to treat documents as things that 'transform, translate, distort and modify the meaning or the elements they are supposed to carry' (Latour in Hull 2012: 253). Anthropological work on documents examines how they often stand for something else, that they do not simply 'reflect' the bureaucratic organization they are attached to but rather are constitutive of bureaucratic rules, practices, knowledge, subjectivities and even the organizations themselves (Hull 2012: 253). Thus, following Riles' discussion of ethnographic approaches to documents, we can see how the document is at once an ethnographic object, an analytical category and a methodological orientation (Riles 2006: 7). Furthermore, and highly relevant for the purposes of this chapter, some anthropological research makes important links between documents, individuals and the state, demonstrating how the state can enter into the life of the community (Das in Hull 2012: 258). More specifically, documents can be characterized as disciplinary and classificatory technologies that render subjects legible to state power (Scott 1998; Torpey 2000). However, as Hetherington demonstrates in his work with Paraguayan peasant farmers who challenge government documents pertaining to land ownership and reform, documents are not stable in their meanings, and 'information' arises not so much from the inscription of documents as their reading: documents thus contain many qualities that can never be completely accounted for (2011).

Keeping in mind documents' complex and ambiguous generative capacities is particularly important when we begin to examine their role and operation in the vast bureaucracies affiliated with immigration and border control of the nation-state. A number of anthropologists have written on the production, circulation and meanings of documents for or about refugees and other categories of immigrants/migrants (Cabot 2012, 2013, 2014; Coutin 2000; Fassin and D'Halluin 2005; Feldman 2012; Feldman and Ticktin 2011; Good 2006; Ong 2003; Ticktin 2011). In Didier Fassin's review of research on the governmentality of immigration in recent decades, he notes the contradiction between the increasing transnational circulation of goods facilitated through international trade agreements and the increasing restrictions on the transnational circulation of persons, and how 'governmentality' (the institutions, procedures, actions and reflections that have populations as object) has developed new strategies of policing and control of human movement across borders. Fassin notes the development of increasingly restrictive and punitive forms of border control, security and deportation, although he does not address how these forms of policing and surveillance may be deployed through documentation with differential effects for different categories of migrants (Fassin 2011: 214–16; however, see Fassin and Rechtman 2009 for a discussion on the role of expert medical documentation in asylum determination processes in France). However, as Heath Cabot demonstrates in her work with Greek asylum claimants seeking 'the pink card' (an identity document through which agents of the Greek state attempt to regulate the movements of applicants seeking protection, but which applicants also desire for the access it provides to material and symbolic protection from those very same agents), migration documents may simultaneously signal both belonging and unbelonging, demonstrating the profoundly ambiguous and unstable nature of documents and their intentions (Cabot 2012; see also Hetherington 2011).

Anthony Good has written extensively on documentation produced by 'expert witnesses' (including anthropologists) who are asked to provide written evidence as 'country experts' in the adjudication of refugee cases in Britain. He notes how the adversarial proceedings in these cases pressurize experts to profess greater certainty than they really feel (2006: 130), and how ongoing participation in this system results in higher levels of self-monitoring as the 'expert' holders of knowledge recognize the ways in which that knowledge must be organized and articulated in order to meet the particular logics of the refugee apparatus (I will discuss expert witnesses in Chapter 6). As will be elaborated below, self-monitoring is an important characteristic of the document brokers I worked with, and changes to processes of documentation reflect constant self-surveillance in order to produce objects that are recognized as 'legitimate' or 'authentic' by the state and therefore maintain the reputation of the document brokers and their organization in the eyes of the state. However, I make the additional observation that this self-surveillance includes anxiety around the 'authenticity' of the refugee subject, which generates somatic, affective modes of assessment that re-inscribe homonormative tropes in the decision about who is genuine and 'deserves' a letter (Cabot 2013).

Fassin and Rechtman make the interesting observation that as asylum decision-making bodies become increasingly suspicious of asylum seekers, the latter's accounts of their experiences have lost credibility, and adjudicators increasingly look to expert opinions of the asylum seeker's body or memory (visible physical or invisible psychological scars) in order to fortify their decision (2009: 273). When we turn to the specific category of SOGI refugee claimants, adjudicators are faced with the additional thorny challenge of finding credible proof of an invisible quality – sexual orientation[1] – and in order to do so, they increasingly rely, at least in part, on the letters of publicly recognized Canadian LGBT institutions and organizations.

As I noted in the introduction to this book, queer migration scholarship directly addresses issues of sexuality in migration by exploring how overlapping regimes of power and knowledge generate and transform identity categories and desires in movement, particularly as they relate to gender and sexuality, revealing the fundamental ways in which sexuality undergirds the organization and boundaries of nation-state, citizenship and national identity

projects. To date, however, queer migration scholars have not focused extensively on the relationship between documents, queer migrants and nation-
states, with the exception of critical analyses of transcripts of SOGI refugee
adjudication decisions in Canada, Australia, England and the United States
(Berg and Millbank 2009; LaViolette 2009; Millbank 2009a; Rehaag 2008)
and White's work on documentation for same-sex family class migrants and
refugees in Canada. White examines 'proof of relationship' dossiers that
binational queer couples and refugee claimants are required to submit to the
Canadian government in order to substantiate their sponsorship applications
or claims of persecution. Her analysis of participants' experiences in producing these 'intimate archives' and 'archives of trauma' reveals how documents
(letters, photos, telephone bills, travel documents etc.) operate as dense transfer points of power, which capture queer subjects within the state's frame of
recognition, enforcing both hetero- and homo-normative identity scripts and
producing what she terms 'affective governance' (White 2013: 42–43, 2014).
As we will see below, the production of documents for SOGI refugee claimants' files is enacted with similar and different effects.

A LIFE DOCUMENTED

Documents are central to a refugee claim. From the moment an individual
applies for refugee status, multiple documents are generated to form the case
file, which is eventually reviewed and assessed by an IRB member in order
to determine if the claimant meets the government's definition of a status
refugee. The primary or initiating document of the refugee claim process during the period when I conducted research was the Personal Information Form
(PIF).[2] This form required the refugee claimants to provide an explanation of
why they were claiming refugee protection and formed the basis of evaluation
by the Board member. It would serve as the key document when the refugee
claimants attended their hearing, in which the Board member would ask them
questions based on the information contained in it and other documents in the
case file.

The 'claimant's guide' on the IRB Refugee Protection Division's (RPD)
website states:

> You must give the RPD documents that support your claim. … You must show
> the RPD evidence of who you are by giving the RPD official documents with
> your name and date of birth on them. … Along with identity documents you
> can submit other documents that you feel are relevant to your claim, includ-
> ing proof of membership in political organizations, medical or psychological
> reports, police documents, business records, news clippings, visas and travel
> documents.[3]

For most of the SOGI refugee claimants I worked with, a crucial set of 'other documents relevant to their claim' were those that could help substantiate or verify their sexual orientation or gendered identity, as membership in this particular social group is now recognized in the IRB's definition of what constitutes a refugee.[4] However, the Claimants Guide provided no further information as to what specific types of documents might be considered helpful in establishing one's membership in this particular social group. The lack of information on this issue caused a significant amount of anxiety for many of the refugee claimants I worked with; most of them were dependent on their legal counsel, support group workers and one another to find out what types of documents should be submitted to help substantiate their claim.

As we saw in Chapter 2, when lawyers came to speak to the support groups, they would often spend a significant amount of time explaining how to go about documenting one's sexual orientation or gendered identity and what types of documents would help to substantiate claims of persecution based on that identity. One lawyer said to the group that 'you have to have proof of your life as gay. ... Proof of socialization is important.' He went on to say that sexual orientation claims were more difficult to prove than transgender ones (no explanation was provided as to why, although I surmised that he was implying that this was due to purportedly more 'visible' evidence of transgender claims). He would urge his clients to 'join (Toronto-based) LGBT groups such as the 519 Community Centre, Black Coalition for Aids Prevention or Supporting Our Youth if you're under 25'. All of these organizations provided 'great support and good proof of your orientation' and could be viewed as evidence that the refugee claimant was 'participating in the community' and establishing a new life in Canada. Other forms of documentation were discussed as well, including letters from friends and family members, photocopies of profiles from gay cruising/dating websites such as 'Gay.com' or 'Adam4Adam.com' ('not enough on their own to prove anything' according to another lawyer) and photographs of romantic/life partners of the claimant in LGBT groups or at the Toronto Pride parade. One lawyer told the group that while photos could be helpful, a single photo of a claimant watching the Pride parade with friends was not going to work: 'I'm gay 365 days a year, not just one. ... You must show how your life is this way every day.' At some of these meetings, successful refugees (those whose hearing had resulted in a positive decision) would endorse the lawyers' comments, noting that they were asked questions about these documents by the Board member at their hearing, indicating their importance and possibly suspicion.

Thus, SOGI refugee claimants were repeatedly told of the need to assemble documentary evidence that would substantiate their life narratives. In most cases, the narrative would need to be honed so that it 'fit' the UN definition of 'refugee', which required proof of membership in a particular social group

(SOGI) and evidence of persecution based on that membership. Therefore, a diverse range of documents ranging from identity certificates to photos to personal and institutional letters were recommended to be added to the application file, which resulted in claimants spending a substantial amount of pre-hearing time obtaining as much documentary evidence as possible. One claimant told me how she had coached her grandmother back in St. Lucia on what to write in the letter, and what incidents should be included and what should not. A number of claimants used their smartphones to take pictures of themselves with peer support group leaders or with visiting LGBT public figures after the meetings, and they would then submit these photos to their lawyers. However, a letter attesting membership in an LGBT refugee support group was promoted as one of the key components of the overall documentation package, with the implication that it carried great weight in terms of legitimizing a credible 'LGBT' identity through membership and participation in publicly recognized Canadian LGBT community organizations.

Much more could be said about the inherent problems of legitimizing an 'authentic' sexual orientation or gendered identity primarily through letters confirming participation in a limited number of publicly recognized LGBT community organizations, some of which will be outlined at the end of this chapter and in Chapter 5.[5] At this point, I want to emphasize how the relatively consistent and insistent promotion of the importance of letters confirming membership in LGBT community organizations for refugee case files helps to contextualize the support group leader's comment at the beginning of this chapter in which he stated that the increased in support group membership was due to the strategic self-interest of refugee claimants and not necessarily due to the quality of leadership or support provided by the volunteers. In fact, he added, many group members stopped attending meetings after a successful hearing in which they received convention refugee status.

HOW TO WRITE A LETTER

Returning to the discussion on how to improve the process for writing letters at the meeting for refugee support group volunteers, the group leader reminded us that 'we have to think about the integrity of (this organization) when we're writing these letters,' particularly as these letters were viewed by the IRB as 'the gold standard', indicating his perception of and concern about the group's relationship to and reputation with the refugee apparatus of the Canadian nation-state. Improvements to tracking attendance was one of the first areas of discussion, as a number of volunteers felt that the current format of recording members' attendance (passing around a sheet of paper at the beginning of the meeting in which each individual printed his or her name, phone number and email address) wasn't working. The problem with this set-up was that people who arrived late often didn't sign the form. Also, one volunteer said that he'd seen some people writing two names on the sheet and some members leaving after they had written down their information. Finally, the volunteer letter-writers were finding that some group members disputed their attendance record at the letter-writing meeting, that is, they claimed to have attended more meetings than was on the official record.

However, when the group leader asked for alternative solutions, the volunteers weren't able to come up with many ideas; none of the volunteers wanted to walk around the group with the sheet watching each individual sign it, and when one member suggested that we take attendance at the end of the meeting, others felt it wasn't fair to allow those who came in late to sign the sheet. In the end, it was agreed that attendance sheets would be distributed towards the middle of the meeting, which would allow latecomers (but not the 'really late' latecomers) to sign in and prevent people from leaving early. One volunteer was assigned to maintaining and updating the attendance records on Excel spreadsheets and regularly posting updated sheets to a cloud file sharing site so that all volunteer letter-writers could access attendance records. The revised spreadsheet would contain the following categories: Member's Name, Email, Phone, Country of Origin, Date of Birth, Immigration Case #, Date of Arrival in Canada, Lawyer, Hearing Date, Status (outcome of hearing), Letter (date written) and (overall attendance) Count.

We then moved on to discuss the process for writing the 'confirmation of group membership' letter, which up to now had followed a rather informal procedure whereby at the end of each meeting, any refugee claimant who had received confirmation of their IRB hearing date was told to meet with one of two volunteer 'letter-writers' after the meeting in order to work out a date on which the claimant would bring her/his refugee claim application and be interviewed by the letter-writer, who would then go home, write the letter and leave it at the support group centre to be picked up. As noted above, the primary complaint about this set-up was in regard to the number of last-minute requests from group members who needed the letter to be written and sent to their lawyer immediately (the lawyer would then forward the letter, along with other documents, to the IRB) and disputes over the number of meetings attended. Volunteer letter-writers were feeling overwhelmed by these last-minute requests and disagreements and wanted a more systematic process. After much discussion, the group agreed that they should create a new form for requesting a meeting with one of the volunteer letter-writers, and that this form would contain clear instructions about the procedure and time frame. The volunteer letter-writers indicated that this new form needed to clearly state the following information: (1) No letter would be written for any member who had attended less than three meetings, based on the 'official' attendance record. (2) The meeting between claimant and letter-writer could take up to two weeks to set up. (3) The letter could take up to two weeks to be written and returned to the claimant. (4) It was imperative that the claimants bring all their refugee claim application documents with them to the meeting so that the correct information could be entered in the letter.

At this point, people began to discuss statements in the letter confirming sexual orientation.[6] One volunteer said he tried to get a sense of claimants' sexual orientation when he asked them questions based on his reading of their PIF, and that sometimes he 'gets the sense that something isn't true'. Others added their doubts about certain claimants' sexual orientation,[7] so it was agreed that letter-writers were not obliged to make any statements attesting to an individual's sexual orientation if they felt uncomfortable or unsure about it. Throughout the meeting, there were a number of references to and questions about the validity or authenticity of some refugee claimants' (sexual orientation) identities and the organization's responsibility to write letters that were 'accurate' and 'truthful', as the group leader had heard that IRB adjudicators were relying more heavily on letters from LGBT refugee support groups such as this one, so 'the pressure is on' (this was the context in which he made the comment about relying on one's gaydar). He noted that other groups were addressing similar problems, that is, members asking for letters after attending only a couple of meetings, so they too had implemented more stringent rules, for example, requiring all members to show their refugee identity documentation at the door in order to be admitted to a meeting, and a mandatory orientation session for new members in order to understand the group's rules and protocols.

These conversations and actions of LGBT refugee support group volunteers convey a sense of responsibility for retaining the organization's reputation in the eyes of the IRB, an arm of the state's immigration apparatus, but they also convey anxiety around the production of documentation for validating refugee claimants' credible sexual orientation. Feedback from successful refugee claimants and lawyers reinforced the idea that these support groups' letters were of crucial importance in a Board member's assessment of a claimant's identity, that is, his or her 'credibility' as a member of this particular social group. Group leaders, volunteers and facilitators were increasingly concerned about writing letters for members who didn't regularly attend meetings and/ or who they believed might not be telling the truth about their sexual orientation because they did not want their organization's perceived 'gold standard' reputation besmirched by letters attached to individuals who did not meet that organization's standards of 'good membership' (defined minimally in terms of attendance) or worse, to individuals who weren't 'really' gay, lesbian or bisexual.[8] This double-edged anxiety pertaining to the maintenance of a good reputation and not writing letters for claimants whose stated sexual orientation was in doubt, resulted in a protocol in which volunteers were encouraged to apply informal and implicit somatic, affective conventions such as the gaydar in making decisions about what kind of content the letter should contain. Thus we witness a moment in which social aesthetics are intimately tied to the production of documentary and bureaucratic forms created for and demanded by the state's immigration apparatus (Cabot 2013: 456). Whether or not these organizations were comfortable with the IRB's use and interpretation of their letters, leaders and volunteers perceived their responsibility not only in relation to refugee claimants' interests but also in relation to the interests of the state. Thus, in revising attendance recording procedures and the letter writing process – due, in part, to feedback from lawyers and former refugees indicating the state's reliance on these documents to authenticate SOGI identity claims and in part to mounting concerns that they were being exploited by possibly bogus refugee claimants – support group volunteers were developing more elaborate processes of self-monitoring and surveillance in order to ensure they (and their material products, the letters) maintained respectability, legitimacy and, possibly, government funding.[9]

Producing more documentation to protect the status of existing documents demonstrates how these groups become further imbricated in the state's increasingly paranoid biopolitics of determining who is allowed to stay within its borders and who is not. This production effectively contributes to legislative and policy reforms that are transforming the refugee determination apparatus into one premised on suspicion and removal rather than support and resettlement, demonstrating Ticktin's point that humanitarian organizations dedicated to 'non-political, non-interventionist' forms of support and care are often accompanied by a form of policing or surveillance such that the moral imperative to act out of love and compassion is accompanied, implicitly or explicitly, by practices of violence, containment and/or exclusion (Ticktin 2011: 4).

Furthermore, these documents and their increasingly regulated modes of production (such as increased surveillance of the refugee claimant via more detailed attendance records) and affective assessments (the gaydar) become enfolded into the nation-state's relatively new acceptance of homonormative sexual identifications – identifications that are highly delimited and normalized along racialized, classed, and gendered axes of difference and thus operate as templates for 'model' immigrants, refugees and/or citizens. That is, documents in SOGI refugee claim files now operate as a set of 'authenticity filters' through which a claimant's credibility as an LGBT-identified refugee (and future Canadian citizen) is evaluated by the adjudicator (and by extension, the state). As we have seen, some of these documents are based on a set of assumptions about what an 'authentically' gay, lesbian, bisexual or transgender person should look and sound like, but these assumptions reflect the experiences, beliefs and affective registers of the volunteers, most of whom were white, middle-aged gay-identified Canadian males, and therefore inadvertently end up supporting homonationalist agendas of the nation-state (Puar 2007).

CONCLUSION

While many scholars have noted the problematic nature of refugee adjudicators' evaluation methods (Berg and Millbank 2009; Jordan 2010; LaViolette 2009; Millbank 2009a, b; Miller 2005; Ou Jin Lee and Brotman 2011; Randazzo 2005), in this chapter I have tried to draw attention to the ways in which the production of documents like attendance records and membership letters by SOGI refugee support group volunteers involves anxieties and affective labour that enact the regulatory structure of the state such that specific formations and performances of sexual orientation are rewarded while other possibilities go unrecognized or are punished. Document brokers in regimes of care, despite, or in addition to, 'best intentions', become participants in the production of homonationalist scripts through which queer migrant bodies are evaluated. Some pass, but many do not.

The cruel twist in the heightened securitization and regulation of SOGI refugee support letters lies in their unwitting enforcement of the state's policing technologies and increasing suspicion of the fraudulent refugee. While the letters are written in order to support an SOGI refugee's claim, the increased regulation and regimentation of their production – attained through the creation of more documents and reliance on the affective register of the letter-writer in order to maintain the organization's reputational status for writing 'gold standard' letters offering 'credible' proof of sexual orientation – reflects the increasingly restrictive and repressive policies of the state premised on the assumption that all refugees are potential frauds (Fassin 2011: 218), and thus makes these letters complicit with other activities associated with increased border control.

Furthermore, these documents often end up as sites of interrogation at the hearing, and thus become another form of testing (and therefore potentially failing) SOGI identity credibility. In a number of the hearings I attended, Board members asked refugee claimants a series of questions based on these letters; often the questions were in relation to the location, date and time of the support group's meeting or the names of the group facilitators; some Board members asked questions about what was discussed at the meetings. Many refugee claimants answered these questions easily, but in one hearing a claimant had a great deal of trouble answering the Board member's questions about the support group facilitator's name (he could only remember the first name) and how he travelled from his home to the support group meeting site (he couldn't remember specific subway stops or the names of intersections where he boarded the streetcar). That hearing resulted in a negative decision, and although it was likely due to a number of other problematic issues in the claimants' testimony, the fact that he had not been able to 'accurately' respond to the Board member's questions derived from a SOGI refugee support group letter likely contributed to the member's decision that his claim was not credible. However, in an interview with a Board member who has dealt with a number of SOGI refugee claims, she informed me that she didn't, 'give much credence to (a SOGI refugee support organization's) letters – anyone can go to meetings and get a letter. They give little insight into their credibility as a LGBT person.' Thus the presence of these letters in SOGI refugee claimants' case files may end up having the opposite of their intended effect by increasing suspicion among adjudicators about their legitimacy, that is, their ability to authenticate claims of sexual orientation identity, revealing their ambivalent, if not duplicitous potential. As Hetherington observes, documents are duplicitous, containing many qualities that can never be exhaustively accounted for, as these qualities are actualized as information through multiple readings in which they are introduced (2011).

As the word of asylum seekers has lost credibility over time (Fassin and Rechtman 2009: 269), letters from medical experts, country experts and other authorities such as LGBT refugee support organizations become the evidence on which credibility is partially determined, and thus form part of the increasingly complex array of instruments developed to scrutinize and assess the truth of applicants, many of whom are rejected and end up added to the pool of illegal aliens after they have exhausted every possible appeal (Fassin 2011: 221), while simultaneously contributing towards the state's ever-changing rules, regulations and policies about who can legally belong and who cannot. The paradox is that in a system of surveillance and suspicion, the ever-increasing amount of documentation (and affective labour) associated with proving the 'authenticity' of the refugee claimant produced by regimes of care may end up being dismissed or viewed suspiciously by the powers that demanded these documents' creation in the first place: the document that supposedly proves the credibility of a claimant's sexual orientation becomes a site for further interrogation, demonstrating the state's underlying assumption of the refugee as a fraud. Queer refugee claims are taken up by mainstream LGBT groups and humanitarian organizations who, despite their best intentions of caring for 'fellow queers', perpetuate homonationalist discourses. The anxiety surrounding the production and unintended effects of SOGI refugee documents illustrates the increasingly exclusionary dynamics of asylum processes and their critical role in underpinning the securitization and privilege of the neoliberal state.

NOTES

1. Among the SOGI claimants and support groups that I worked with, sexual orientation was considered more difficult to 'prove' than gender identity, the latter of which was assumed to be more 'visible' to adjudicators.

2 Due to changes to the Canadian refugee apparatus initiated in December 2012, documentation formats and processes have also been altered: the PIF has been replaced by the Basis of Claim form. All of the research participants in this project had filed their applications using the PIF.

3. http://www.irb-cisr.gc.ca/Eng/RefClaDem/Pages/ClaDemGuide.aspx#_Toc340245815 (accessed 14 August 2013).

4. http://www.irb-cisr.gc.ca/Eng/RefClaDem/Pages/ClaDemGuide.aspx (accessed 16 August 2013). This definition follows the United Nations definition of a convention refugee: One's sexual orientation or gender identity may be considered to form 'a particular social group' who have a well-founded fear of persecution and are in need of protection because if they return to their home country they will face a danger of torture, a risk to their life or a risk of cruel and unusual treatment or punishment.

5. For example, while there appears to have been some recognition among lawyers and support workers that becoming a refugee required learning an overly inscribed identity narrative, comments like 'I'm gay 365 days a year ...' indicate that there was little reflection on sexual identity/orientation as a similarly learned narrative or performance. Sexuality was viewed as an inherently natural, and all-consuming quality of the body, mind and soul. See Chapter 2 for further discussion of how the Canadian refugee apparatus operates with particular Western, classed and racialized ideas about sexuality.

6. It should be noted that not all SOGI support organizations would write letters containing affirmations of group members' sexual orientation or gendered identity. In fact, the vast majority of volunteer organization letters that I read in the files of research participants (those who allowed me to look through their documents) only confirmed the individuals' membership in that organization, their duties (if any) and attendance. Some letters would include 'moral value' statements attesting to the individual's commitment or dedication to that organization and/or the quality of their work.

7. Some members were silent throughout this discussion, so I don't know if there was general consensus on this issue.

8. I heard no discussions about 'fake' transgender refugee claimants, which once again may be due to the (highly problematic) assumption that (trans)gendered identification cannot be 'hidden' like that of sexual orientation.

9. Two of the SOGI refugee support organizations I participated in received some operational funding from the federal Department of Citizenship and Immigration.

Chapter 5

Discourse and Emotion in SOGI Refugee Hearings

For most of the Toronto-based refugee claimants that I worked with, the part of the refugee determination process they wanted to learn most about was 'the hearing'. On the Canadian Immigration and Refugee Board website, the hearing is described as 'an important moment in the refugee protection process because (it) is usually when the RPD (Refugee Protection Division) decides whether you are a convention refugee or a person in need of protection. ... (The hearing) is a non-adversarial process at which the member or the RPO (refugee protection officer) will ask the claimant questions about the facts supporting the claim in order to establish the truth of the story. No one argues against the claim.' However, another page of the IRB website states that 'the refugee claimant has the burden of proof,' indicating that the process may indeed contain adversarial moments.[1] We see further hints of adversity in the description of the sequence of events at a hearing: The sequence is outlined on the website:

1. You will testify: Before you testify, you must make a solemn affirmation, which is a promise to tell the truth. You will then be asked questions first by the member, and then by your counsel.
2. If you bring any witnesses, they will testify after you have testified.
3. After you and any witnesses have testified, the member will ask you or your counsel to explain why you think the evidence shows that you are a convention refugee or a person in need of protection.
4. The RPD member will decide whether you are a convention refugee or a person in need of protection.[2]

Thus, while the hearing may be described somewhat benignly in some sections of this government portal, other sections construct a different image via a description that conveys a structure and format premised on formal Euro-American juridico-legal terminologies and logics, such that the RPD member is, in effect 'a judge', who is gathering 'evidence' to determine if the 'plaintiff's' case is true or false based on his or her (and any witnesses) 'solemn affirmation' to tell 'the truth'. Evidence is gathered at the hearing through cross-examination of the claimant's story, in which particular incidents, locations and people presented in the written version of that story (known in IRB parlance as the 'Personal Information Form' and more recently, 'Basis of Claim' form)[3] are broken down into a series of questions from the Board member who then evaluates the oral testimony in relation to the written documentation. Thus, for the refugee claimant, the hearing may feel more like an episode of the American television drama 'Law & Order' than a 'non-adversarial' conversation.

In previous chapters I have explored how SOGI refugee claimants learn about and prepare for the hearing. I have argued that most claimants learn about the importance of credibility from their legal counsel, immigration support workers and other refugees. More specifically, they learn how to speak, respond and perform in order to persuade the member they are authentic (and therefore credible) Lesbian, Gay, Bisexual or Transgender (LGBT) refugees. In this chapter I focus on the training, words and performance of the key player who evaluates the SOGI refugee claimant's documents and performance – the IRB Member. The Board member (or 'Member'), as noted above, is the individual at the hearing who decides if the claim for refugee protection is accepted or rejected. On the one hand, this is an extraordinary responsibility, the determination of whether an individual is telling the truth or not, with extraordinary consequences for that individual if it is decided that he or she is not telling the truth. On the other hand, this is a mid-level bureaucratic position in a vast and growing immigration apparatus where hundreds of Board members across Canada make hundreds of decisions on refugee claims daily (the IRB states that there are, on average, 40,000 hearings per year). As Didier Fassin observes, the governmentality of immigration in many twenty-first-century nation-states has resulted in a large 'street level bureaucracy' in which the state's dirty work of selecting good from bad immigrants has been downloaded to local bureaucrats, who sometimes experience moral dilemmas between their obligations as civil servants implementing state policy and their emotions when confronted with tragic situations (2011: 218).

While there is now a substantial body of research in refugee and immigration studies that elucidates the deeply problematic logics and assumptions in the policies and decisions of this 'street level bureaucracy' in relation to refugees, and SOGI refugees more specifically (Berg and Millbank 2009; LaViolette 2009; LaViolette 2010; Millbank 2009; Miller 2005; Rehaag 2008), it is important to find out what we can about the training and decision-making *process* of these bureaucrats and their perspectives on their duties and responsibilities. In so doing, we can challenge the tendency to construct and render the state as an impersonal force that often appears to operate with its own logic and rationale. However, my goal is not to 'humanize' the state in the sense of trying to develop an empathetic analysis – rather, I am following anthropologist Laura Nader's now classic entreaty to 'study up' (1972), that is, to study individuals and groups in greater and lesser positions of power in order to better understand the (il)logical, (im)moral and often contradictory organization of power, with a particular focus on the intersections of discourse, terminology, emotion, sexuality, nation and citizenship as they form a powerful nexus through which some migrant bodies are allowed to pass and many more are not.

In an effort to learn more about the training, processes and practices of Board members, I met with three current and former members,[4] three IRB staff and one outside consultant who conducted training workshops and developed guidelines for questioning sexual orientation refugee claimants at the hearings. They provided me with important insights on adjudicating processes and practices along with some of the material (including guidelines for sexual orientation and gendered identity refugee claims) that has been distributed at IRB member training workshops. I also attended nine SOGI refugee claimants' hearings at the IRB offices in Toronto over a ten-month period from November 2011 to September 2012. Finally, I consulted a book written by Peter Showler, former director of the IRB, which consists of 'a collection of thirteen fictional vignettes ... exposing the dilemmas and choices faced by refugees and those who decide their fates', according to the description on the back cover. While the cases in the book are 'fictional' (as are the examples I provide below[5]) because of the confidentiality requirements of all hearings, I found them to be a fruitful site of analysis based on Showler's attempt to portray the inner voices of IRB officials as they negotiate various cases.

In sifting through these various sites, events, interviews and documents, my goal in this chapter is twofold: first, to identify the discursive contours through which SOGI refugee cases are assessed, that is, to examine the discourse and terminology utilized in the hearing by the member to assess the credibility of the claimant. In all refugee hearings, the claimants must provide 'credible evidence' to prove that they are eligible for refugee protection. For sexual orientation and gendered identity claimants, 'the burden of proof' that must be demonstrated is generally twofold – first, they must prove to the Board member that they are members of a 'particular social group', who in the Canadian context are generally defined as individuals who identify as lesbian, gay, bisexual or transgendered in their sexual or gendered orientation. Second, the claimants must prove that as members of this social group, they face persecution in their country of origin. As I have pointed out in previous chapters, sexual and gendered desires, practices, identities and prejudices are organized in deeply different ways within and across social, cultural and national borders. Proving credible sexual or gendered orientation and proving credible persecution based on membership in this social group become deeply entangled in sexual and gender identity terminologies with pre-existing socio-cultural determinate concepts, which may be well understood by the member but not by the claimant (McConnell-Ginet 2006: 228); misunderstanding and/or misinterpreting the meanings of sexual and gender identity terms may influence a negative evaluation of the latter by the former.

An additional challenge in the hearing is that much of the adjudication is based on the personal narrative and oral testimony of the claimant; unlike claims based on political opinion, race, nationality or religion, which tend to have some form of independent verification of group membership, sexual orientation claims depend mostly on the presentation of internal, often unspoken, or unspeakable qualities, desires and practices such that extremely private experiences infuse all aspects of the claim (Berg and Millbank 2009: 196). Once again, complex, intimate and traumatic experiences may be difficult to articulate or render 'credible' if they do not 'make sense' in relation to the members' conceptualizations inherent in their use of particular sexual identity terms, and the members may utilize a social aesthetics of eligibility similar to support group volunteers who write letters, outlined in the previous chapter.

My findings support Berg and Millbank's arguments that in SOGI refugee cases, adjudicators often make evaluations based on sexual identity terms that reflect their training and/or 'common sense' understanding of sexual identities, which are based on a staged model of sexual identity development derived from specific cultural, gendered, raced and classed experiences and operate with particular assumptions about sexual identity as fixed, discover-able and moving from a position of closeted to 'coming out', in which the hearing serves as the apotheosis to this narrative (Berg and Millbank 2009: 207–15). However, I want to extend this argument by locating its key points in the IRB training documents and guidelines for these types of claims, which thus extends the discursive terrain beyond the bureaucratic event of the hearing itself and connects it to wider chains of socio-legal discourses of migration and sexuality. This discursive terrain produces an institutionalized speech genre (oral evidence-based evaluation techniques) which produces linguistic inequality through pretextuality, that is, the member's socially pre-conditioned meaning assessments influence communicative behaviour and reinforce the privilege of those who are trained in and familiar with those preconditions (Maryns and Blommaert 2002: 12–14).

My second goal is to identify adjudicators' non-linguistic, affective or emotional registers which may influence the decision-making process and to consider the relationship between these non-linguistic registers and the hegemonic linguistic evidence-based process of adducing the truth of a refugee claimant's story. That is, in interviews with IRB members and staff and in Showler's book, there is often reference to the importance of nonverbal, corporeal or emotional cues, which Board members utilize to help underscore or validate their linguistic evidence-based decision-making framework. I argue that this affective dimension of the decision-making process is both similar to and different from the social aesthetics employed by SOGI refugee support group letter-writers discussed in the previous chapter: it allows the Board members to humanize their relationship to the claimant, and creates, in their view, the potential for an 'empathic' bond (or lack thereof) that helps to validate their decision. However, this empathic bond may be based on assumptions of universal, essentialist emotive capacities and displays, particularly in relation to love, desire and fear. These assumptions about being able to 'sense' the truth about feelings and emotions in others are potentially problematic when applied in the hearing in which persons from diverse cultural, racial, class and/or economic backgrounds are performing and assessing a difficult story that is full of violence, fear, shame and rapid life transitions in an environment that is tightly structured through a juridico-legal framework, which utilizes terms and discourses privileging a particular set of relationships between truth, identity, sexuality, gender, culture and nation that are well understood by some and possibly not understood at all by others. In line with the previous chapter, I argue that affective labour in assessing SOGI refugee credibility invokes particular incarnations of nationalism and citizenship, which are themselves freighted with moral valences of proper assemblages of sexuality, gender, race and class, thus contributing to the hegemonic affective economy of the nation-state.

A PAUSE IN THE PROCESS

All IRB hearings in Toronto take place on the 4th and 5th floors of a nondescript office building in the downtown core. Each floor has a waiting area; the 4th floor waiting area has one wall of thick glass, with the refugee claimants, lawyers, friends and family on one side and the IRB staff on the other. The rest of each floor is divided into identical small rooms in which the hearings take place. It is a strange experience walking down hallways peering into room after room with exactly the same placement of furniture, lighting, computer, Canadian flag, coat of arms and security camera mounted in the ceiling. Each room has four desks arranged to form a square, and two doors, one opening into the hallway where the refugee claimant and legal counsel enter, and one opening into a private hallway that is only accessible to IRB staff. One desk has a computer and telephone – this is the Board member's desk, and the other desks are bare except for microphones used to record voices. These other desks are for the claimant, legal counsel and other IRB staff. In most rooms there is also a box of tissues on the refugee claimant's desk. The refugee claimant and the member face each other directly. Friends, witnesses or observers sit in a row of chairs behind the refugee claimant, so no eye contact can be made.

Every hearing I attended followed the same general format. The Board member would enter the room from the door located behind their desk. We would stand up as he/she entered, and once seated, the member would announce that this was the hearing of (claimant's name), followed by asking the claimant if he or she understood English (if no translator was present) and then asking him or her to take an oath 'to solemnly affirm the evidence you give today is the truth'. The Board member and legal counsel would then engage in a discussion about the organization of documents in the file, confirming that, for example 'item C1' is the Personal Information Form, and 'item C4' is the letter submitted by a psychologist. In a number of cases, additional 'last minute' documents, such as a letter from an overseas family member, were submitted by counsel, which then had to be accepted by the Board member and given a specific file number. The refugee claimants would sit quietly observing this conversation, and a number of them told me afterwards that they had no idea what was going on other than that they recognized 'their' documents were being discussed in some manner.

Showler aptly describes these opening formalities as 'more priestcraft ... (that) were mainly for the record to satisfy the procedural requirements of the Federal Court. Claimants rarely understood the legal folderol. ... It simply confused and alienated them' (Showler 2006: 187). Opening the hearing with a required oath to 'solemnly affirm' telling the truth, followed by a conversation in which documents are identified by combinations of number and letters in a sequence known only to the legal counsel and Board member immediately crystallizes the moment as both a bureaucratic event and formal judicial ritual utilizing an institutionalized, procedural and technical discourse that the claimants have little to no familiarity with, thus rendering them marginal and unequal by virtue of their 'illiteracy' in relation to the other participants in the ritual who, through their relaxed familiarity with the proceedings and bureaucratic discourse, can be perceived to be occupying the roles of priest and ritual expert (Maryns and Blommaert 2002: 19).

Following this opening ritual discourse, the Board member normally identifies the key 'issues' for the claimant and counsel, that is, the areas of the claim that are problematic and/or require further clarification through questioning. For many of the SOGI refugee claimants, two key issues are identified: their credibility as members of a particular social group (the veracity of their claim to being gay, lesbian, bisexual or transgendered), and the credibility of their claim to being persecuted as a member of that social group (is their story of why they left their country of origin true, and if so, does it meet the UNHCR Convention and Protocol Relating to the Status of Refugees definition of 'persecution'?). The refugee claimants are then reminded to answer all questions as accurately as possible, and if they don't know or forget a particular date or location, to say so instead of making something up. After identifying the issues, questioning begins, often with a few benign background questions like 'how many members are there in your family' or 'how big is the village you grew up in?' These questions are often short in length, seeking out 'factual' information, and most claimants answered them with relative ease. In most cases, there would then be an abrupt switch in the form and content of questioning, from factual details to a completely different topic like 'Are you a homosexual?' or 'When did you realize you were gay?' followed by, 'What does the acronym LGBT stand for?' In another case, a claimant might be asked a series of detailed questions about his or her son's birth certificate (e.g., 'Why is there no middle name initial on the certificate when you provide this middle name on your Personal Information Form?'), immediately followed by a series of questions about his or her first boyfriend in high school.

Prior to attending hearings, I wrongly assumed that the member's questions would be ordered in the same sequence as the events outlined in the claimants' PIF, which usually began in adolescence and progressed chronologically through to adulthood, highlighting events and actions relevant to the claimant's (perceived) sexual orientation/gender identity that eventually forced them to leave their country. I was therefore surprised by the highly detailed and apparently random order of questioning at the hearing, in which the sequence and timing of a particular event would be cross-examined in minute detail and then the member would suddenly switch to asking detailed questions about a particular personal document such as a college transcript. Refugee claimants would often confirm feeling confused and disoriented by the member's questions when I spoke with them after the hearing. In an interview with a member, I asked whether rapid shifts in question topics was a specific strategy for eliciting evidence, and she responded that because there is only a limited amount of time in which to assess the claim, and because most claims contain a few key issues that require cross-examination in order to determine credibility, she could not afford the luxury of asking questions chronologically. However, the effect of these multiple temporal and topical jumps was disorienting to say the least, and while some claimants were impressively adept at adjusting to these rapid shifts, others became visibly agitated and increasingly unfocused or vague in their answers, which could lead the member to infer that there was inconsistency in the testimony, which could in turn lead to a decision that the claim was not credible.

In addition to the random order and movement of questioning, the wording of the questions itself warrants close examination in order to better understand what kind of information or knowledge the Board member is trying to elicit and/or considers a 'good' answer. I am particularly interested in members' questions that utilize terms referring to the claimant's sexual identity,[6] as they form a critical component of the overall assessment of the credibility of the claim. As noted above, questions about sexual experiences, sexual identification and/or knowledge about sexual cultures could come 'out of left field' at any point in the hearing. One minute a claimant might be asked if she knows about the laws pertaining to sexuality in her country of origin and the next question might be about where the LGBT refugee support group meets in Toronto. Despite the (apparent) random order of questions assessing the credibility of the claimant's sexual identity, I often heard the same questions being asked in the hearings I attended. Not surprisingly, the appearance of similar questions about sexual identity in multiple hearings is not a random coincidence. In interviews with Board members and IRB staff, I was repeatedly told that SOGI refugee claims are now a standard component of all Board members' training. One staff member reminded me that the IRB has come a long way since the first lesbian and gay refugee claims were lodged in the early 1990s (see also LaViolette 2010): Whereas it used to be the case that some Board members dismissed a claim if the person didn't 'look' gay or lesbian, now all members get three weeks of in-class training, and SOGI claims are a standard module in the training package. This module was developed by staff members in consultation with national lesbian and gay rights groups such as EGALE and expert consultants in sexuality, gender and migration law. One of these consultants gave me a copy of the guidelines[7] that are provided to Board members to help them better understand the particularities of these claims. The guidelines begin by noting that 'assessing the veracity of a refugee claimant's homosexuality is a very difficult, sensitive and complex task in the context of an administrative or quasi-judicial hearing' (LaViolette 2004: 3). They then outline some 'general principles' such as 'there are no universal characteristics or qualities that typify sexual minorities' (2004: 4) and that many factors may intersect with the sexual orientation of an individual (the primary example provided is gender, that is, sexual minorities often challenge dominant gender values) (2004: 6). The guidelines emphasize the centrality of 'credibility' in the determination of a claim, that the onus of proof is on the claimant, and that in rejecting a claimant's testimony regarding his or her sexual orientation, members must be careful to clearly identify the contradictions, inconsistencies, omissions or implausibilities that support a negative conclusion on the issue of membership in the particular social group. This is followed by a note indicating that members have to be careful when it comes to implausibility: 'The Federal Court has cautioned that because refugee claimants come from different cultures, actions which appear implausible when judged from Canadian standards might be plausible' (LaViolette 2004: 10). As will be seen below, the challenge of determining (im)plausible sexual desires, identities and relationships based on written and oral testimony can be extraordinarily difficult, if not impossible, given the potential for mistranslation and/or misinterpretation based on privileged definitions and meanings utilized in the institutionalized discourses of the hearing.

The guidelines include 'a proposed model of questioning claimants about their sexual orientation', and it is in this section that we see the possible origin of the similar questions that I heard in various hearings. It is somewhat telling that this section begins with the statement, 'It cannot be stressed enough, however, that there are no true answers to these questions' (LaViolette 2004: 12), which, I would argue, reveals more about linguistic inequality in the refugee determination process than perhaps any other sentence in the guidelines, and which I will return to below. There are three general 'Subjects of Inquiry' in this section, each containing a series of suggested questions[8]: (1) Personal & Family (When did you come to realize your homosexual orientation? What did you personally believe about homosexuality when you realized you were lesbian or gay? Have you been involved in a relationship with someone of the same sex in the past? Have you told anyone about your sexual orientation?), (2) Lesbian and Gay Contacts and Activities in the Country of Origin & Canada (Where do gay men or lesbians go to socialize in your country of origin? How do they meet each other? Did you know of any lesbian or gay groups in your country of origin? What do you know about gay and lesbian communities in Canada? Do you socialize in gay and lesbian bars? Which ones? How different are lives of gays and lesbians in Canada compared to back home?), and (3) Discrimination, Repression & Persecution in the Country of Origin & Canada (What do you fear if you return to your country of origin? What are the official laws on homosexuality in your country of origin? Do you know the legal status of gays and lesbians in Canada?) (LaViolette 2004: 13–16).

I would like to focus on the sexual identity terms utilized in these questions (which may be asked in the hearing) and the claimants' answers to these questions in order to better grasp how pre-existing knowledge (or the lack thereof) and (un)familiarity with these terms produce linguistic inequality, with potentially severe consequences for the refugee claimant. In some hearings, a claimant might be asked a question like 'When did you first realize you were homosexual?' followed by 'Where did you realize this?' Some claimants would answer the first question with a specific age like '14', but in one hearing I attended, a claimant paused long enough for the member to ask, 'Did you understand the question?' The claimant then hesitantly answered, 'When I was in university'. The claimant's pause could have been interpreted to be problematic by the member because this question is included in the SOGI guidelines, which implies that the claimant should be able to provide an answer in a relatively straightforward and decisive manner. Someone who is pausing could be lying because someone who is telling the truth is assumed by the member to be able to quickly recall such a significant moment, based on the member learning from the guidelines that self-consciousness of one's sexual orientation is a significant event. But the question 'when did you realize you were a homosexual' is freighted with particular socio-cultural assumptions about sexual identity development because of the presence of terms like 'homosexual', which have been identified in sexuality research as socio-cultural concepts located in Euro-American colonial worlds, which now have extensive transnational mobility and interpretive variability.[9] Ethnographic research has demonstrated how connections between sexual practices, desires, relationships, identities and terminologies are histori- cally and culturally variable, so terms like 'homosexual' and 'gay' may be unfamiliar and/or have different meanings related to different socio-cultural contexts. Not all societies may have sexual identity terms that easily equate to 'gay' or 'homosexual', and even in societies with identity terms for people who engage in same-sex relationships, there may be significant temporal and/or cognitive gaps between the memory of initial desire for someone of the same sex and realizing that one's desires are associated with a particular sexual identity term. There is also evidence demonstrating that those who engage in same-sex sexual practices may not identify with a same-sex sexual identity term even if they are aware of that term associated with that practice in their own language.[10]

If we return to the claimant's pause after the question posed above, it could be the case that he was pausing to figure out what the Board member was ask- ing; perhaps he had same-sex relationships when he was younger, but hadn't thought of himself as 'a homosexual'; perhaps he hadn't thought of himself as 'a homosexual' until he was accused of being one by someone else; perhaps he hadn't thought of himself as 'a homosexual' until he arrived in Canada and filed a refugee claim because in his country of origin he had married a woman and had a child while he continued to have sexual relationships with men and didn't therefore perceive himself as 'that kind of person'. It is also possible that the answer to the member's question was written in the claim- ant's PIF, where these kinds of events and moments are usually noted with details of specific dates and locations, so the claimant may have been pausing to remember what was written there.

The possible pause to remember the details of one's own life written in a document utilizing a particular format and style reveals how, in addition to assumptions about sexual desires being attached to a particular moment of self-consciousness about identifying as 'a homosexual', sexual identity terms in the hearing are also defined and evaluated through spatial and temporal grids through which the claimant and their antagonists move. Complex mental, emotional and sensorial processes become precisely timed and located facts written in chronological order on the PIF (and in other documents), which the claimants are expected to be able to reproduce exactly in their oral testimony. In most cases, it was impossible to know how the Board member interpreted the claimant's answer as they would not give an opinion on how well the question was answered. However, in one case, when a claimant told the Board member that she realized she was lesbian when she was 14, the member responded, 'That's very young to have that kind of realization,' simultaneously conveying his pre-existing knowledge/bias about 'lesbian' sexual identity formation and his moral judgement about when one *should* know their sexual identity.

I also found that questions pertaining to the claimant's knowledge of 'lesbian and gay contacts and activities in Canada' contained similar pre-existing conceptualizations of and connections between sexual desires, identity terms and cultural practices associated with those terms. In hearings, claimants could be asked if they knew what the acronym 'LGBT' stood for. While some had no problem with this, others struggled with the terms. One claimant only remembered 'gay', and then started to mumble words to himself as he searched for the other terms. Finally he said, 'the other words have jumped out of my head.' Members might move on to a different set of questions, but then return to the acronym again later in the hearing (often there was no change in the answer). Other claimants could be asked whether or not they went to LGBT bars and clubs in Toronto, and if so, where they were located. In some cases, a Board member might hold up a photo of a claimant marching down Yonge Street with another woman during the annual Pride parade in Toronto and ask the following questions:

Board Member (BM): What day was that?

Refugee Claimant (RC): Pride was in ... I think June?

BM: In June?

RC: June ... I don't remember the exact dates.

BM: It's not that long ago. ... You don't remember the first time you had physical contact with this woman?

RC: It was at night after Pride.

BM: But you don't know when it was?

RC: I don't know the date.

BM: You think it was June.

RC: I think it was.

BM: Beginning, middle, or end of June?

RC: (sighing) I think between the middle and end ...

This line of questioning could have been derived from the guidelines, which state, 'Many gay men and lesbians find it easier in Canada to meet other gay people, to get involved in social activities, to go to bars or access gay and lesbian culture' (LaViolette 2004: 18). While this may be true for some refugee claimants, it may not be the case for others. A number of the refugee claimants told me that they did not spend much time in the bars and clubs on Church Street, the centre of Toronto's 'gay village'. One woman, Anna, said that she would like to go more often, but she lived in Etobicoke, a suburb of Toronto, and it would take her too long to get home on public transit; further- more, she was working long hours at a nursing home, and was usually too tired to go out. Alimi, a bisexual-identified man from Nigeria, had recently attended his first ever Pride parade, and while he had been amazed at how 'open' everyone was, he was also intimidated by the very public display of sexuality, and he tried to stay away from cameras because he was worried that a photo of him might be seen 'by the wrong people'.

While most of the people I interviewed were aware and appreciative of the openness of sexual diversity in Toronto and the relatively easy and safe access to queer spaces and social life (compared to where they came from), there were other factors that caused them to not feel safe or secure. Most of the interview- ees could not afford to live in queer-friendly downtown neighbourhoods, and were often finding accommodation in shelters, homes of family members who did not know about their sexual orientation or apartments in the outer suburbs where significant numbers of people from similar ethno/national backgrounds lived, resulting in what many felt was a need to continue to be discreet about where and with whom they were seen. The precariousness of accommodation and work, combined with long internalized feelings of fear and distrust of any queer space or gathering meant that a number of interviewees did not have a well-developed sense of mainstream Toronto LGBT topography and culture in the way that the guidelines imply they should.

Furthermore, we might want to question what and where exactly is 'LGBT culture' and who participates in it. In other words, the Board member's (and training guidelines') assumption that queer people congregate in the same spaces and at the same events, or that queer people should be knowledgeable of these spaces and events, elides significant racial, gendered, sexual and ethno-national differences that produce multiple 'queer' sites and communi- ties across the greater Toronto area. In other words, to assume a particular knowledge of certain clubs, groups and locations associated with the 'LGBT' acronym is once again an example of socially preconditioned meaning assessments that impose a homonormative vision of queer life. The fetishization of time and place in questions aiming to determine the credibility of sexual identity is a manifestation of a juridico-legal framework operating with Euro-American conceptualizations of socio-sexual identities, that is, a specific set of terms that are premised upon a staged model of sexual identity development and belonging that is raced, classed and gendered.

DISCIPLINARY COMMENTS AND SIGHS

My examination of the refugee claim hearing up to this point has focused on procedural ideology and terminology in questions posed by the Board member, that is, how sexual minority terms in questions often contain socially preconditioned meanings about sexuality that are connected to particular socio-cultural, historical and political formations. However, while most of the discussion in the hearing was organized around a question and answer format, in which the member asked questions and the refugee claimant provided all the answers, there were occasional moments when the member would comment on an answer, indicating doubt regarding its veracity, thus revealing the member's perspective on what a good answer should sound like. I have already noted one instance above, in which a Board member indicated her disbelief that a claimant could know she was a lesbian at age 14. In another case, the member held up a photo of the claimant's girlfriend from Jamaica and asked the claimant how old the girlfriend was when the photo was taken. She responded, '36'. The member was silent, looking intently at the photo, and then replied, 'She looks much younger than 36.' She then stood up and walked around the room showing the photo to the claimant's legal counsel and me saying, 'Don't you think she looks younger than 36?' (We remained silent.) In another case, a claimant was explaining why he returned to Kenya after living in the United States for two years, where he had an ongoing relationship with another man. The member asked the claimant if he had any sexual relationships after he returned to Kenya, to which the claimant said no, and the member responded, 'How do you go from having a partner in the USA for two years to nobody in Kenya for five years?' In both cases, the members expressed their disbelief in the veracity of the claimant's answer and at the same time conveyed their belief or opinion as to what the right answer should sound like. In one case, the member assumed she could tell the age of a stranger from a different ethno-racial background based on a photograph. In the other case, the member indicated his belief in what the normal sexual appetite of a young homosexual male should be. Once again, the likely negative assessments that were derived from these exchanges appear to be based on the assumption of a universal 'common sense' about how we look as we age in one case, and how often we need to have sex at a certain age in the other case, assumptions that gloss over a vast range of other potential interpretations or explanations.

In some hearings, particularly the ones that were not going well and were taking a long time (sometimes three to four hours), there could be unspoken signs from the members indicating that they were not pleased with the claimant's answers. These sometimes took the form of a sigh. For example, at one hearing, the member was cross-examining the claimant's educational background and finding discrepancies between the claimant's answers and the documentation in her file in relation to particular dates and locations. After a series of questions regarding discrepancies between the claimant's different home addresses during her high school and university studies, the Board member was silent for almost a minute as he made notes, and he then sighed heavily before taking up a different line of questioning. While I didn't remember to ask the claimant if she'd noticed this sigh after the hearing, I interpreted it to be a clear sign of the member's displeasure with her answers and a non-verbal cue that he had made a negative decision as to the credibility of the claim thus far.

THE SIXTH SENSE

Non-verbal cues like sighing give potential insight into a member's emotional state during the hearing, and I became interested in finding out if members were conscious of feelings or emotions that might influence their linguistic evidence-based decision-making process. Perhaps the best example of the dialogue between a linguistic evidence-based decision-making process and an emotional sense-based decision-making process appears in Showler's (2006) fictional vignettes of refugee hearings, in which he sometimes narrates the case from the member's perspective. I was particularly interested in one vignette, which takes us through a case involving a Russian man claiming asylum based on sexual orientation persecution. The chapter begins with a description of the Board member, Hester Laframboise, going to work with 'an armful of books, all pertaining to homosexuality, a topic that had consumed her interest for the entire weekend' (Showler 2006: 183).[11] Laframboise discusses with her staff how she has found some problems in the story of the Russian claimant, such as the fact that he lodged a complaint with the Russian police after he was beaten when he should have known that the police were notoriously homophobic, and that she would focus on these issues in the hearing.

When Laframboise enters the hearing room, Showler writes that she is surprised by the appearance of the claimant: He is 'not at all what she expected' as he's 'surprisingly tall with unruly hair, and a face that was closed to the world' (2006: 186). It is notable how an individual's body type and facial features make a first impression on this (fictional) Board member – while she is clearly not making a decision based on these features, the fact that she is surprised indicates there could already be particular assumptions at work, that is, big men aren't intimidated as easily, or a 'stone-face' makes it harder to believe the claimant's story. Based on her first impression, Laframboise thinks, 'this could be an act,' indicating her doubt of the claim's veracity based on physical features and demeanor. Later in the hearing, she returns to reflecting on the size of the claimant as she has trouble believing that this 'large man' was afraid of fellow workers and skulked about the halls of his building fearing physical confrontation. 'Also, he didn't look gay, not in any of the ways she understood, although the literature of the weekend had educated her on that point. Gays came in all shapes and sizes, eluding the stereotypes as often as matching them.' (Showler 2006: 191). While this passage indicates how Board members may be self-aware of their heterosexist or ethnocentric tendencies, it also reveals how awareness of limits of knowledge may induce reliance on decisions that are partially based on other registers in addition to linguistic evidentiary-based assessment techniques.

Following these feelings of doubt based on her appraisal of his appearance, Hester re-asserts her belief in the deductive process of cross-examination of oral testimony:

> Hester believed she could use reason, knowledge and intuition to drill through the claimant's story. With patience and the right questions you could discover the truth. Most often truth was discovered in the details, the small facts surrounding the large event. Small facts spontaneously rendered, that could not be prepared in advance. You had to look for the little things. She had to believe that, otherwise she would be the fraud, supplanting her reality for theirs. (Showler 2006: 192)

Yet, a few paragraphs later, when Hester is questioning the claimant about being beaten in a dormitory room where he was caught having sex with another student, she becomes frustrated by his vague answers, and after asking him to 'provide more details about the beating', she sees 'a strained look' pass over his face and wonders if she had seen 'a flash of pain in those dark eyes. ... She had seen something, pain, possibly fear, but real, the briefest opening of a curtain' (Showler 2006: 194). Once again, this passage speaks to the investment in finding emotional, sensorial cues such as 'pain' or 'fear'. Much of the rest of the chapter oscillates between these two deductive processes, the emotional-sensorial and the linguistic-evidentiary. By the hearing's mid-point Showler writes, 'She had no gutsy interior emotions at the moment. This fellow wasn't giving them anything. Nothing. He was shut down and she couldn't find a way to pry him open. She also couldn't pick up any hint of homosexuality, not a whiff. Not that she would know. She had to be honest.' (2006: 196). Showler repeatedly illustrates the ways in which deductive logic through questioning and intuition based on 'gutsy interior emotions' are combined to determine the truth of a claim, and how, when a Board member is aware of his or her limits of knowledge, he or she may rely more heavily on sensorial cues. The chapter ends without a formal decision (Hester indicates that she will provide a written decision), but it is quite clear that it will be negative based on credibility, that is, lack of sufficient evidence that this man is gay and that he suffered the alleged acts of persecution (2006: 208).

While my interviews with Board members did not reveal the same level of intimate detail about their own feelings or emotions during the hearing, some provided me with similar anecdotes from sexual orientation refugee cases, which indicated a similar calculus of the emotional-sensorial and linguistic evidentiary techniques at work: these anecdotes were from cases where the claimants, both men, had witnesses who were lovers or ex-lovers testify before the Board members. One member said that when the witness walked into the hearing room, the two men looked at each other and blushed deeply – it was clear to the member that they were in love. Another Board member said that 'accessing the emotional is critical', and that if the claimant's partner was in the room, 'you can tell its genuine'. While the members noted that they couldn't use these moments or cues as the primary rationale for their decision, they indicated that they nevertheless made each case easy to decide. One member summed up this approach by saying, 'you need head and heart to be a good Board member'. I heard similar comments in interviews with other IRB staff who are involved in training Board members. One stated that 'You can't dismiss your sixth sense, but you can't rely on it alone without testing conclusions objectively'. Another noted that she thinks the best members utilize a combination of 'empathy and evidence' in making their decisions.

But how much should a member trust his heart? How sure can one be about her 'sixth sense'? How much can be deduced from corporeal cues, especially in highly organized and charged moments in which the misinterpretation of bodily signs is possible because of the constraints and structures of this bureaucratic and judicial event and the diverse socio-cultural backgrounds of the various participants? The examples that members provided me with indicate an assumption of universal emotions associated with particular corporeal displays, that is, we all recognize 'true love' or 'real fear' when we see it. Furthermore, there is an assumption that these universal emotional displays provide a momentary glimpse into the deeper truth of the refugee claimant's story: Beneath the written/spoken testimony lies an authentic emotional core connected to individual experiences. This emotional core cannot be controlled or consciously manipulated, hence its appeal as a conduit to what a person 'really' is. Conversely, as Showler's vignette about the gay Russian refugee claimant illustrates, if the claimant is 'hard to read' and doesn't display any emotions while recounting traumatic or intimate moments, the Board member may become suspicious of the story's veracity.

Thus, it would appear that sensing and deciphering emotions is a key component in the assessment of refugee claims in addition to the juridical deductive framework based on oral examination of texts and narratives. However, as Catherine Lutz and Geoffrey White note in their review of anthropological research on emotions, significant tensions exist between psychobiological theories that argue for universal human emotions (sometimes referred to as a hardwired/materialist perspective) and a theoretical framework that views emotions embedded in socially constructed categories in which the importance of cultural systems or worldviews is fundamentally important to emotional experience. Lutz and White outline significant socio-cultural variation in notions of privacy, valuation of emotional displays and ideas of appropriate self-conduct in public arenas, any/all of which may impact the ways in which emotion is conceptualized and performed in social activities (1986: 420). More recently, research on emotion has focused on its political dimensions and the ways in which power and authority may be organized through and by particular attachments of emotions to objects. I find Sara Ahmed's discussion of how emotion works on surfaces of bodies in order to define and align some within a 'proper' community such as the nation-state and others abject to and outside of that community to be particularly applicable to the context of the hearing (2004). Like Ahmed, I am concerned not with what emotion 'is' but rather with what it 'does', or rather what is done with perceptions of emotion in a quasi-juridical state event that prioritizes linguistic evidence-based testimony. In contexts of intense cross-cultural translation located within the structure of a highly charged quasi-judicial setting where the refugee claimant's future is being decided, emotions may be displayed, repressed or performed in relation to a multiplicity of factors. The Board member's interpretation of emotional cues or the lack thereof is presupposed upon reliance on his or her own emotional register and the assumption that he or she can accurately perceive the emotional register of the refugee claimant, an assumption that I am arguing may lead to misrecognition, misinterpretation and misjudgement. Even though these emotional interpellations do not appear to be formalized in the evaluative process (or training) of the adjudicator, they appear to undergird or legitimize linguistic evidence-based assessment techniques, thus revealing how particular arrangements of discourse, terminology and emotion do the work of gate-keeping for the nation-state.

CONCLUSION

In this chapter, I have examined how Canadian refugee claim adjudicators assess the credibility of sexual orientation refugee claimants by asking questions that contain terms imbued with particular socio-cultural, historical and political meanings. As Miller notes, the particular kind of identity created, named and rewarded in these hearings is one constrained by asylum's historically specific development and role in the modern regulation of the movement of people:

> Articulating gayness within the asylum process, bringing queer sexuality into the national consciousness of who is here, or who should be here, can be seen as part of a broader engagement with multi layered legal principles, national prejudices, and struggles for public space involving not only asylum seekers but their advocates including NGO champions. All are caught up in the process of making meaning for one's national and international audience at the same time as an individual subject seeks refuge. (Miller 2005: 144–45)

Over the last 20–25 years, the Canadian refugee apparatus has increasingly recognized sexual orientations and gendered identities as particular kinds of social groups worthy of protection under the refugee laws of Canada. One of the outcomes of such recognition is increased attention to and assessment of the definitions and meanings of sexual orientation and gender identity terms, that is, determining appropriate modes of questioning that will help adjudicators determine the 'credibility' of sexual orientation or gendered identity of the claimant. While training guidelines indicate that adjudicators must be careful in their assessment of the 'implausibility' of sexual orientation and gender identity claims and that, in fact, there may be 'no true answers', the order and content of questions in the hearings I attended revealed the application of Euro-American socio-sexual identity terms with socially preconditioned (historic, geographic and political) meanings about sexual identity development, culture and community, which manifest gendered, raced, and classed experience and/or knowledge that privilege the member and work against the refugee claimant. The member's questions, based on guidelines derived from recommendations of some LGBT scholars and activists, assume a particular kind of 'queer literacy', and assumptions about what constitutes a correct answer belie how sexual and gender identity terms are embedded with particular forms of knowledge in juridical bureaucratic events and enable authority to be claimed and retained. What is relatively new here is the way in which a particular discourse about 'authentic' desire, sexuality, gender and identity is now being utilized by the bureaucratic machinery of the nation-state as a form of gate-keeping, such that learning and understanding this discourse and its key terms improves one's chances of being recognized as an 'authentic' SOGI refugee, opening the door towards 'legitimate' citizenship. Yet, while some refugee claimants demonstrate competency with this discourse, others do not, and in hesitating or stumbling over an answer they risk losing credibility, having their claim rejected, and being deported to their country of origin.

I have also tried to demonstrate that the determination of credible sexual orientation in refugee hearings is simultaneously influenced by non-linguistic, non-verbal cues. Conversations with IRB members and staff indicate reliance on an ability to perceive and interpret emotional cues pertaining to questions about intense events or relationships. Interpreting corporeal signs such as blushing upon seeing a lover and relying on 'the heart' to help determine if a story is true reveals an emotion-based evaluative framework that is at least partially applied alongside the linguistic evidence-based framework in determining credibility of claims to be lesbian or gay. This reliance on an emotional register may reflect adjudicators' moral dilemmas over the limits of their knowledge, but these officers in charge of one component of immigration control are responsible for interpreting and applying the policies of the nation-state (Fassin 2011: 218), and they evaluate emotional displays as a mode of accessing the truth (or falsity) of a claimant's story. This somatic or affective dimension of evaluation helps to illustrate how the bureaucratic machinery of the nation-state produces a discursive moral network of terminological, corporeal and sensorial registers in order to define and sort out good migrants from bad ones. In other words, the nation-state's gate-keeping policies and practices are organized around a moral core of the good/bad immigrant/refugee and manifested in part through discourses and terminologies that are enhanced through an assemblage of emotional and sensorial assessments gleaned from individual stories of love, loss and trauma (Ahmed 2004; White 2013, 2014).

In his overview of the governmentality of immigration, Fassin observes a paradox: that as asylum is increasingly disqualified both quantitatively and qualitatively, nation-states develop increasingly sophisticated instruments to scrutinize the 'truth' of applicants who, in the great majority of cases, will be rejected and end up added to the pool of illegal aliens after they have exhausted every possible appeal (2011: 221; see also Fassin and Rechtman 2009: 250–74). Similar to the social aesthetics of eligibility employed by SOGI support group volunteers when writing letters, adjudicators' terminological and sensorial registers are employed to assess the credibility of sexual orientation of refugees, and operate as some of the instruments of this 'truth finding' machinery. However, the Board members wield greater power with their ability to support or reject refugee claims and must be recognized as one of the key nodes in the gate-keeping mechanisms of the nation-state.

The effect of heightened suspicion and scrutinization and the application of multiple assessment registers (linguistic, corporeal and somatic) results in an inevitable increase in the number of rejected asylum seekers, which then confirms the nation-state's claim to need to further increase security and surveillance of asylum because of the increased number of 'bogus' asylum seekers. It is a pernicious circular logic, indicative of the heightened securitization and gate-keeping mechanisms of the late-liberal nation-state and the subtle, yet powerful, techniques through which forms of citizenship are granted in ways that privilege and give life to particular racial, gendered and classed formations while rendering others illegitimate, unworthy and ultimately disposable. In the next chapter, I pursue this logic as it operates in two other forms of documentation that are crucial to the refugee claim and the hearing: the expert witness report, and the National Documentation Package (NDP).

NOTES

1. http://www.irb.gc.ca/Eng/brdcom/references/procedures/proc/rpdspr/Pages/rpdp.aspx (accessed 24 October 2011) and http://www.irb-cisr.gc.ca/Eng/tribunal/rpdspr/ClaDem/Pages/ClaimGuideDem12.aspx (accessed 25 January 2013).

2. http://www.irb.gc.ca/Eng/brdcom/references/procedures/proc/rpdspr/Pages/rpdp.aspx (accessed 24 October 2011) and http://www.irbcisr.gc.ca/Eng/tribunal/rpdspr/ClaDem/Pages/ClaimGuideDem12.aspx (accessed 25 January 2013).

3. The Immigration and Refugee Protection Act has undergone substantial revisions, implemented in December 2012, which have changed the refugee claim process and documentation standards. My fieldwork concluded prior to the implementation of these revisions. See Conclusion for a brief discussion of some of these changes.

4. As Nader observes, the ethnographic work of 'studying up' can be challenging, as powerful individuals and institutions are often literally and figuratively well guarded. I found it difficult to access Board members. I submitted a request to the IRB to interview Board members, but was granted access to interviews with 'policy and procedure' staff members. I met Board members through other networks of contacts.

5. I am employing Showler's approach to writing about hearings (2006: xi): I have fictionalized all examples from hearings by combining conversations and events from separate hearings and changing all identifying details of refugee claimants and Board members (i.e., age, gender, profession, country of origin, family background). Therefore, the following examples from hearings do not refer to or portray any individual, whether refugee claimant or any other person involved with the refugee claim process. My interest is not in identifying IRB members, refugee claimants or specific cases, but rather in analysing the organizational framework and process of the hearing and the underlying knowledge that is applied in the decision-making process.

6. In interviews with Board members, issues and concerns focused on 'sexual orientation' but not 'gender identity'. While I introduced myself as someone who was interested in 'SOGI refugee claimants', Board members only commented on and

provided examples of cases involving sexual orientation cases, and the majority of these involved 'gay male' applicants.

7. 'Sexual Orientation and The Refugee Determination Process: Questioning a Claimant About their Membership in the Particular Social Group' (LaViolette: 2004).

8. What follows are just a few examples of questions for each section.

9. See, for example Boellstorff (2007), Leap and Lewin (2002, 2009), Murray (2009) and Weston (1993).

10. While controversial, the term MSM (men who have sex with men) was developed in HIV/AIDS research as a way of identifying men who engage in same-sex practices but do not identify with a socio-sexual identity term like 'gay', which imputes exclusive male-male sexual relationships and/or identification with a social group with similar behaviours and values.

11. We are not told the titles of the books or if they pertain to homosexuality in Russia or Canada, or some other aspect of the topic of homosexuality.

Chapter 6

National Documentation Packages and Expert Witness Reports

Over the last few years, I have been asked to submit affidavits or 'expert witness' reports on behalf of SOGI refugees and asylum seekers who have lodged their claims in Canada and the United States, which are then submitted as evidence to be reviewed and assessed by a Board member (Canada), asylum officer or immigration court judge (United States) at a hearing (Canada), interview or court appointment (United States). Mostly I have been asked to write about general social conditions for gay and/or transgendered people who live in English-speaking Caribbean nations like Grenada and Barbados, because of my prior anthropological research in this region, which has focused on homophobia and sexual rights (Murray 2009, 2012). For example, one request came from a lawyer in Buffalo, New York, asking if I could write a letter of support for her client, a citizen of Barbados who was in deportation proceedings. The lawyer intended to prove that because her client was transgender, HIV positive, and, in her words, 'a large flamboyant individual', and given Barbados' laws, which criminalize buggery, and social attitudes, which stigmatize HIV positive and transgender individuals, the government would fail to protect her client from private actors who would likely suffer no consequences if they were 'to torture and/or do worse to her client'. The lawyer hoped that I could write a report substantiating her claims of the likelihood of torture if the client was extradited to Barbados.

In a different but related area of refugee documentation utilized in hearings, I have discovered that some of my published research on sexual rights and homophobia in Barbados was quoted in the IRB's "National Documentation Package" (NDP) for Barbados. NDPs are compiled by the Refugee Protection Division of the IRB and 'contain a selection of documents on issues that are relevant to the determination of refugee protection claims'.[1] These collections of documents are publicly accessible and may be utilized by the refugee claimants and/or their lawyer to substantiate claims of systemic persecution in their country of origin. They may also be accessed and used as evidence by the IRB member responsible for making the decision on a claim. There are, at the time of writing, approximately 175 NDPs available on the IRB website, forming what we might think of as an archive of sexual orientation and gender identity, albeit one that is organized in highly delimited ways.

Anthropologists and social scientists are regularly asked to submit 'expert witness' reports focusing on social, cultural or political conditions in refugee-producing nation-states on behalf of human rights organizations or lawyers representing refugee claimants (see Cohen 2009; Good 2006; Good and Kelly 2013; McGranahan 2012; Offord 2013; Swink 2006). In addition, their published research may be knowingly or unknowingly employed by various actors in the refugee apparatus (refugee claimants, lawyers representing refugees, government lawyers, judges, and/or refugee/asylum bureaucracy staff) as evidence to help ascertain the existence of risk of persecution in the claimant's country of origin, assess a claimant's credibility as a member of a particular social group, or assess claimants' accounts of their experience of persecution (LaViolette 2009: 438). In this chapter I want to think about the cumulative effect of this other set of SOGI refugee documents (that is, distinct from documents like letters written by SOGI support groups, discussed in Chapter 4), which are central to the adjudication process as they accrue in the paper and electronic folders of courts, government immigration and refugee departments, and other legal and bureaucratic archives of the nation-state, producing a governmental archive of sexual orientation and gendered identity. Do North American governments' bureaucratic archives of 'other' nation-states' sexual and gender rights, abuses and discriminatory practices re-inscribe or trouble hegemonic discourses of national sexual cultures and gendered subjectivities, which may carry within them older colonial tropes and their deeply entrenched racialized and classed hierarchies? How are gendered identity and sexual orientation being written into discourses of national belonging, rights and citizenship in documents written by 'experts'? What are the effects of these archives on those who come into contact with them – lawyers, academics, expert witnesses, refugee claimants and/or the general public?

In order to address these questions about governmental bureaucratic archives of 'other' nation-states' legal statutes, criminal codes and social attitudes towards sexual and gender minorities, in this chapter I explore sections of the IRB's NDP for Barbados, which contains excerpts from my research about sexual rights and discrimination. I will also discuss the impact of NDPs in the decision-making process of refugee claim adjudicators at the hearings of some SOGI refugee claimants in Toronto. I will then explore some issues that have arisen when I have been asked to write expert reports about social conditions for sexual and gender minorities in Caribbean nation-states, which are submitted to lawyers representing SOGI refugee clients in the United States, and finally, I will consider the broader impact of refugee archives as formations of governmentality and citizenship.

I suggest that expert reports and NDPs contribute to the formation of a bureaucratic archive of sexuality that reinforces homonationalist discourses and narratives, which I have argued throughout this book can be found in numerous nodes of the refugee apparatus. As we have seen in previous chapters, the new wrinkle in this homonationalist discourse is the figure of a grateful homosexual or transgender victim of a foreign nation-state with repressive, homo- or transphobic laws, practices and attitudes, who is rescued and given the 'gift' of citizenship in an 'enlightened' democratic nation-state like Canada or the United States.[2] In certain state institutions and their archives, a 'normative' SOGI refugee or immigrant has emerged as a potentially acceptable citizen, but those who come from nation-states without adequate documentation demonstrating persecution of 'LGBT' groups and/or who don't fit the normative SOGI definition run the risk of rejection, deportation and/or incarceration.

In these archives of governmentality, 'culture', 'sexuality', 'nation', and 'rights' are framing concepts that assume cross-cultural intelligibility such that 'civil servants and politicians reflect, draw on or manipulate popular notions of national versus alien culture to develop policies and manage state institutions (which, in turn, serve to reinforce popular notions of national and alien cultures). In these ways, we can say that issues surrounding migration stimulate, manifest and reproduce (national) cultural politics.' (Vertovec 2011: 242). In this chapter, I am arguing that it is within refugee courts' and immigration departments' bureaucratic archives of sexuality that we can identify another node in the production of homonationalism, a discourse that relies on a highly delimited conceptual triad of sexual and gendered 'identity-border-order' that undergirds the social imaginaries of the nation and its other (Vertovec 2011: 245).

While this book focuses on Canada, it is by no means the only nation-state receiving SOGI refugees. Australia, the UK, South Africa, a number of Western European countries, and the United States have also been popular destinations for individuals who make refugee claims on the basis of sexual orientation and gendered identity persecution. This chapter focuses on individuals who apply for asylum *within* Canada or the United States, because of my ethnographic research focus (Canada) and my limited experience as an expert witness in Canada and the United States. This discussion of governmental archives does not address individuals who apply for refugee status and/or are identified as refugees outside American and Canadian borders, and are then re-settled in Canada or the United States as officially recognized or 'status' refugees. Re-settled status refugees are processed through a different bureaucratic arrangement that operates through multiple national and trans-national governmental and non-governmental organizations, and would thus require studying different and/or additional documents and archives.

DOCUMENTS, ARCHIVES AND REFUGEES

As noted in Chapter 4, anthropologists are paying greater attention to the mediating role of documents, making important links between documents, individuals and the state, demonstrating how the state can enter into the life of the community. In that chapter I presented a case study illustrating documents' complex generative capacities in labour affiliated with immigration and border control of the nation-state, arguing that the creation of new forms of documentation by support group volunteers employed affective registers reflecting increased levels of surveillance and suspicion about the bogus SOGI refugee. While that chapter focused on documents written by one particular set of agents (volunteers and staff in SOGI refugee support groups), which primar-ily attested to a claimant's membership and participation in a support group, in this chapter I am focusing on a set of documents that speak to other issues in the assessment of a refugee claim such as social conditions in a particular nation-state and/or persecution experienced by members of a particular social group in their 'origin' nation-state. Ostensibly, these latter documents carry great weight in the determination process because of their authors' 'expert' status.

In the field of refugee studies, Good has written extensively on documen-tation produced by expert witnesses like anthropologists who are asked to provide written evidence as 'country experts' in the adjudication of refugee cases in Britain. He notes how the adversarial proceedings in these cases pressurize experts to profess greater certainty than they really feel (2006: 130), and that ongoing participation in this system results in higher levels of self-monitoring as the 'expert' holders of knowledge recognize the ways in which that knowledge must be organized and articulated in order to meet the particular logics of the refugee apparatus.[3] As we will see below, self-moni-toring is a key component of the production of my reports – my awareness of the politics of documentation in relation to SOGI refugee claims constitutes a form of self-surveillance resulting in the production of documentary objects that are recognized as 'legitimate' or 'authentic' by the state, but simultane-ously re-inscribe problematic tropes about national sexual cultures, rights, identities and practices.

In her analysis of documentary evidence outlining human rights conditions pertaining to sexual minorities in their countries of origin (material that is often included in NDPs) used in refugee claims, Nicole LaViolette argues that while there have been improvements, 'existing human rights documentation still fails to provide the kind of information sexual minority refugees need to support their claims' (2009: 439). However, as shall be elaborated below, in addition to inconsistent or unsystematic reporting, which may influence an adjudicator's decision to deny a SOGI refugee claim, when approaching the accumulated documents of SOGI claims as an archive of governmentality, we also need to consider how documentation about SOGI persecution 'is built in relation to (an) acceptable narrative of both violation and responses to violation' in the country of origin (Miller 2005: 139), and how that narrative constructs relationships between sexual identities, attitudes, rights and citizenship in both the country of origin and the refugee-receiving nation-state.

In the emerging area of queer archival studies, some scholars are exploring issues of migration and sexuality in the production of archives: Melissa Autumn White examines 'proof of relationship' dossiers that bi-national queer couples are required to submit to the Canadian government in order to substantiate their sponsorship applications. Her analysis of participants' experiences in producing these 'intimate archives' reveals how documents like letters, photos and telephone bills operate as dense transfer points of power, which capture queer subjects within the state's frame of recognition, enforcing both hetero- and homo-normative identity scripts and producing what she terms 'affective governance' (White 2013). More recently White explores LGBTQ refugee claimants' challenges in creating 'archives of trauma', documentation of past violence that will substantiate their claims to persecution based on their sexual orientation or gendered identity, but simultaneously reify and essentialize refugees' and refugee home nation identities (2014). Martin Manalansan challenges assumptions of what constitutes the queer archive (and by extension, queer identity) in his exploration of 'undocumented' queer immigrants' households in New York City (2014). While the documentation that I am working with is clearly not part of a 'queer archive' like that outlined by Manalansan, my analysis is influenced by analytical frameworks that 'queer' the archive, that is, research which is 'about recalling and renewing the historical imperative to apply critical pressure to the type of knowledge we inherit in relation to sexuality and gender and the manner through which we inherit it' (Marshall, Murphy and Tortorici 2014: 3).

NATIONAL DOCUMENTATION PACKAGES

As we have seen at numerous points throughout this book, documents are integral components of a refugee claim. From the moment an individual applies for refugee status within the United States or Canada, multiple

documents are generated to form the case file, which is eventually reviewed
and assessed by an IRB member in Canada or an asylum officer of the US
Citizenship and Immigration Services Department (USCIS) in order to determine if the claimant meets the government's definition of a status refugee.[4]
As I have noted in previous chapters, the documentary evidence required to
make a successful SOGI asylum claim mostly involves two areas: (1) credible
proof of 'membership of a particular social group', that is, proving that one
is homosexual, transgendered, lesbian, gay or bisexual and (2) demonstrating
persecution based on membership in that group. Documentary evidence such
as NDPs and expert reports play a central role in shaping the legal reasoning
and rhetoric in the second area (Miller 2005: 145).

In the Canadian refugee determination process, while the refugee claimants
are responsible for providing evidence at the hearing (such as evidence of
their country's human rights record, evidence confirming their identity and/
or evidence of persecution in their country of origin), the RPD also gathers
information drawn from governmental, non-governmental and media reports
(LaViolette 2009: 439–40), which are compiled into NDPs. In the United
States, asylum claimants may also submit articles from newspapers, books
or human rights reports that help to explain the situation in their country
and what had happened to them in their initial application for asylum. While
the USCIS does not compile publicly accessible NDPs like the IRB, asylum
applicants are encouraged to obtain information from other US government
websites that contain information on countries' human rights records like the
Department of State and the Central Intelligence Agency's World Factbook
website.[5] In the following paragraphs I focus on Canadian IRB NDPs as this
is where my research has been used.

As noted above, an NDP is a compilation of publicly available documents
that report on country conditions such as political, social, cultural, economic
and human rights conditions. Recognizing that these conditions are subject to
change, the IRB regularly reviews and updates country packages, but notes
that 'NDPs are not, and do not purport to be, exhaustive with regard to conditions in the countries surveyed or conclusive as to the merit of any particular
claim to refugee status or protection'.[6] Nevertheless, one should not under-
estimate the potential importance of these documents: while oral testimony
and the personal narrative of the refugee claimant are the central 'evidence'
in Board members' assessment of a refugee claim, their understanding of a
claimant's country of origin conditions 'weigh(s) heavily in the final analysis
of the likelihood that an applicant will face persecution if returned to the
country of origin' (Swink 2006: 256).

All IRB NDPs share the same general organization and categories. I will
briefly outline some of the content of the NDP for Barbados, a country in
which I have conducted research on sexual rights, homophobia and social

change (Murray 2012). Each NDP 'folder' begins with a 'List of Documents' organized into different sections with each section containing links to various documents. These sections include 'General Information and Maps' (for Barbados, the main links in this section are to the Central Intelligence Agency's World Factbook, and the Ministère des Affaires Etrangères, France), human rights related issues, (i.e., 'sexual minorities' and 'gender, domestic violence and children'), 'identification documents and citizenship', 'criminality and corruption', and 'exit/entry and freedom of movement'.[7]

For this chapter's purposes, I focus on Section Six in the Barbados NDP, 'Sexual Minorities', which, at the time of access (December 2013) contained links to three documents, one produced by the IRB, a second written by the International Lesbian, Gay, Bisexual Trans and Intersex Association (ILGA) entitled, 'State Sponsored Homophobia: A World Survey of Laws', and a third written by Maurice Tomlinson, a Jamaican lawyer and LGBT rights activist. The ILGA document and Tomlinson article are brief in content, and present somewhat contrasting views about social conditions for sexual and gender minorities in Barbados. In the ILGA document, Barbados occupies a half page consisting of a small map of the Southern Caribbean region with two images above the map, one with two generic 'bathroom figure' males and the other with two generic bathroom figure females. Each image is framed by the words 'male/male illegal' and 'female/female illegal'. The text consists solely of excerpts from the 'Sexual Offences Act' (1992, Chapter 154–265) focusing on 'Buggery' (Section 9) and 'Serious Indecency' (Section 12), giving the impression that homosexuality is illegal according to the laws of the nation, and that gays and lesbians are subject to persecution under these laws (Itaborahy and Zhu 2013).

Tomlinson's article is titled 'Progress in Barbados despite harsh anti-gay laws', and states:

> Barbados has the harshest penalty for homosexual activity in the Western hemisphere on its books, but overall enjoys a culture of tolerance. … Barbados has recorded very few of the savage homophobic attacks of its fellow Caribbean Community country, Jamaica. This is perhaps a function of a tolerant culture where people in this small densely packed territory are quite likely to know at least one gay individual. (Tomlinson 2013)

In noting that Barbados has a 'tolerant culture' despite harsh penalties for homosexual activity, Tomlinson introduces an important distinction between legal statutes of a nation-state and its socio-cultural attitudes towards sexual minorities.

The longest and most detailed document in this section, 'Treatment of sexual minorities, including legislation, state protection and support services', is written by staff in the Research Directorate of the IRB. It contains a more detailed discussion of the Criminal Code, societal attitudes and support for sexual and gendered minorities,[8] but overall, makes a similar point to Tomlinson's article, namely that 'there have not been any criminal prosecutions for same-sex activity between consenting adults in the region "in recent time",' based on reports from and personal correspondence with 'local LGBTI organizations' and that '(while) Barbados does not have any legislation that protects against discrimination based on sexual orientation in employment, housing, education or health care, the government states that it is "committed to protecting all members of society from harassment, discrimination and violence regardless of sexual orientation"' (Research Directorate 2012). This portrait of a national culture of tolerance towards sexual and gendered minorities is further reinforced by a reference to some of my research on sexual diversity and attitudes in Barbados. It reads:

> An article about sexual diversity in Barbados by an associate professor of Anthropology at York University published in the University of the West Indies, *Caribbean Review of Gender Studies,* explains that 'queens' (effeminate homosexual men, some of whom dress and act like women) are visible in the public culture of Barbados (Murray 2009, 1, 3). The same source notes that while queens have been subject to discrimination, harassment, and physical violence, many appear to have achieved greater public acceptance, or at the very least are more publicly visible, and they are at the forefront of queer community organization and activism whereas lesbians and gays appear to be the problematic group who are less socially acceptable and visible and are not well-integrated into the queer community of Barbados.

This summary, based on what appears to be the first three pages of my article, gives the impression that I am also making an argument for a culture of tolerance for at least one group of Barbadians who refer to themselves as 'queens'. However, if the report's author(s) had read further, they would have seen that my statement regarding the 'appearance' of greater public acceptance of queens and invisibility of gays and lesbians was a straw-man argument: my objective was to challenge taken-for-granted assumptions about the content and meaning of these sexual-gender identity terminologies, that is, to problematize assumptions that these terms are homologous with their Euro-American counterparts. I argue that for some Barbadians, 'gay' and 'queen' are used interchangeably for any cis-male-identified individual who desires another cis-male-identified individual, and that same-sex desire and gender performativity are often intertwined, demonstrating ways of organizing bodies and desires that, at the very least, trouble Western mainstream LGBT categories that are presupposed upon particular distinctions between gender performance, desire and sexual identity (Murray 2009: 12). In other words, I caution against assuming transnationally uniform meanings of socio-sexual identity terms like 'gay', 'lesbian' and 'transgender', as assumptions about these meanings impact how a range of related human rights issues like 'visibility', 'invisibility', 'tolerance' and 'discrimination' are perceived and evaluated.

Furthermore, and perhaps more directly related to the interests of an IRB hearing, this summary of my article states, '*many* (queens) appear to have achieved greater public acceptance' (my emphasis); however, the adjective 'many' does not appear in that sentence from the article. In fact, I state on the same page that 'discrimination and harassment, ranging from being denied housing to verbal epithets and physical violence, are part of everyday life for many queens, and many feel that life in Barbados has become more difficult for them over the past 20–25 years', due to a variety of factors including the HIV/AIDS epidemic, the increasing presence of evangelical churches and the circulation of popular dance hall music from Jamaica containing homophobic lyrics (Murray 2009: 3, 8–9), but this information is not mentioned in the summary. Also missing from the summary of my article is what I considered to be a significant observation about how socio-economic position or class structures socio-sexual networks in Barbados and has a direct impact on one's ability to maintain privacy and anonymity in relation to sexual partners and social activities, which in turn impacts one's ability to safeguard against potential discrimination and harassment (Murray 2009: 14–15).

In noting these oversights of and problematic summaries of key arguments in my writing about sexual and gender minorities in Barbados, my objective here is to draw attention to the different epistemic frameworks, interests and objectives in my research versus the IRB staff who contribute to and assemble the NDP. Whereas the goal of my research has been to challenge popular North American media descriptions of the Caribbean as a uniformly homophobic region by providing insight into the socio-sexual diversity of one nation in this region and some of the complex social, political and economic forces operating at local, national and transnational levels, which produce a range of sexual and gendered identifications and ideas about those identifications in post-millennium Barbados, the goal of the IRB's Research Directorate is to create a report containing a brief synopsis of key findings about particular issues relevant to a refugee claimant's nation of origin. The refugee claim and NDP are structured through frameworks that premise the nation-state as the primary entity through which citizenship, identity, and culture are organized – thus sexual orientation and gendered identity are constructed assuming that culture, gender, sexual identities and attitudes are uniform and contiguous with national borders.

That some of the documents in the Barbados NDP note differences between laws on homosexuality and social attitudes is not an insignificant point, but one potential problem of this form of cultural shorthand lies in the potential for an IRB member to dismiss a Barbadian SOGI refugee claim based on his or her interpretation of the NDP documents (including the problematic summary of my research), which emphasize societal tolerance of sexual and gender diversity.[9] While it is important to keep in mind that members do not base their decisions solely upon information contained in NDPs, these documentation packages can nevertheless influence a member's decision. For example, LaViolette outlines how a lack of reliable information about conditions in the country of origin can lead the IRB to use inadequate resources (such as gay tourism websites) and/or make problematic assumptions about country conditions, that is, documentation that alludes to 'tolerance' of sexual/gender minorities or an absence of documentation of abuses against SOGI individuals means that they are not persecuted (LaViolette 2009: 449).

At the hearings of two Barbadian SOGI refugee claimants that I attended in Toronto in early 2012, both were cross-examined extensively on their knowledge of Barbados' laws pertaining to homosexuality and the level of protection (primarily from the police) they could obtain after they had been physically attacked and/or threatened (in addition to many other questions pertaining to other aspects of their file). Both received positive decisions; however, these were rendered prior to the addition of my research and the Tomlinson article to the Barbados NDP.[10] Approximately six months later, I was informed that another Barbadian SOGI refugee applicant (whose hearing I did not attend) was not successful, and they believed that the IRB member who assessed their claim was not persuaded that they had been subjected to persecution, but rather decided that they faced the less serious harm of discrimination. As LaViolette has documented, this follows a pattern in Canadian SOGI refugee decisions, particularly for claimants coming from countries where social, legal and political situations of sexual minorities are changing, and criminal laws against homosexuality are being challenged. Lack of evidence or unclear, contradictory information, such as that found in the Barbados NDP, may allow an adjudicator to decide that the country conditions constitute 'discrimination' rather than 'persecution' and therefore the claimant does not meet the standard definition of refugee (LaViolette 2009: 451).[11]

Perhaps even more troubling is the cumulative effect of NDPs as archives of gendered identity and sexual orientation circulating through various levels of the Canadian immigration and refugee apparatus, contributing to a particular configuration of nation-state, sexuality, gender and citizenship. When a region of nations is summarized through statements like, 'There is widespread social discrimination against homosexuals and few openly gay people in Saint Lucia' (St. Lucia NDP), 'LGBT organizations (in Jamaica) reported scores of cases of attacks, harassment and threats against lesbians, gay men and bisexual and transgender people' (Jamaica NDP), and 'in St. Vincent and the Grenadines there is no safe space for homosexuals to go' (St. Vincent and the Grenadines NDP), we see a region constructed through the framework of the nation-state, defined and imagined in terms that assume coterminous geographic, socio-sexual, gendered, and cultural boundaries. The English-speaking Caribbean is, for the most part, produced as a singularly homo- and transphobic region of nation-states, in which discrimination, violence and death are daily threats faced by gendered and gender and sexual minority populations. While I am not in any way disputing the facts of violence and discrimination experienced by these populations, I want to draw attention to the way in which documents that form SOGI refugee archives reduce the complexity of everyday social life to a set of coterminous sexual, cultural and political borders, an essentializing act that occludes the multiple ways in which contemporary forms of global capital, development aid and funding, and international political, economic, security and military alliances simultaneously re-inscribe and transform sexual, gendered, racial and numerous other inequalities in this region (Cruz-Malave and Manalansan 2002; Luibheid and Cantú 2005). In other words, the narratives of NDPs are predicated on generalized statements about nation-states and their coterminous sexual and gendered cultures and identities, narratives that obscure diverse, complex, socio-sexual practices, attitudes and behaviours, thus reinforcing a homonationalist narrative that portrays mostly non-western, Global South nations as the barbaric, uncivilized, undemocratic 'other' through their uniformly homo- and transphobic laws and attitudes and Global North nations as bastions of democracy, equality and liberty.

EXPERT WITNESS REPORTS

Expert witness reports form another body of documents in which we can see similar patterns of homologous configurations of the nation-state, culture, and sexual and gendered identities. As noted in the introduction to this chapter, anthropologists and other social scientists are regularly asked (usually by SOGI claimants' lawyers in my experience) to write 'expert' reports documenting social conditions pertaining to sexuality and gender in clients' home nations. The lawyer in Buffalo who asked me to write a statement about country conditions for her Barbadian HIV positive transgender asylum claimant would add this report to her claimant's file, which would then be submitted to a US immigration court as part of the evidence to support the claim that extradition of this individual would result in torture. In her email, the lawyer informed me that due in part to 'her client's serious identity conflict' she was 'extremely unstable and insecure prior to her sexual reassignment surgery, resulting in unlawful behavior leading to a detrimental criminal record'. According to the lawyer, this criminal record barred her client from all forms of relief in the U.S. Immigration Court except, perhaps, under 'Withholding and/or Deferral Of Removal under the Convention Against Torture (CAT)'. The lawyer said that if a person can show that removal to his or her home country will result in torture and/or death at the hands of government officials and/or private actors acting with the government's acquiescence, such a person may be entitled to have his or her removal deferred or withheld. The lawyer intended to prove that because her client was transgender, HIV positive, a criminal deportee, and dependent on government assistance to manage her HIV, and because Barbadian laws criminalize buggery, she would likely be denied government aid for her medications, thus depriving her of essential life-saving treatment, which would amount to torture under CAT. The lawyer also planned to argue that the government would fail to protect her client from private actors who, because of the laws that criminalize and thus stigmatize 'her lifestyle', would more likely than not 'feel emboldened and immunized from retribution to torture and/or do worse'.

I responded to this request by informing the lawyer that based on my knowledge of Barbados' criminal laws, HIV/AIDS policies and societal attitudes towards 'transgender' persons, I would find it problematic to support the claim that her client would face the equivalent of 'torture' were she to return to Barbados. I never heard this term or its equivalent used during my conversations and interviews with sexual and gender minorities in Barbados, whereas other terms like discrimination, homophobia and prejudice were more commonly employed. I also informed the lawyer that I highly doubted any Barbadian citizen would not receive HIV medications based on their gendered identity or sexual orientation; however, I could write a statement about homo- and transphobia, social conditions for gendered and sexual minorities and HIV stigma in Barbados, which she agreed to.

I tried to write a report that began to address some of the intersectional dynamics that produce discrimination and hardship in differing degrees for sexual and gender minorities in Barbados depending on factors such as socio-economic status, education, HIV status, religious affiliation, transgressive gender performativity and transnational life experiences. However, the report did not address larger structural forms of gendered and sexual violence that are produced through Barbados' participation in transnational neo-liberal forms of economic restructuring, which result in greater economic precarity for many Bajan citizens (Freeman 2000) that in turn results in some accusing minorities (sexual, immigrant or other) as the source of economic upheaval or the cause of social and moral decay (Murray 2012). Nor did I speak about the tourist economy, which re-inscribes racialized heteronormative tropes of servile, sensuous natives to be consumed by white, middle-class European and North American citizens (Alexander 2005; Kempadoo 2004). I did not speak of the ongoing discrimination faced by racialized and sexual minorities within the United States, nor of the structural violence of the US government's immigration apparatus, increasingly suspicious of and hostile towards 'unwanted' outsiders, often defined in terms of ethno-national and/ or racialized identities (Puar 2007), which forces individuals who are trying to migrate for various reasons (possibly because of American military or political actions) to sometimes take desperate measures in order to get past the borders or stay within them.

Upon receipt of my report, the lawyer requested me to 'strengthen' the language around issues of stigma and discrimination faced by HIV positive and/or transgender individuals to bring my report more in line with CAT definitions of torture, which I found troubling and refused to do. The lawyer made some further minor edits, which I accepted, and the report was then added to the client's file. At the time of writing, the client's court date had been delayed twice and she had been told that her trial would be rescheduled for some time in mid to late 2015.

What was said and not said in my report was very much influenced by the structural and political parameters of the refugee determination apparatus. In their analysis of writing on medical certificates issued to refugee appli-cants, Fassin and Rechtman note how the wording of the certificate conforms to standards defined by the organization issuing it and testifies to the writer's effort to meet as closely as possible the imagined expectations of the bodies responsible for adjudicating the case (Fassin and Rechtman 2009: 251). They report how doctors, as expert witnesses, are put in a difficult position – many do this work in order to provide care and advocate for patients, but in order to produce 'respectable' evidence for the asylum court, they must structure accounts of psychological and physical trauma in particular ways that they feel will meet the expectations of judges (ibid., 260–64). In other words, what is, in fact, a complex and nuanced range of bodily and psychological reac-tions to a variety of forms of harm is often reduced to meet a standard defi-nition of 'trauma' in the asylum determination process. In writing on social conditions for gendered and sexual minorities in Barbados, I faced a similar challenge of trying to meet a judge's expectations (or what a lawyer imagined to be a judge's expectations) of what constitutes a 'persecutory' nation-state that will endanger the life of asylum claimants if they are forced to return to that nation, while at the same time attempting to avoid problematic, essential-ized national caricatures of that society.

In asylum claims, adjudicators are working within a domain in which Euro-American legal and judicial frameworks structure procedures and decision-making processes, that is, objective evidence must be produced to prove a claim of persecution (LaViolette 2009: 439–40). However, as Good notes, and as we saw in the previous chapter, asylum courts also operate with presupposed unspoken assumptions of 'common sense', that is, beliefs, identities and relations between beliefs and identities that speakers assume are known and shared by all competent members of the culture. Yet, asylum narratives challenge assumptions of 'common sense' shared by all members in the adjudication process because of potential cultural and experiential differences between the teller and the listener, hence the increased reliance on expert reports, which are assumed to help the claimants and their legal representatives structure their accounts according to the 'common sense' expectations of the judge (Good 2006: 193).

The problem for many social science 'experts' is that, for the most part, we are all too aware of the problems of 'common-sense' assumptions about identities and beliefs in cross-cultural contexts. Whereas much critical social science emphasizes the intersectionality, contextuality or situatedness of knowledge production and truth claims, the refugee determination process emphasizes knowledge production based on certain forms of 'admissible evidence' consisting of provable essential or evidential facts, which fulfil the legal burden of proof. While the critical social scientist operates from a perspective emphasizing that 'facts' are relative as they are produced in particular socio-cultural, political and historical contexts and/or embedded in subjectively produced knowledges (i.e., challenging the 'fact' that the nation-state is *de jure*, the container of culture, identity, morality and rights), this does not translate easily into the legal-juridical domain where such reflexive critique is antithetical to its sense-making processes. The refugee determination bureaucracy operates with a logic of being (or aspiring to being) a unified system of knowledge control, while the critical social scientist asks questions about the location, structure and power of knowledge and the moral, cultural and historical underpinnings, locations and subjectivities of its producers. In other words, we see profoundly different ontological agendas at work in these professional fields, resulting in challenges of strategic translation and interpretation for all those involved in a refugee claim.

In writing my report for the lawyer, I was thus engaged in a game of strategic translation, in which I attempted to depict some of the complexities of socio-sexual and gendered life in Barbados, which demonstrated the importance of intersectional frameworks and locally produced gendered and sexual knowledge in order to understand discrimination, homophobia and inequality. However, I also wrote a report that tried to meet the lawyer's objectives, such that it would help her persuade an immigration judge that this asylum claim was genuine in that it met the definition of refugee contained in the 1951 United Nations Convention Relating to the Status of Refugees (to which the United States is a signatory), that is, someone who has fled his or her country because of a well-founded fear of persecution based on his or her membership in a particular social group and is unable to obtain the protection of his or her home country.[12] In other words, my report was written in a context in which sexual and gender identity (membership in a particular social group), nation (country of origin) and 'persecution' were assumed to be contiguous, homologous, and cross-culturally translatable concepts that would meet a standard definition of SOGI 'refugeeness'.

CONCLUSION

In this chapter I have argued that NDPs and expert reports contribute to bureaucratic archives that re-inscribe homonationalist narratives, which contain descriptions of 'good' and 'bad' gendered and sexual identities and attitudes, and by extension, good nations and bad nations: within Canadian and American national borders we find 'good' attitudes towards these identities; within 'other' national borders like those of mostly Global South nation-states we find 'bad' attitudes towards these identities. These homologous borders of sexual orientation and gender identity, nation, and culture contribute to the formation of a normative homosexual or transgender refugee, construed primarily as a victimized citizen of his or her former home nation-state, and now a grateful potential citizen of his or her new home nation-state. While documents in SOGI refugee archives may offer hope and security to a small number of individuals, the process of eliciting, evaluating and recirculating representations of national cultures of persecution and suffering contributes to a governance apparatus that generates racist and colonialist images (Cantú 2009: 69–70). It may be true that the refugee brings the ordinary fiction of national sovereignty into crisis, but the archives of Global North nation-states' immigration bureaucracies and courts work forcefully to re-inscribe homologous national cultures that erase sexual and gender diversity and transnational hierarchies of inequality while simultaneously imposing assumptions and meanings based on triumphalist narratives of gendered and sexual liberation.

While legal scholars of SOGI refugee claims may argue that more reliable information on gender and sexual rights, state protection and general social conditions for sexual and gender minorities in nation-states around the world will lead to 'improving the evidentiary burden of sexual minority claimants' (LaViolette 2009: 462), the underlying violence of homonationalist narratives of Global North nation-states, and their silence on issues such as domestic racism, sexism, homo/transphobia, heightened border security, detention and deportation of increasing numbers of migrants, and/or transnational political-economic alliances, which negatively impact diverse local and migrating populations, remain unchallenged. It is important to acknowledge the contributions of different agents within the refugee apparatus struggling towards achieving fair and just results for SOGI and other categories of refugee claimants, but it is equally important to critically engage with documents in archives and the effects of these archives, which contribute toward the subjugation and subjectification of individuals and populations (Fassin 2011: 214–16).

Can NDPs and expert reports be written 'ethically', without furthering the symbolic violence through which national 'others' and their gendered and sexual lives are produced in ways that re-inscribe homonational tropes? Anthony Good has little sympathy for this quandary: 'When experts complain about the ways in which their evidence is treated by courts, they lose sight of their own complicity in such distortions. By agreeing to work within legal conventions and restrictions, they themselves contribute to the "de-reflexification" of their expert knowledge which inevitably results' (2006: 259). For him, the moral imperative trumps any other concerns: 'They have chosen ... to view involvement as the lesser evil, and have decided that the troubling of their own professional consciences is a price worth paying if victims of persecution are thereby occasionally saved from the bleakness of refoulement' (ibid).

In terms of my own participation, I have chosen a compromised path: I hope that my 'expert' reports will assist individual claimants in their attempts to remain in their new home nation-states, which are increasingly suspicious or hostile to certain categories of classed, gendered and racialized immigrants, but I am equally aware that these reports reproduce troubling homonationalist features, in which nation, culture, sexual and gendered identities and attitudes are linked in ways that downplay transnational political-economic linkages, their attendant classed and racialized inequalities and local socio-political injustices. Expert reports, along with other social and behavioural research, end up as pieces of evidence in refugee files and NDPs, which accrue in the archives of Canadian and US immigration bureaucracies and courts, contributing towards reified, essentialized portraits of gendered and sexual social lives in 'other' nations premised upon a problematic conflagration of nation, sexual/gender identity and culture emphasizing homophobia, discrimination and intolerance in these mostly Global South nation-states, and implicitly endorsing the United States or Canada as nations embracing sexual and gendered diversity and freedom. My moral counter-weight to writing reports and (unintentionally) contributing to NDPs is to contribute to the critical academic archive: to write this chapter and give presentations that draw attention to the larger inequities of the refugee apparatus in nation-states like Canada and the United States, which continue to exclude vulnerable gendered, sexual, ethno-racial and classed groups of people from crossing or staying within national borders, but I continue to wonder about which of these archives carries more clout in terms of audiences and their attendant political effects.

NOTES

1. http://www.irb-cisr.gc.ca/Eng/resrec/ndpcnd/Pages/index.aspx (accessed 6 January 2014).

2. See Canaday (2009) for a discussion of shifting American state policies on sexual citizenship over the course of the twentieth century. Canaday outlines how homosexuality emerged as a category to be regulated over the course of the twentieth century in various state institutions such as immigration, the military and welfare.

3. Good notes that 'most anthropologists are likely to feel somewhat squeamish about having their evidence labelled (as expert witnesses), because many of the most important things they have to say arise out of the hermeneutic interpretation of intersubjective understandings communicated to them by individual informants' (2006: 13). In other words, most anthropologists are more comfortable engaging with the context-dependent nuances, political complexities and shifting terrains of socio-cultural spaces and experiences. However, American asylum courts and Canadian refugee claim hearings operate with different assumptions about and processes for determining knowledge, facts and truths about social-cultural experience, resulting in what could be viewed as an inter-cultural, inter-textual gap or problem of translation for the anthropologist as he or she tries to interpret, translate and communicate his or her knowledge about an issue, behaviour, person or moral code. Asylum courts and refugee claim hearings are juridical-legal environments where different conceptual frameworks and processes for determining and defining 'facts' and 'truths' are at play, resulting in what Povinelli (2001) calls a problem of incommensurability for the anthropologist (as well as the refugee claimant, albeit through different registers), worlds that do not speak to each other, but are forced to do so, and in the process lose something in translation.

4. There are a number of different routes through which a refugee application may be lodged and/or processed in Canada and the United States, and the format and content of documents submitted to USCIS and IRB are not identical. However, there are some broad similarities between the two systems such as the requirement for claimants to be able to provide documentary evidence substantiating their gendered orientation or sexual identity (i.e., membership in a particular social group) and per-secution in their country of origin.

5. http://www.nolo.com/legal-encyclopedia/how-prepare-affirmative-asylum-application.html (accessed 8 January 2015).

6. Ibid.

7. There are a number of other sections in the Barbados NDP that do not con-tain any documents or links to documents. These include 'judiciary, legal and penal systems', 'media freedoms' 'religion', 'nationality, ethnicity and race' and 'labour,

employment and unions'. http://www.irb-cisr.gc.ca/Eng/ResRec/NdpCnd/Pages/ndpcnd.aspx?pid=6395 (accessed 12 December 2013).

8. This report also includes sections on 'Treatment by Society', 'State Protection', 'Treatment by Police' and 'Support Services', and thus provides the most extensive and detailed information of the three documents listed in this section of the NDP.

9. The argument put forward in my research was that tolerance may apply to some Barbadian citizens but not to others, depending on a number of different factors including socio-economic status, education, religious and/or political affiliation (Murray 2012).

10. As noted above, NDPs are updated regularly (approximately every six to twelve months); the date of revision is listed on all NDPs.

11. According to the UN High Commissioner for Refugees Handbook on Procedures and Criteria for Determining Refugee Status, while discrimination may amount to a violation of human rights, it will not necessarily amount to persecution. As LaViolette notes, the notion of persecution lies at the heart of the definition of refugee, but it is a poorly defined concept (2009: 450).

12. Immigration and Refugee Board of Canada Claimant's Guide. http://www.irb-cisr.gc.ca/Eng/RefClaDem/Pages/ClaDemGuide.aspx#_Toc340245779 (accessed 7 January 2015). In this case, the lawyer was also trying to employ language from another legislative policy, 'Withholding and/or Deferral Of Removal under the Convention Against Torture (CAT)' as it was likely that her client's past criminal record might render him ineligible for refugee status.

Chapter 7

The Challenge of Home

'Home' is a popular topic in refugee research, although it is sometimes difficult to discern how much of the talk about home is determined by the researcher's assumption that home *should be* the focus of conversation, and how much home is genuinely something that refugees want to talk about. For example, I have noticed that in many of my interviews with SOGI refugees, towards the end of the intake interview, I would start to ask questions about settlement in Toronto, and I would ask how Toronto compared to the interviewees' former 'home' and/or what they missed about 'home'. Similarly, in some LGBT refugee support group meetings I attended in Toronto, the theme of the meeting, determined by the facilitator, would focus on feelings, memories or ongoing relationships with refugees' former 'home-lands' and the people there. The answers to my questions and comments in these meetings were diverse and ran the gamut from deep nostalgia to ambivalence, and hostility. Some individuals in these discussions made it clear that this was not a topic they wanted to spend much time on, as they preferred to 'look forward rather than backward', (Janine) and focus on their future here in Canada. However, if home risks the possibility of being a topic that is overly determined by the researcher or support group facilitator, we cannot ignore the fact that it is also a critically important, if not overly determined, component of the refugee claim process itself, as particular depictions of home(s) must be presented in the queer migration to liberation nation narrative.

Home thus has multiple meanings and feelings in sexual minority refugee claimants' memories and their experiences of the Canadian refugee apparatus. This final chapter begins to unpack the layered, complex and sometimes contradictory narratives of home for SOGI refugees and their complex connections to discourses of national belonging in 'home' and destination nations. I begin this chapter with a brief discussion of the ways in which home operates as a central yet troubling concept in both refugee and queer studies. I then focus on the role and significance of home in SOGI refugee narratives presented to the IRB in documents and at the hearing. I demonstrate how representations of home in these 'official' narratives re-inscribe the homonationalist queer migration to liberation nation narrative undergirding the refugee apparatus, in that Canada is construed as a new, liberated, home nation for sexual and gender minorities, while former home nations (mostly from the Global South) are construed as backward and primitive because of their rampant homo- and transphobia. 'Old' and 'new' homes are constructed in ways that re-inscribe racialized colonial tropes emphasizing the binary opposition of the civilized, socio-sexually inclusive white Canadian nation-state versus the uncivilized, homophobic non-Western racialized nation-state. The final section of this chapter focuses on more informal discussions about home with SOGI refugee claimants in different social contexts. I observe that the queer migration to liberation nation narrative is articulated by many participants in more informal contexts, which may be due in part to their investment in articulating a narrative that meets homonormative definitions of SOGI refugee identity demanded by their engagement with the refugee determination apparatus. However, despite the possibly strategic claim to be grateful to have 'a new home' where gendered identity or sexual orientation is accepted and protected, most interviewees continue to communicate with friends and family in their countries of origin and have diverse, intense and complex feelings about their former homeland(s), resulting in 'ambivalent homonationalisms' (White 2013), observed also in Chapters 1 and 2. In this exploration of the diverse experiences and meanings of home for SOGI refugees, I argue for a reconceptualization of home that recognizes simultaneous, complex attachments to multiple homes constituted across transnational fields while simultaneously co-opting and undermining homonationalist discourses in the refugee determination apparatus, which attempt to forge privileged chains of attachment between nation, desire and particular racialized, classed and gendered identity formations.

HOME/WORK: RESEARCH ON HOME, MIGRATION AND SEXUALITY

Research on refugees has had a significant impact on the conceptualization and meanings of home. Researchers have noted that government and media discourses of refugees often emphasize their homelessness or in between-ness in relation to belonging to a particular nation, and the concomitant tension between the need to return them to their country of origin or integrate them into their new home nation. From this perspective, they are unsettled, transitional, and 'risky' bodies out of place (Sirriyeh 2010: 215; Feldman 2012; Mannik 2013). However, anthropologists working with refugees and other immigrant or transnational groups have argued that identities cannot be defined simply in terms of physical, spatially bounded locations, and for these groups home is understood less as a fixed place and more as a matter of where one best knows oneself (Gupta and Ferguson 1992; Malkii 1995; Rapport and Dawson 1998; Simich, Este and Hamilton 2010). Home is better understood as a fluid process that is reconstructed through mobility and place, and can be conceived as a broad fusion between spatial, social, psychological, temporal and affective domains (Sirriyeh 2010: 215). Some social constructionists argue that home can be constituted through cultural practices and daily routines (Dyck and Dossa 2007; Berger 1984), whereas others argue that these routines and practices are always enacted in relation to material surroundings, such that space remains important. The shift towards recognizing the possibility of creating home through and in movement, or from roots to routes (Clifford 1997), produces more open-ended and creative possibilities for thinking through the relationships between identity, space and belonging. Thus, feeling 'at home' for an immigrant or refugee may be a product of a complex interaction between space, location, social relations, security, intimacy, privacy, choice and control (Sirriyeh 2010: 215).

Levitt and Glick-Schiller argue that it is also important to acknowledge simultaneity, or living lives that incorporate daily activities, routines, and institutions located both in a destination country and transnationally. Incorporation into a new land and transnational connections to a homeland or to dispersed networks of family or persons who share a religious or ethnic identity can occur at the same time and reinforce one another (Levitt and Glick-Schiller 2007: 182; see also Al-Ali and Koser 2001). Levitt and Glick-Schiller identify this as a transnational social field approach (185). As we will see, simultaneity, or the ways in which home is constituted transnationally, figures prominently for sexual orientation and gender identity refugees even when they are rendered immobile because of travel restrictions placed upon them while their refugee claim is being processed. However, we may need to exercise caution with theories like the transnational social field approach, which champion 'home in movement': As Al-Ali and Koser observe, ' people engaged in transnational practices might express an uneasiness, a sense of fragmentation, and even pain. Everyday contestations of negotiating the gravity of one's home is particularly distressing for those who are vulnerable, for example the poor, women, illegal immigrants and refugees.' (2001: 7). Furthermore, the refugee's relationship to home is different from other transnational immigrant experiences because of the former's placement into the refugee apparatus upon arrival in the 'receiving' nation. In our contemporary world system, defined and delineated through the geo-political figure known as the nation-state, there are particular nodes through which identity and home are legislatively and juridically defined and recognized as il/legitimate. Refugees are a particular category of migrants who must seek protection in a destination nation and claim they are persecuted in their home nation, thus calling into question the laws, morality and sovereignty of both origin (often referred to as former or old home-land) and destination (often referred to as new home-land) nation-states.

Feminist, anthropological and queer migration scholarship has made a significant contribution towards a better understanding of the ways in which gender and sexuality intersect with other forms of difference and inequality in movement across borders. Queer migration scholarship critically engages hetero- and homonormative arrangements of homelands, borders, bodies, desires and movements, which are generally upheld by the bureaucratic institutions of the neo-liberal nation-state and capitalist discourses such as mainstream media and advertising (Cantú 2009; Carillo 2004; Decena 2011; Epps, Valens and Johnson-Gonzalez 2005; Espin 1999; Gopinath 2005; Hart 2002; Luibhéid 2002; 2008; Luibhéid and Cantú 2005; Manalansan 2003, 2006; Patton and Sanchez–Eppler 2000; Weston 2008; White 2013, 2014).

In challenging hetero- and homo-normative components of home in the queer migration to liberation nation narrative below, I apply some insights from queer migration scholarship, in particular, Ahmed, Castañeda, Fortier and Sheller's arguments about home and migration (2003), which challenge reductionist theories and assumptions about the meaning of migration and home[1] by 'blurring the distinctions between here and there' and consider how processes of homing and migration take shape through 'experience in broader social processes and institutions where unequal differences of race, class gender and sexuality are generated' (2003: 5). At the same time, I remain attentive to the influence of homonationalist narratives as hegemonic fantasies of legitimation and a desire to belong (White 2013).

In much writing on LGBT lives and communities, the relationship between desire, difference, marginalization and migration has been closely examined and home often occupies a prominent yet fraught role. It is often represented as a site of shame, silence and violence, something to be left as soon as possible, in order to find a new home in a queer utopia, often figured as a dense, urban space full of people with similar desires. As Kath Weston observes in her seminal ethnography on gay and lesbian families in the San Francisco area, 'get thee to the big city' was a common sentiment among her informants (1997). Weston argues that there has been a 'great gay migration' from rural to urban areas throughout much of the twentieth century to form new communities and new places where one could belong and feel 'at home'. According to Weston, this great gay migration puts LGBT people in a similar position to refugees:

Across the globe the movements of refugees, immigrants, wanderers, and work-seekers have contributed to what Edward Said has described as a 'generalized condition of homelessness'. ... Sexuality as well as ethnicity or nationality can be harnessed to a search for 'roots' and shaped through a symbolic of place. (1995: 269)

However, if we take some of the above arguments of feminist and queer migration scholars into account, we might begin to ask if the 'homelessness', 'search for roots' and 'symbolic of place' of North American gays and lesbians is identical to that of individuals from St. Lucia, Nigeria or Iran who experience discrimination and violence because of same-sex desires or non-conformative gender practices and are forced to migrate to Canada to place a claim for refugee status with the IRB. Does movement away from home/lands that are considered dangerous and unfriendly towards new home/lands that are imagined to be welcoming and safe make the North American 'great gay migration' and transnational movements of SOGI refugees identical socio-historical events? How might the great gay migration of North America operate as a privileged narrative that impacts an SOGI refugee's narrative when the latter is being assessed to be credibly gay, bisexual, transgender or lesbian by an IRB member? Do SOGI refugees bring different perspectives and investments to the queer migration narrative and quest for home? As we listen to the diverse ways in which SOGI refugees navigate and negotiate variously embedded narratives of home below, I argue that we see a tense, complex and fluid arrangement between space, identity and belonging, rendering possible multiple or simultaneous homes (albeit not always aligned complementarily) that track towards and away from dominant homonationalist discourses (White 2013).

HOME AT THE HEARING

As outlined in Chapter 2, soon after refugee claimants lodge their claims with the IRB, they must submit their Personal Information Form, or PIF, which includes a section called 'the narrative', where they must set out in chronological order all the significant events and reasons that led them to claim refugee protection in Canada. In this form, the applicant must 'indicate the measures taken against you and members of your family, as well as against similarly situated persons, and by whom these measures were taken. Include dates wherever possible'.[2] This form becomes the key source of examination at the hearing, and, in particular, the written narrative of events operates as the baseline of evaluation for the credibility of the claim. As we saw in Chapter 5, at the hearing, the refugee claimants' oral testimony is assessed for accuracy in relation to the PIF narrative, and significant discrepancies between the written document and oral testimony may be used as evidence that the claim is not credible. While Chapter 5 focused on the ways in which sexual and gender identity terminologies are deployed and evaluated in hearings along with affective, somatic evaluative registers, in this chapter I focus on the significance of home in the PIF narrative as a crucial component of evaluation in the Board member's determination of a credible SOGI refugee claim at the hearing.

As noted in Chapter 2, in preparation for the hearing, claimants are reminded repeatedly by their lawyers, support group leaders and one another that there are a number of criteria and definitions utilized by IRB members at the hearing to determine the credibility of an SOGI refugee claim, and that if they understand these criteria and definitions, then they stand a better chance of being successful. One of these criteria involves creating a narrative of consistent homo- or transphobia throughout personal life histories, which are then connected to depictions of systemic, national cultures of homo- or transphobia. In other words, the narrative of life 'back home' must be presented in a particular way that meets a relatively rigid definition of persecution presented in the IRPA, which mobilizes essentialized, reductionist conflagrations of 'other' nations and national cultural attitudes pertaining to gender and sexuality (as well as other forms of social difference). Most of the refugee claimants I interviewed had legal counsel who worked with them in varying degrees to ensure their personal narrative in their PIF followed a particular format. While the personal narratives I saw ranged from 2 to 10 pages, most followed a similar storyline, which begins with the establishment of the claimant's sexual or gendered identity (for example, 'When I was 14, in approximately July 1994, I had my first sexual experience with a man in a park near my home in Kingston, Jamaica',) and also notes their awareness of local or national attitudes towards people who engage in same-sex or transgender practices (for example, 'In my school in Lagos I heard negative things about homosexuals'). Narratives would generally move from a discussion of same-sex experiences and/or memories of sexual/gendered difference during youth, adolescence and adulthood, which established the 'identity' of the claimant, to detailed discussions of the moments in which these identities were discovered or witnessed by someone, and the fallout from this discovery, which often included physical and verbal violence, and sometimes hospitalization or imprisonment. In some narratives there might only be one 'incident' that puts the claimant's life in danger and/or forces him or her to leave the country quickly. In other narratives, there would be a series of incidents over a number of years in which the claimants faced continuous or escalating levels of hostility and finally reached the conclusion that they could no longer live in that place and must leave. Most narratives ended with a statement that the claimants were afraid to return to their country of origin because they feared they would be targeted for persecution by their homophobic community because of their sexual orientation or transgender identity, and they did not think they would receive protection from authorities in their home nation-state as they were equally homo/transphobic. Thus, in most narratives, the underlying message was one of fear and/or violence in all facets of the individual's life back home, whether from family members at home, the wider community or the institutions of the state such as schools, hospitals and the police. The majority of narratives that I read made a clear connection between an unsafe domestic home space, home community and home nation-state.

A final component of most PIF narratives was the intentionality of the SOGI refugee claimants seeking out Canada as their new home and chosen safe haven. There was often a statement towards the end of the narrative indicating that the individual came to Canada to escape persecution and be free, implying awareness of and gratitude towards his or her new home nation and its liberating opportunities, thus reiterating the queer migration to liberation nation narrative in which old and new homelands were divided into simple binaries of liberated/oppressive (and by extension, civilized/uncivilized, modern/primitive, and developed/undeveloped).

At the hearing, home spaces[3] sounded to me like crime sites from a police investigation, in which experiential, spatial and temporal dimensions of particular incidents were interrogated by the members in order to determine if they should believe the claimant's story or not. I was struck by how often claimants were required to remember very specific and intimate details of traumatic events occurring in their homes, like the distance between the house where the claimant was caught having sex and the house where they ran to hide, or the time at which they phoned the police after they were beaten by a family member who had discovered their transgendered identity. In the hearing, home spaces and the often traumatic events that occurred within them were clinically dissected into spatial and temporal grids through which the claimants and their antagonists moved, and became precisely timed events which the claimants were expected to be able to accurately remember and reconstruct. Not surprisingly, during this intense scrutiny of what were often extraordinarily difficult experiences and memories, some claimants had trouble answering questions accurately (from the member's perspective), while others answered with clarity and precision.

However, a traumatic life 'back home' was not the only focus of the hearing. In most of the hearings I attended, the member also examined the claimants' knowledge of their new homeland, specifically, their activities and participation in LGBT spaces in Toronto. As noted in Chapter 5, this was usually done as part of the member's inquiry into the credibility of the claimants' sexual orientation or gendered identity; if the claimant could accurately identify specific LGBT spaces and organizations that had been named in their narrative and/or package of documents, then this would help to verify their

identity as a 'gay', 'lesbian', 'bisexual' or 'transgendered' person. I have previously argued how this is a problematic way to establish a credible sexual or
gendered identity, but here I want to focus on the ways in which belonging to
a new home-land were framed, assessed and connected to an authentic, and
therefore credible, LGBT identity.

Assessment of knowledge of the SOGI refugee claimant's new home-land
by the Board member was sometimes conducted through a series of questions
that tested the spatial and temporal knowledge of the claimant. For example,
a member might focus on a document in the claimant's file indicating
that the claimant was a member of the Toronto Metropolitan Community
Church (MCC), which serves a primarily LGBT congregation. The line of
questioning could go something like this:

Member: And where is that (church)?

Refugee Claimant: Is on ... um ... is on ... somewhere on ... Danforth and ...

M: Do you go there often?

RC: Yes, twice a month.

M: And since when are you going there?

RC: I've been going since January this year.

M: Almost a year now, twice a month and you can't tell me where it is?

RC (sighing): I have memory problems sir ... of how to get there ... I take the
subway to Bayview ... to Broadview ... then I take a streetcar.

M: To where?

RC: I stop at at ... at ... Danforth and ... Danforth ... and ... Danforth and ...
I stop at an intersection and I walk ... about 2 blocks to church ... is at Broadview, from the Broadview station is 10 minute walk ...

M: So are you walking or taking a streetcar?

RC: Sometimes I walk and sometimes the streetcar.

M: But you don't know where the streetcar takes you.

RC: It takes me on Broadview. ... I think it ... (exasperated sigh) ... Danforth
and ... uh. Gerrard ... is the intersection ... so when I come ... when I drop on
the intersection I walk to the church.

M: And what time is the church service?

RC: One for 9 o'clock and one for 11.

M: Which do you go to?

RC: I started with 9, and then later, I switch to 11 o'clock.

M: Why do you switch?[4]

There are a number of reasons why SOGI refugee claimants might not accurately remember the public transit route from where they are residing to a downtown church, ranging from high levels of anxiety at the hearing, which may make it difficult to remember detailed information, to unfamiliarity with a new urban environment and its various neighbourhoods. However, when a refugee claimant is unable to clearly describe (what are assumed to be) well-knownToronto LGBT sites and/or routes to those sites identified in their PIF or other documents, they may be assessed as not credible based on the member's assumption of an association between particular geographical sites as the home-space(s) of sexual/transgender community/ies. In this line of questioning, there appears to be an assumption that knowledge of Toronto LGBT community spaces as home spaces is a 'legitimate' test of credible LGBT identity, and thus should be examinable through questions focusing on spatial grids and locations.[5]

Thus, in the hearing, we see how particular incarnations of 'home' in the homonational queer migration to liberation nation narrative are instantiated through the questions asked by the IRB member. In fact, we might consider home and the homonational are conflated in that normative definitions of both 'old' and 'new' home spaces are an integral component in the construction of the normative homosexual or transgender refugee, thus producing the hom(e) onormative: both home(s) and the homosexual, bisexual or transgender person are built upon a model constructed out of contiguous nationalist, cultural, racial, gendered and classed boundaries and assumptions. While I am not arguing in any way that these SOGI refugee narratives are fabricated, I am stressing that their privileged and oft-repeated status in the hearing produces a highly limited representation of the claimant's former home community and nation as violent, oppressive and homo/transphobic, thus contributing to hegemonic discourses, which reinforce national, cultural, racial and other hierarchies on transnational scales such that 'old home' countries, which are often (but not always) located in the Global South are demonized, and 'new home' countries, which are often (but not always) located in the Global North are sanctified (Ou Jin Lee and Brotman 2011: 246).

SIMULTANEOUS HOMES: INFORMAL DISCUSSIONS OF OLD AND NEW HOMES

While the IRB hearing was perhaps the most important event after SOGI refugees' arrival in Toronto, they faced numerous other challenges in settling into their 'new homeland'. Almost all of the participants I worked with were in the pre-hearing stage of the process, that is, they had arrived in Canada mostly from Caribbean and African countries, and either made a refugee application at the airport or at a Canada Citizenship and Immigration Office (CIC) soon after arriving. The majority were still waiting for their hearing date with the IRB when I first met them. Up until 2013, this could be a long wait, anywhere from eight to twenty-four months.[6] The settlement period involved spending a lot of time working through various levels of legal, provincial and federal bureaucracies, beginning with visits to the CIC Offices to fill out refugee claim forms, applying for legal aid, visiting law offices, taking medical exams, applying for a work permit and then looking for a job, applying for Social Assistance (Ontario Works) and a Social Insurance Number, and trying to obtain relevant documentation for the hearing.

The participants I worked with were also searching for accommodation that was affordable, safe and comfortable, but this was an elusive combination – some were currently staying with family, some were in shelters, some were sharing apartments with room-mates who they were not 'out' to, and a number were changing their arrangements every few months. Latoya, the transgender claimant from Barbados whom we met in Chapter 1, had moved at least four times in the six months since her arrival in Toronto. She provided me with a number of reasons for these moves: she had gotten into a fight with a former friend with whom she shared her first apartment, so she had moved to another apartment with a group of Barbadian queens and gay men, but it was too crowded and someone was stealing her food, so she moved again to the apartment of another friend, but they got into a fight over a boyfriend, and so she then moved into a youth shelter where she felt scared to be trans, so she dressed as a boy, and wasn't happy there. At the time of our last interview prior to her hearing, she had moved into a shared apartment with a group of gay and trans people from different Caribbean islands. Latoya hoped that she would soon find herself a boyfriend so that they could move in together and 'settle down'.

With so many of the refugees facing a sustained period of unsettlement in their initial months in Toronto, perhaps it is not so surprising to find that when 'home' was the topic of discussion, current accommodations were rarely mentioned. In fact, material or physical space often was *not* the key factor in response to the question 'what does home mean to you?' Jo, an older woman from St. Vincent who self-identified as a lesbian, responded to this question by simply stating, 'My dad'. Janine, the self-identified bisexual woman from Jamaica whom we also met in Chapter 1 said, 'It's where I feel comfortable. It could be an organization like the 519 (an LGBT community centre in Toronto). It's where my friends are, it's where I find acceptance and support'. Support groups and organizations that were either SOGI refugee-specific or queer/LGBT focused were often identified as spaces where one could feel at home,[7] because, as Lorraine, a young woman in her 20s, said:

It's about being accepted ... (this organization) is my home away from home ... Home is where the heart is too. Right now, I feel like Canada is my home, because my heart is here now. I could never do some of these things (back in Jamaica). Like, this program here, the support group ... you get free medical. I can see a therapist now to try and solve all those problems that I had. You know, it's just like, okay, Jamaica's my home and my family are there, but that's on paper.

Many of the participants I interviewed noted how important the SOGI refugee support groups and organizations were for them, describing them in similar ways to the above quotes. For many, these groups and organizations were the first time they had been in a safe space with 'people like me', as several participants put it. They could talk with each other, get information about the hearings, listen to how other lawyers were treating their clients, and find out what jobs other refugee claimants were getting. In addition, the support groups were social spaces in which people made new friendships, flirted and sometimes started up new romantic relationships, although as we saw in Chapter 2, these could also become spaces in which questions and doubts about 'authentic' gay and lesbian identities could arise.

In Lorraine's comment above, as well as other participants' answers to questions about home, there was often a conflation of 'Canada' and queer spaces such as the 519 Community Centre when talking about 'feeling at home'. Canada was often acknowledged as 'my new home', because the participant could be himself or herself or 'do things here' that he or she couldn't do in his or her former home-land, but the specific site of where one felt at home (that is, a space/moment in which one felt free, socially connected and safe) was often the SOGI refugee support group and/or an LGBT-focused organization. Thus, in these discussions, a kind of 'site specific homonationalism' was produced through the conflation of claiming Canada to be a new home space where one had a sense of safety and freedom in relation to one's sexuality or gendered identity, but the actual locations of these feelings were specific and limited to the spaces of particular groups and organizations that were dedicated to supporting SOGI refugees, LGBT and/or queer of colour newcomers.[8]

While these comments reveal a form of homonationalism that is site-specific, they also resonated with homonationalist narratives of Canada found throughout the refugee apparatus, in which Canada is represented as a nation that embraces LGBT communities, supports LGBT rights and is part of progressive liberal democratic nation-states. Once again, it is important to keep in mind the temporal, social and political context in which these claims were being made. As discussed in Chapter 4, in some SOGI refugee support group meetings, members were attending not only to obtain information about the refugee process and life in Toronto, but also to obtain a letter from the group facilitator confirming their membership in the group, so articulating homonationalist sentiments might be a strategic move to ensure one is viewed as a model group member, and thus deserving of a strong letter of support.

As much as specific sites in Toronto were acknowledged to evoke home-like feelings, discussions of home would often also include memories or thoughts of people, places and events 'back home' in the participants' country of origin. In one conversation with former refugee claimants who had successfully obtained official refugee status, the topic turned to what the participants missed about home. Jo missed a spot 'back home' where there was 'great food, amazing fish, an atmosphere of relaxed, where we could play dominos, smoke a little weed and drink; I had a relationship with the owner there, if I didn't have money she'd say pay next time ... Canada don't offer that at all.' Other participants missed family members and friends. Peter, a quiet man in his 30s from Nigeria, was very specific in his description of what he missed: He said, 'I miss the body marks, the familiar marks on my Mum's body, which her mother had, and I have ... I miss seeing that'. In these comments home was articulated through remembered locations, bodies, smells, touches, and sensations that were often connected to deep and long-term relationships with family, friends or lovers.

However, some participants did not feel nostalgic for the places they had left. Stefana, a young woman in her 20s from Russia, stated, 'I remember the bad things, so I don't wish to go back – it's good to remember the bad and why you left. I ran away, from my family, and I don't want to forget that.' Peter spoke in a way that combined feelings of anger *and* nostalgia: 'I don't miss anything; only when I talk to Mum, I miss her. And I miss one ritual from back home, which was where I would visit my dead boyfriend's grave every week; I feel bad that I can't keep doing that.' Others talked about how leaving their home country was like a 'bad breakup', or that they still loved their home country but were deeply saddened and/or angered by the behaviour and attitudes of the people there. As Stefana said, 'The same thing I miss is the same thing that makes me angry: the people.'

Latoya, Janine and Joe, whose life-stories were presented in Chapter 1, displayed very little sentimentality or nostalgia as they talked about leaving Barbados, Jamaica and the Middle East. Janine was very clear about her feelings on this issue:

Janine: I think life has made me into a chameleon. I can blend into anywhere, into any environment easily.

David: Mmhmm.

Janine: And I don't have to be, 'Oh, I miss Jamaica, I miss the beaches and I miss the ackee and salt fish and the food.'

David: [laughing]

Janine: If only ... I don't have that kind of nostalgia.

David: No.

Janine: That other people have.

David: Right ...

Janine: I just only know that I'm comfortable and happy.

David: Yeah, you want to be comfortable in your own skin. Yeah ...

Janine: So, I don't have that kind of ... that kind of trauma that others have had.

Joe said he had absolutely no interest in returning home or communicating with his mother there, as it was she who had caused him so much grief and terror. Likewise, Latoya was more interested in focusing on things that mattered in the here and now, such as finding a job, a boyfriend and a permanent place to reside.

Nevertheless, while thinking about people and places 'back home' evoked diverse, often ambivalent emotions and memories, almost all of the participants I worked with kept in touch with friends or some family members in their country of origin. This was mostly done via computer and smart-phone technologies such as Facebook, Skype, BBM, Twitter, or MSM, but some participants said they made landline phone calls to elderly parents and relatives who didn't have or use computers. Thus intimate relationships with people from 'back home' were maintained and highly valued by most participants, even when memories or feelings of that homeland were often vexed or deeply ambivalent. The importance of keeping connected to even just a few friends and family members back home speaks to simultaneity, or the ways in which home is constituted transnationally, and figures prominently for SOGI refugees even when they are rendered immobile because of travel restrictions placed upon them while the refugee claim is being processed.

These comments begin to reveal the complexity of memories and feelings about life in former and current home-lands and how they are articulated in relation to the powerful parameters of the homonationalist 'queer migration to liberation nation' narrative. Participants often affectionately recalled people, places, and experiences 'back home' alongside remembered moments of fear, anger, shame and secrecy. In many cases, there was ongoing communication with friends and family in the country of origin, sometimes with the intention of eventually helping them to move to Canada, sometimes to make arrangements for money transfers and sometimes just to keep up to date with the news of what was happening in the lives of loved ones. In the end, we witness 'ambivalent homonationalisms', that is, 'a fundamental ambivalence

towards nationalized forms of belonging' (White 2013: 44), in relation to
Canada and countries of origin, but we also see simultaneous homes formed
in relation to fluid and multiple locations, registers, scales and relations, ranging from LGBT community groups to the smells of a fish fry or the marks on
a mother's body.

CONCLUSION

I end this chapter with a quote from a letter to the editor responding to a
2012 online story in 'Xtra' (a Toronto gay and lesbian newspaper) about a
'gay man from St. Vincent' who recently had his refugee claim rejected by
the IRB:

> How many of us, even Canadian born, have sought refuge in larger cities in
> order to escape the abuses we either suffered or anticipated in our home towns?
> In our effort to counteract the impacts of bullying, we've been telling our kids,
> it gets better, but in too many places, that simply isn't true, not unless you
> leave and wipe the dust from your feet when you go. I know that I'm a refugee;
> I didn't leave the country, but I most certainly fled. But I don't have to prove it,
> do I? I don't have anyone telling me that my native city is safe, that it's not so
> bad where I'm from, or judging my credibility as a witness to my own history.
>
> B. B. Toronto[9]

This comment resonates with some of the themes I have been working with in
this chapter: the letter-writer, who I assume identifies as 'a Canadian LGBT'
individual, makes a connection between a 'gay man from St. Vincent' who
has unsuccessfully applied for refugee status in Canada and her/his own flight
from a home town (presumably rural) in Canada to the 'larger city' in order
to find a safe and accepting space that he/she can call home. He/she makes
an explicit link between LGBT Canadians and SOGI refugees as the former
seek refuge in the big cities for the same reasons as the latter. However, as the
letter-writer notes in the final sentence, when the small town Canadian LGBT
persons arrive in Toronto, Montreal or Vancouver, they don't have to prove
who they are to anyone nor do they have to worry about anyone telling them
that their native city is safe to return to. Here lies a crucial difference between
the transnational SOGI refugee and the LGBT Canadian citizen-'refugee':
The latter is not scrutinized by the Canadian nation-state's refugee apparatus,
which has the power to determine if a person's claims about his or her sexual
or transgendered identity and life back home are credible and to decide
whether or not a person can stay in their new home city and nation. In other
words, the Canadian LGBT citizen-refugees never face a refugee apparatus in

which their experience and knowledge of sexual and gendered identities (and laws about and social attitudes towards these identities), and their intimate, sometimes traumatic personal experiences are examined by a government bureaucrat working within a Euro-American juridical legal framework, which employs homonationalist discourses about sexual and gendered identities and their relationships to national cultures of homophobia or freedom.

Many of the refugee claimants I worked with learned that a particular incarnation of their old 'home' (their country of origin) must be constructed in the narrative presented to the IRB and supplemented by other documentation and their own testimony at the hearing. For the most part, this is a representation of home that conflates violent, unsafe domestic, community and national spaces, cultures and identities. Home, whether it be house, community or nation, must be systematically and uniformly rendered homo- or transphobic in order for a SOGI refugee claim to be credible. Conversely, the claimants must demonstrate that in their 'new home' of Canada, they are consistently, openly, publicly gay, lesbian, bisexual or transgendered; that is, they must show knowledge of and participation in socially recognized LGBT events, relationships and spaces in order to render their sexual or gendered identity credible, based on Euro-American hegemonic definitions of these socio-sexual identity terms. These contrasting formations of old and new homelands constructed in tandem with 'closeted' and 'out' LGBT identities (the latter of which are attached to publicly recognized LGBT organizations and spaces) reflect the deployment of a homonationalist narrative that privileges racialized, classed and gendered arrangements of sexual identities, cultures and values into attachments of national disidentification or identification organized around 'old' and 'new' homelands.

Yet, when SOGI refugee claimants talk about home outside the official contexts of the hearing, a more complex and diverse spectrum of feelings, attachments and memories emerges. While Canada is identified by some to now be their home because of the safety, freedom and security that they have found here, the specific sites of that feeling of safety and freedom are generally limited to SOGI refugee support groups and related LGBT organizations. Home is often not defined in terms of a material space, but rather in terms of multiple spaces defined through affective ties (past and present) connected to a sense of safety, security, belonging and inclusion. Furthermore, when 'home' arises in informal discussions, there are both good and bad memories of 'life back home', and connections with people back home are often maintained despite these fraught memories.

SOGI refugee migration to urban centres like Toronto is therefore fundamentally different from the urban migration of Canadian LGBT citizens in terms of borders crossed, the nation-state's intimate presence in the evaluation of the refugee's ability to follow a homonational script and the nation-state's ability to forcefully incarcerate and/or remove the failed refugee claimant 'back home'. While some Canadian LGBT citizens are now enfolded into a highly delimited narrative of national belonging (and the socio-economic rewards that go with it), SOGI refugee claimants must occupy a national narrative in which their role is that of deserving victims who are rescued by the benevolent state and are thus transformed from oppressed to liberated subjects by virtue of their movement across national borders in order to pass their hearing (Grewal 2005). However, in informal conversations, we find a messy multiplication of home(s), in which complex, fraught memories of and ongoing connections with 'old' home-lands and people there are maintained as new memories and connections are forged in home spaces defined through affect, security and likeness, underscoring Ahmed et al.'s reminder to be attentive to the process of homing, which emphasizes the interdependence between migration and home: 'making home is about creating both pasts and futures through inhabiting the grounds of the present' (2003: 8–9), and may strategically incorporate elements of homonationalist narratives while simultaneously undermining them through forms of multiple belonging.

NOTES

1. See, for example, Cohen and Sirkeci (2011).

2. Under the federal government's 'Protecting Canada's Immigration System' Act, the Personal Information Form (PIF) was replaced by the Basis of Claim (BOC) form in December 2012. All the research informants had submitted refugee applications that contained the PIF. The BOC questions follow a different organizational format from the PIF form, although their content and objectives are similar.

3. While 'home' is not a term used in IRPA or the UNHCR Convention, there are references to having fear of persecution in the 'country of nationality' and to persons 'outside the country of former habitual residence' who are unable to return to that country. In some of the IRB hearings that I attended, Board members asked the claimants what they feared if they were made 'to return home'; lawyers and support workers would also talk about 'getting your documents from home' or 'getting in touch with your family back home', such that 'home' and 'country of nationality' or 'country of former habitual residence' were often conflated.

4. This conversation is an amalgamation of different questions and comments by Board members and claimants. It is therefore fictitious because of confidentiality requirements of the hearing.

5. This knowledge may be due in part to the Board member's training on how to assess the credibility of SOGI refugee claims (see Chapter 5).

6. Once again, this period has been reduced substantially after the refugee reform legislation enacted in December 2012.

7. See Ou Jin Lee and Brotman (2011: 261) for similar findings.

8. As we saw in Chapter 2, some interviewees stated that they were wary of these groups, as they felt there were individuals from their home nations in attendance who the interviewees 'knew' were not lesbian, gay, bisexual or transgendered, and, in fact, were homophobic towards them back home. Thus, even 'home-like' SOGI refugee-focused spaces in the new home nation of Canada were not entirely safe.

9. http://www.xtra.ca/public/National/Canada_denies_another_gay_refugee_claimant-12652.aspx (accessed 20 October 2012).

Conclusion

The New Normal

In Chapter 1, I presented the migration experiences of Joe, Janine, Odu and Latoya, arguing that they both cleaved to and diverged from the hegemonic queer migration to liberation narrative found in much public discourse on SOGI refugees. The following two chapters explored the ways in which SOGI refugees learn about, prepare for and perform 'SOGI refugeeness', that is, they learned how to occupy an 'authentic' refugee narrative that contains particular assumptions about what a SOGI refugee should look and sound like and what elements the story of a SOGI refugee should contain in order to appear 'credible' to an IRB member. I argued in these chapters that this was a learning process that involved, for many, the acquisition of new knowledge about and interpretation of social aesthetics based on homo-normative assumptions. Chapter 4 shifted the focus from SOGI refugee claimants to support group volunteers who wrote letters attesting to refugee claimants' membership and participation in these groups. In the anxieties over producing letters of 'respectable' quality, we saw the ways in which another component of the refugee apparatus (humanitarians, caregivers and support workers) become enmeshed in state surveillance and border anxieties through the social aesthetics of eligibility employed in letter-writing by volunteers. The following two chapters shifted focus to the prime event for most Canadian inland refugee applicants, the hearing, and the documentation produced by 'experts' for the hearing. We witnessed again the ways in which homonormativity operated through the terminologies, patterns of questions and affective registers of the Board members and their use of refugee case file documentation. 'Expert' witness reports and governmental archives of sexuality also contribute towards homonationalist discourses in the refugee apparatus. Chapter 7 took up a broader theme in refugee research – home – and demonstrated the ways in which home has multiple meanings for SOGI refugees, who must present former and current homelands in particular ways that reproduce a homonationalist narrative of Canada as a nation of freedom to which the refugee 'victim' must be eternally grateful. However, many SOGI refugees maintain ongoing relationships with friends and family in their former 'homelands', and have complicated feelings of attachment to and disengagement from these people and places, resulting in fluid homes and multiple belongings.

I present this brief summary, in part to remind the reader that this book has only covered a relatively short but intense period of time (anywhere from a few months to a few years for most of the people I worked with) in the lives of a group of migrants who are labelled refugees because of the particularities of their migration experience, international legislation defining these forms of migration as 'seeking asylum' and the bureaucratic policies and practices of the immigration and citizenship apparatus of the nation-state, which create and enforce these particular definitions and time frames. Thus the previous chapters scrutinized most intensely the period that begins with lodging a refugee claim (in Canada) and ends with the hearing, a period that I found to be a troubling, dense and complex moment in which to explore meanings of and relationships between sexuality and gender identities, the qualities of 'refugeeness' and formations of nationalism produced, expanded, tested and sometimes resisted by various participants (refugee claimants, lawyers, support group workers and volunteers) enmeshed in the refugee apparatus. However, in focusing on this particular 'moment', I have run the risk of re-inscribing a static, essentialized identity upon the very subjects for whom I endeavoured to render a more nuanced and complex depiction. In other words, by spending the majority of this book on a particular moment in which these individuals are placed into a bureaucratic and legislative process designed to evaluate the credibility of their claim to being SOGI refugees, we end up viewing them primarily or only as 'SOGI refugees', without much attention to the rest of their lives before or after the refugee determination process. I began the book by trying to trouble popular narratives that contain assumptions about how people 'become' SOGI refugees and what those stories are supposed to look like, so I would like to end by briefly following up on some of the people whose migration stories I presented in Chapter 1 in order to once again illustrate the diverse and unevenly unfolding lives of this particular group of migrants.

Joe: Two years after my first meetings and interviews with SOGI refugee claimants in Toronto, I was still in touch with Joe and Janine, but I had lost contact with Odu and Latoya. On a rainy day in June 2013, I met Joe at a café in a north Toronto neighbourhood. He and his girlfriend had recently moved there and he didn't want to walk far from his apartment as he was recovering from a gender reassignment-related operation. It had been difficult to get the surgery, Joe said, as there had been problems with provincial health coverage and billing because of inconsistent gender markers on his identity cards. Joe also had to go to the Centre for Addiction and Mental Health (CAMH) for an interview in order to get approval for surgery – he was dreading the interview as he'd heard terrible things about CAMH's Gender Identity Unit from other trans people, but he had no problems. One unexpected outcome of the surgery was that it left Joe feeling very vulnerable, and it stirred up some of the trauma of his past – he still had fears of what might happen if certain people from his family or community showed up. Even though everything was 'much more manageable now', Joe wondered if these fears and nightmares would ever disappear completely.

Joe said that his operation had helped him to make a decision about his career choice. He had been thinking about careers for a while – 2012 was spent getting academic upgrading at a local community college, so Joe now had a 'Canadian high school credit'. He was doing this because he didn't want to transfer any educational documents/transcripts from his 'old identity' to Canada – he wanted a completely fresh start, with no connections to his life 'back there' – he referred to this as 'making a clean break'. While in the hospital, Joe identified with the nurses' work – it had some similarities to his previous work as a scientist and he wanted a job with more interpersonal elements. His girlfriend had also decided to become a nurse, so in the fall of 2013 they enrolled in a pre-health sciences program at a local college, following which they would apply for a Registered Practical Nurse Program (two years), possibly followed by a Bachelor of Science in Nursing, which would make them Registered Nurses.

Joe's successful hearing, which had taken place just before we first met in 2011, was 'intense' – it went on for about three hours – but was ultimately successful, and more recently he had obtained his permanent resident status[1] in February 2013. He figured it had taken longer than usual because of the 'discrepancies' on his identity documents (all his federal documents still identified him by his birth name and sex). Joe couldn't have the gender/name categories on his federal documents changed until he obtained citizenship, which at the time of our interview was still two years away. All of his provincial cards had been revised, so he was frustrated that he had to wait another two years, but at least it was there 'on the horizon'.

Joe now spent most of his free time with his girlfriend. He had joined some trans groups after he arrived in Canada but had become frustrated with them: 'I don't have time for the "we are oppressed" view' that pervades these groups', he said. Joe felt this had become an identity based on a political position, and he didn't like it when people tried to impose that identity on him. He also didn't visit the local LGBT community centre much anymore. It had helped him a lot when he first went there but now he felt there was too much focus on how 'we must stand up for our rights ... but you've already got them', at least compared to where he came from.

He and his girlfriend (who is white, about the same age as Joe and from a small rural town in Ontario) were finding it difficult to make friends in Toronto – 'people aren't approachable here and don't like to just hang out with friends'. However, after three years, Joe now felt more comfortable in Toronto in that he better understood the 'social aspects': 'I know how things work. ... If I'm on the TTC, and someone is doing something strange, I know it's normal to pretend it's not happening.' He had become more involved in Canada Day celebrations and he noticed that on Canada Day, most of the people wearing Canada's colours and celebrating were immigrants – 'Immigrants are more Canadian than Canadians.' Even though there are ongoing challenges in Toronto, 'I'm so lucky; here, I'm safe. ... I can go to an emergency ward and not worry about my safety. ... I don't ever want to forget that I'm really, really lucky. ... I'm proof of a living miracle.' At the same time, he knows Canada isn't perfect – 'I don't like (Rob) Ford (the mayor of Toronto at the time) or (Steven) Harper (the Prime Minister of Canada at that time)' – but he had experienced life in other countries like the United Kingdom, 'which is good at some things and bad at others, just like Canada'.

We ended the interview by discussing 'the next big step' for Joe, reconstructive surgery 'down there' (constructing a penis), but he didn't want to have this operation in Canada as he didn't like the Canadian surgeons' methods or results. He had been doing a lot of research and was very impressed by a surgeon in San Francisco, but this would mean waiting until he obtained his citizenship and doing some saving as the operation would cost him from $27000 to $30000.

Janine: I met Janine at an uptown café around the same time as Joe (July 2013). She had moved to an apartment in that area the previous August, and was incredibly thankful that she no longer had to live with her relatives in Scarborough. She was as energetic and talkative as always and seemed to me even more confident and articulate: 'life has changed for the better' since her hearing in early 2012. The hearing lasted 'just 27 minutes' and Janine remembered it very clearly. She'd heard that the Board member for her case was gay (which could work for or against you, she reminded me). He had asked Janine how she identified, and she had replied, 'bi'. She was expecting some trouble based on that claim (this is what others had told her), but there was none. The Board member asked her to tell him about her involvement with the LGBT community. Justine responded by asking, 'Do you mean personal or professional?' The member smiled, and said, 'Let's stick with professional' so she told him about her volunteer work and membership in a number of local LGBT and SOGI refugee groups. He then asked her for directions from her residence to a bar on Church Street that she had mentioned in her

PIF, and so 'I directed him'. His last question was 'What would happen if you returned to Jamaica?' and Janine had replied that there would be corrective rape or worse. Very shortly after that the Board member said that he accepted her claim. Janine couldn't believe how quickly it was over.

Because of her bail conditions after being placed in detention at 'The Milton Hilton', Janine had to live with relatives, but she spent most of her time away from their home, as she didn't get along with them. As soon as she received her letter confirming she was a convention refugee, she notified everyone about her change of address – she moved out and was living with a friend in a bachelor apartment in the neighbourhood near the café we were chatting in. She and her friend got along, but Janine found her difficult at times: 'She's on planet X (X being the friend's name) and is messy and not responsible.' A couple of months ago they moved into a one bedroom apartment in the same building, so at least now Janine had her own room.

Like Joe, Janine wasn't spending as much time in 'the gay village', although she would still go there occasionally: 'I've got a hangover from it,' she said, as she had spent so much time there for the first couple of years, and she was now wanting a change of scene. She was also spending a lot of time looking for a job, but said she had faced numerous hurdles and barriers. She had signed on with an employment agency, and they had helped her tailor her CV for particular jobs and prepare for interviews; however, 'It's a real problem here because people don't want to hire newcomers.' A couple of months prior to the interview, Janine landed a job as a receptionist at a small business near her apartment. Janine was enjoying the work so far, but was already planning to start looking for something more challenging once she had built up her reputation. Janine made a remark similar to Joe's when she said that after a couple of years in Canada, 'I'm learning about human nature, Canadian style.' When I asked her what this meant, she said, 'Canadians are polite and diplomatic, but they often try to sell you something by putting icing on shit; they don't tell it straightforward. … Jamaicans are much more straightforward.' Janine continued to do a great deal of volunteer work and really enjoyed it. Recently, she'd been appointed to the board of directors of an LGBT organization, and she felt this was a great opportunity to learn a number of skills.

Janine's permanent residency (PR) application was submitted in August 2012 (almost twelve months before our interview), and she thought it 'should be coming through very soon', although it was a bit more complicated than the usual PR application as her lawyer had to send in a form from Virginia police saying her shoplifting case had been closed/abandoned. She wasn't too worried about getting PR status, but was getting tired of the wait.

Janine was dating both a girl and a boy at the time of our interview, but the girlfriend had got drunk during Pride and really embarrassed her, so she was not sure whether or not that would continue. She was really enjoying her boyfriend as he accepted her as she was: 'Bisexuals are usually misunderstood, especially by straight men but he's curious in an open way; I can be myself with him, he's being very respectful … so it's all cool right now.'

Odu: Odu and I had met intermittently since the first interview. Most of the time, I would drive to a suburb in northwest Toronto and meet Odu at a Tim Horton's (a Canadian coffee shop chain) located a few minutes' drive from his apartment. Odu had purchased a car, which he needed for his job as personal support worker that required him to work in different locations around the city.

Odu's hearing had been postponed twice, and when it was finally held in March 2012, it did not go well. He said it felt like the Board member didn't believe anything he said, and in addition he didn't believe some of Odu's documentation, such as his school certificates from Nigeria. The Board member even questioned the validity of his Nigerian passport because it had expired. He asked Odu 'strange questions' like 'How many semesters are there in the Nigerian school system?' Odu said it took him a couple of minutes to answer because he wasn't prepared for this question, and the member asked him why it was taking him so long; he did this repeatedly, which made Odu feel that the member thought he was lying, when he was just trying to get the dates or answers correct in his head. The Board member asked about a relationship Odu had with another man for a number of years, and why Odu couldn't contact his ex-lover – Odu said he hadn't been in touch with him for a while and didn't know how to get hold of him. Odu felt that the member had come in ready to fail him and had made his decision before the hearing began. Afterwards, his lawyer said that this Board member had a reputation for failing these types of claims, and that he would request an audio copy of the hearing as he felt the member had made a lot of mistakes. His lawyer then lodged an appeal with the Federal Court. Over the next six months, waiting for the outcome of the appeal, Odu became less and less communicative when we met. He said he was just focused on working, 'living in the present', and waiting to see if the appeal would be successful. Odu was now having to check in with the Canadian Border Services Agency once every few weeks, and he said his lawyer had also launched a compassionate and humanitarian leave appeal, so he was preparing more documentation for that. During one particularly difficult meeting, in which he seemed very uninterested in talking, I mentioned how a few people we both knew from the church he had been attending were asking how he was doing. He smiled, and said he really enjoyed going to church, and then he started to sing the song from the weekly communion ritual. I hummed a bit with him, and he kept smiling and singing with his eyes closed.

I lost touch with Odu soon after this meeting, towards the end of 2012. When I called him one day, the cell-phone number was no longer valid, and I did not receive any further communication from him. Our mutual contacts at the church and SOGI support group had not heard from him either, so we assumed that he had either lost his appeal and been deported or had gone underground in order to avoid deportation by the authorities.

Latoya: As noted in Chapter 7, Latoya had been moving between shelters and friends' apartments in the first few months after her arrival in Toronto. At the time of her hearing, which I attended in March 2012, she was living in a community home for LGBT youth. She was still looking for a 'steady job', but in the meantime she was doing occasional drag shows and 'other things' (which may or may not have referred to sex work).

Latoya's hearing was scheduled for an early afternoon in March and she invited me to attend it. Latoya arrived at the IRB downtown offices wearing a form-fitting pinstriped business suit, which she had made, accentuating her thinness and tallness. Latoya said she had been up all night trying to finish it and make it look 'like I saw it in my mind'. She was wearing a wig with short straight hair in a sort of bob, and she had kept in her signature piercing blue contact lenses. A couple of women sitting near us in the waiting area kept giving Latoya sideways glances, but Latoya didn't notice them and/or was focused on the matters at hand. Latoya's fellow support worker from her community home also showed up. Her lawyer arrived a few minutes before the hearing was scheduled to start, and we went to the hearing room. The lawyer reviewed the procedure of the hearing with Latoya, what to say if she didn't understand a question (always ask the member to clarify or repeat), and that if she felt overwhelmed she could ask for a break and/or ask everyone (i.e., the support worker and me) to leave. The Board member arrived about thirty minutes after the scheduled start time, and after some consultation with the lawyer, began asking Latoya a number of questions, most of which focused on a series of violent incidents involving her ex-boyfriend in Barbados, which had been reported to the police and had resulted in the ex-boyfriend being jailed temporarily. The questioning continued for about forty-five minutes, and was followed by a few additional questions from Latoya's lawyer focusing mostly on her voyage to Canada and her involvement with Toronto LGBT organizations since her arrival. The Board member then requested a break, during which Latoya broke down and cried, saying it was 'too much'. The Board member re-entered the hearing room after about ten minutes and said she was prepared to render a positive decision. She noted that this was a well-documented claim in terms of sexual orientation and incidents that occurred to Latoya; also the letters from support groups here in Canada confirmed that she was an active member of the LGBT community. Latoya smiled and said 'thank you'. The Board member left the room, and everybody hugged one another.

I also lost touch with Latoya a few months after the hearing for the same reason as Odu – her cellphone number was no longer working, and she did not contact me with her new number. However, she continued to check in with some of the SOGI support group workers who I knew, and according to them she was 'doing fine' and was now enrolled in a hair styling and makeup school downtown.

***

In these brief follow-ups of just a few of many SOGI refugees in Toronto, we witness the profound significance and effects of the refugee application process on the lives of these individuals, particularly the impact of positive and negative decisions of the hearing, but we also see ongoing dilemmas, desires and choices that existed before and after the refugee determination process, which resulted in diverse feelings and actions towards the present and future. We see, from my perspective, how some individuals 'live on' in Toronto, while others fade or disappear abruptly. As someone who is marginal to the migration apparatus from the perspective of these refugee claimants, maintaining contact with me to provide updates on their lives was not a priority for most of them. At the same time, the abrupt 'endings' and subsequent silence from some of my research participants like Odu speak to the harsh reality of the refugee apparatus, and its necropolitical powers: Odu may or may not still be in Canada, he may or may not have returned to Nigeria, and he may or may not be in hiding here or there. But in terms of his 'identity' in the legal and bureaucratic components of the apparatus, he had been deemed 'bogus', and therefore he had disappeared either by going underground[2] or by being incarcerated and/or deported.

Through Odu's story we thus see the refugee apparatus operating in a permanent state of exception (Agamben 2005), continually reexamining itself for 'faults', 'failures' and 'blockages' that allow what it deems 'illegal and dangerous' bodies to pass through national borders or allow those same bodies to stay within its borders longer than necessary. The refugee apparatus continually reviews and revises, with the impossible goal of creating a 'system' that gives approval only to select bodies as genuine refugees. This nervous, distrustful, labile apparatus awards legally recognized life to some (through convention refugee status), but takes life from others (by declaring them illegal or criminal, based on their failed refugee application). We see one element of apparatus operations in a state of exception, where legislated rights can be diminished, superseded and rejected by a government in the process of refiguring power (Agamben 2005)

As I noted in the Introduction, the refugee apparatus, a device of population control and economic management composed of otherwise scattered elements (Feldman 2012: 15), is never stable. It acts and reacts to changes in national

and transnational migration patterns and laws, and to changing public moralities pertaining to immigration and/or particular classes of immigrants – a process of constant adaptation, or what Foucault calls 'normalization' (Feldman
2012: 14). Throughout this book I have made numerous references to policy
and procedural changes that have occurred to the refugee apparatus following
the conclusion of my fieldwork, which have created new normalizations and
impacted SOGI refugee claimants' experiences and/or outcomes. While it is
still 'early' days in terms of assessing the impact of changes brought about
by Bill C-31, which received Royal Assent on 28 June 2012, and came into
effect in December 2012, there is mounting evidence from the 'front lines' –
reports from lawyers, SOGI support workers, refugee advocate organizations
and refugee applicants themselves – that the apparatus has reconfigured and
tightened itself even further, shrinking timelines and increasing the number
of categories of inadmissibility. Sajnani reports:

> The most important, over-arching element of the changes under Bill C-31 is that
> they create a refugee apparatus that is anti-refugee for all potential claimants.
> The new regime entails a swath of measures that aim to 'crack down' on those
> immigrants who the government has not selected as economically advantageous
> or desirable. The measures, including shortened timelines, the increased use of
> detention, draconian measures for 'irregular' arrivals and boat arrivals, 'safe
> third country' provisions which shift responsibility for refugees between states,
> and measures which off-load governmental responsibilities for protection onto
> civil society, seriously erode the protection imperative in domestic and interna-
> tional law. (2014: 21)

Sajnani examines numerous sections of Bill C-31 that may have adverse
impacts on SOGI refugee claimants. These include the newly established
category of Designated Countries of Origin (DCO): 'DCOs are nations
designated by the Minister as respecting human rights and the rule of law,
and being generally "safe". Claimants from these countries are presumed
to have a lesser chance at a successful refugee claim. They are therefore
afforded shorter timelines, and therefore less consideration, throughout
the asylum process' (2014: 27). The effect of the DCO category on SOGI
refugee claimants is particularly problematic: in the new DCO legislation
there is no mechanism for designating certain groups within a country as
being vulnerable, oppressed or persecuted. Most, if not all, states with 'good
human rights' records could be identified as having numerous 'blind spots'
that (often strategically) overlook or ignore groups within their borders with a
history of oppression. SOGI refugee claimants are one of the groups likely to
be negatively impacted by the DCO list: 'There are significant human rights
abuses against sexual and gender minorities in several countries currently on

the DCO list (CIC, 2014). For example, Mexico, which is currently on the DCO list, reports high levels of anti-LGBT violence, particularly in Mexico City' (Sajnani 2014: 29).

A second major change involves the shortening of time limits in the refugee determination process. During the period in which I conducted fieldwork, claimants had twenty-eight days from making a claim at a port of entry to find a lawyer, start to prepare their case and submit their initial claim to determine eligibility. Refugee claimants, lawyers and support workers reported how difficult it was to complete all these tasks within this twenty-eight-day period. However, under the new provisions, claimants have only fifteen days to do these same tasks. For claimants making inland claims (i.e., at a CIC office after already entering Canada), the timeframe is now generally less than fifteen days. Another change in timing has occurred around the wait period between submitting the claim and the hearing. During my fieldwork period, refugee claimants could wait from six months up to two years for their hearing. As Sajnani observes, the delays were often due to IRB inefficiencies and backlogs caused in large part by the government's decision not to appoint a full roster of adjudicators. While this long wait period could be very stressful, it did allow SOGI refugee claimants the time to obtain and submit necessary documents from their home countries, join and participate in local LGBT organizations, and find some form of work. However, instead of addressing institutional issues causing the delays and backlogs, the new laws have shifted the burden onto claimants by imposing much shorter timelines between claim and hearing: '45 days for DCO claimants and 60 days for non-DCO claimants for port-of-entry claims (claims made at airport or border customs offices), and 30 days for DCO claimants and 45 days for non-DCO claimants for inland claims' (Sajnani 2014: 31–32). Thus, whereas SOGI refugee claimants used to have several months or years to prepare for the hearing (amass proper documentation, get involved with local LGBT groups, and learn sexual/gender identity terms and their associated knowledges, narrative strategies and performative aesthetics), the new process places SOGI refugee claimants in an even more precarious position, in which they have substantially less time to prepare their case file and themselves for the complexities and deeply embedded 'logics' of the refugee determination hearing.

Conversations in early 2015 with a couple of facilitators from the two Toronto SOGI support groups where I had volunteered during my fieldwork confirmed the problematic impacts brought about by Bill C-31, but also noted some other unforeseen (and possibly unrelated) changes: One organization had been forced to change its intake process for new group members: there used to be an orientation session, which was mandatory for everyone who wanted to join the support group; after attending the orientation session, one could then start attending the next support group meeting (usually the following week). However, because of the extremely short wait-times between filing the claim and the hearing, the organization was now having the orientation session on the day before the group meeting, which would allow new refugee claimants to start attending meetings sooner, and build up their attendance record faster, so that letters (confirming membership in the group) could be written sooner.

Another change was in relation to attendance: In both support groups, overall attendance at the regular meetings dropped off significantly from the beginning of 2013 (the Bill came into effect in December 2012); attendance in one group dropped from around 200 to 60–70 per meeting; however, since January 2015, the numbers had started to creep up again, and were now up to about 100–120 at the meetings, according to the facilitator. Both groups were also noticing increases in members from countries that had not figured prominently during my research in 2011–2012: There were now more members from African countries other than Nigeria, such as Uganda, Cameroon, Senegal and Kenya. There was also an uptick in numbers from the Ukraine, Pakistan, the Dominican Republic and the Bahamas. The facilitators said it was hard to explain these increases, but they were, 'usually related to something going on back home', according to one facilitator. For example, he had heard that there had been significant increases in violence against LGBT persons in the Bahamas and the Dominican Republic. However, he noted, these changes could also have to do with LGBT/refugee networks, messages being passed on by friends, border services agents, Googling, and/or workers and residents at local Toronto shelters. At the same time, the number of SOGI refugee claimants from some other countries had decreased since my fieldwork. For example, there were now far fewer claimants from Grenada and St. Lucia since the Canadian government had recently imposed visa restrictions on citizens from those countries travelling to Canada.

Both facilitators also noted that starting in 2013, there seemed to be higher numbers of failed cases among their group members. One facilitator felt that this may be due to the fact that the IRB had instituted a new process for hiring Board members, and that most of the new members were civil servants who were not initially receiving good training on SOGI cases. She heard a number of clients report inappropriate questions and comments from Board members: In one hearing, a member spoke to a claimant about how big his pecs and biceps were, and that someone that big should be able to defend himself from physical harm. The member went on to reject the claim, although it had since been successfully appealed. In fact, it was noted that there also appeared to be increased numbers of appeal cases, mainly as a result of the establishment of a new Refugee Appeals Division (RAD), which provides a more systematic and clearly defined process for claimants and their legal counsel to appeal negative decisions they consider problematic.

Thus the apparatus continues to transform, adapt, rebuild and extend: The Canadian refugee apparatus has, over the last twenty-five years, developed particular modes through which to define, evaluate and reject applications for refugee status based on sexual orientation and gender identity persecution, but these definitions and modes of evaluation are in constant flux as indicated through this brief synopsis of some of the changes brought about by Bill C-31. As numerous migration researchers and advocates have noted, over the last twenty years the trend in most Global North nation-states has been towards increased levels of suspicion, surveillance and extradition of migrants crossing their borders. Refugees are just one of many categories of transnational migrants whose identities are increasingly defined by the national and transnational immigration apparatus as bogus or fraudulent, and thus not deserving of the rewards of citizenship of the receiving state. As the political regimes in many Global North nation-states invest more heavily in global military, political and economic interventions in the name of liberty, economic freedom, security and/or the eradication of 'terrorism', they continue to refuse to acknowledge the ways in which these investments, policies and actions perpetuate or increase violence against already marginalized and vulnerable groups (defined through multiple intersecting axes of gender, sexuality, socio-economic status, ethnicity, race and/or religion) in those locations 'targeted' for 'intervention'.[3] Their actions often force members of these marginalized and/or vulnerable groups to flee and cross national borders in order to seek protection. The silences, gaps and omissions in the homonational queer migration to liberation nation narrative found in multiple segments of the refugee apparatus allow for collective transnational violence to continue without the dots between persons identified as 'refugees', immigration bureaucracies, and national and transnational political, economic and military actions and policies to be connected, but the narrative also shifts the focus away from ongoing local inequalities and new, sometimes different experiences of economic, racialized and/or socio-cultural marginalization and vulnerability in the 'liberation nation', resulting in strategic or 'ambivalent homonationalisms' (White 2013) and fluid belongings to multiple homes that make life bearable for those who are moving within, through and beyond the refugee apparatus.

NOTES

1. A permanent resident is someone who has obtained permanent resident status by immigrating to Canada, but is not a Canadian citizen. Permanent residents are citizens of other countries. A permanent resident gets most of the social benefits that Canadian citizens receive, including health care coverage; they may live, work or

study anywhere in Canada, and apply for Canadian citizenship. They may not vote or work in certain high-level security jobs. In order to obtain Canadian citizenship, a permanent resident must live in Canada for at least two years in a five-year period. If he or she lives outside of Canada for longer, they may lose their permanent resident status. In 2014, the federal government introduced a number of changes to the Citizenship Act including longer 'in-residency' rules that made permanent resident status much less 'permanent' than before.

2. A 2007 Royal Canadian Mounted Police report estimated there were up to 500,000 'undocumented' people living in Canada, many of whom were 'rejected' asylum claimants (Scott 2015).

3. For example, according to a recent report published by the International Consortium of Investigative Journalists and their media partners, over the last decade (2005–2015), projects funded by the World Bank have physically or economically displaced an estimated 3.4 million people, forcing them from their homes, taking their land or damaging their livelihoods. http://www.icij.org/blog/2015/04/new-investigation-reveals-34m-displaced-world-bank (accessed 23 April 2015).

Bibliography

Agamben, Giorgio. 2005. *State of Exception.* Chicago: University of Chicago Press.

Agathangelou, Anna. 2004. *The Global Political Economy of Sex: Desire, Violence, and Insecurity in Mediterranean Nation States.* New York, NY: Palgrave Macmillan.

Ahmed, Sara. 2001. *Strange Encounters: Embodied Others in Post-Coloniality.* London, UK: Routledge.

———. 2004. *The Cultural Politics of Emotion.* Edinburgh: University of Edinburgh Press.

———. 2006. *Queer Phenomenology: Orientations, Objects, Others.* Durham: Duke University Press.

———. 2010. *The Promise of Happiness.* Durham: Duke University Press.

Ahmed, Sara, Claudia Castaneda, Ann Marie Fortier, and Mimi Sheller, eds. 2003. *Uprootings/Regroundings: Questions of Home and Migration.* New York: Berg.

Al-Ali, Nadje and Khalid Koser, eds. 2001. *New Approaches to Migration: Transnational Communities and the Transformation of Home.* London: Routledge.

Alexander, M. Jacqui. 2005. *Pedagogies of Crossing: Meditations on Feminism, Sexual Politics, Memory and the Sacred.* Durham: Duke University Press.

Allick, Chantalie. 2011. The Many Faces of Pride. *The Globe and Mail* p. A14, July 2, 2011.

Annes, Alexis and Meredith Redlin. 2012. Coming Out and Coming Back. Rural Gay Migration and the City. *Journal of Rural Studies* 28(1): 6–68.

Bakan, Abigail and Daiva Stasiulis. 2003. *Negotiating Citizenship: Migrant Women in Canada and the Global System.* Basingstoke: Palgrave Macmillan.

Barrett, Rusty. 2002. Is Queer Theory Important for Socio-Linguistic Theory? In *Language and Sexuality: Contesting Meaning in Theory and Practice*, Kathryn Campbell-Kibler et al. eds., pp. 25–43. Stanford: CSLI Press.

Berg, Laurie and Jocelyn Millbank. 2009. Constructing the Personal Narratives of Lesbian, Gay and Bisexual Asylum Claimants. *Journal of Refugee Studies* 22(2): 195–223.

Berger, John. 1984. *And Our Faces, My Heart, Brief as Photos*. London: Bloomsbury Publishing.

Berlant, Lauren, ed. 2004. *The Culture and Politics of an Emotion*. New York: Taylor and Francis.

Boellstorff, Tom. 2007. Queer Studies in the House of Anthropology. *Annual Review of Anthropology* 36: 17–35.

Boucher, Geoffrey. 2006. The Politics of Performativity: A Critique of Judith Butler. *Parrhesia* 1: 112–41.

Brenneis, Donald L. 1987. Performing Passions; Aesthetics and Politics in an Occasionally Egalitarian Community. *American Ethnologist* 14(2): 236–50.

Bucholtz, Mary and Hall, Kira. 2004. Theorizing Identity in Language and Sexuality Research. *Language in Society* 33: 469–515.

Butler, Judith. 1990. *Gender Trouble*. New York: Routledge.

———. 1993. *Bodies That Matter: On the Discursive Limits of "Sex."* New York: Routledge.

———. 1995. Burning Acts: Injurious Speech. In *Performativity and Performance*, A. Parker and E. K. Sedgwick, eds., pp. 197–227. New York: Routledge.

Cabot, Heath. 2012. The Governance of Things: Documenting Limbo in the Greek Asylum Procedure". *PoLAR* 35(1): 11–29.

———. 2013. The Social Aesthetics of Eligibility: NGO aid and indeterminacy in the Greek Asylum Process. *American Ethnologist* 40(3): 452–86.

———. 2014. *On the Doorstep of Europe: Asylum and Citizenship in Greece*. Philadelphia: University of Pennsylvania Press.

Canaday, Margot. 2009. *The Straight State: Sexuality and Citizenship in 20th Century America*. Princeton, NJ: Princeton University Press.

Cantú, Lionel, Jr. 2009. *The Sexuality of Migration: Border Crossings and Mexican Immigrant Men*. New York: New York University Press.

Carillo, Hector. 2004. Sexual Migration, Cross-Cultural Sexual Encounters and Sexual Health. *Sexuality Research and Social Policy* 1(3): 58–70.

Chase, Steven. 2013. Baird Belies Conservative Image Through Defence of Gay Rights Abroad. *Globe and Mail*, September 8, 2013.

Clifford, James. 1997. *Routes: Travel and Translation in the late 20th Century*. Cambridge: Harvard University Press.

Cohen, Lawrence. 2009. Lucknow Noir. In *Homophobias: Lust and Loathing across Time and Space*, David A. B. Murray, ed., pp. 162–84. Durham: Duke University Press.

Cohen, Jeffery H. and Ibrahim Sirkeci. 2011. *Cultures of Migration: The Global Nature of Contemporary Mobility*. Austin: University of Texas Press.

Cooney, Darren. 2007. Queer Newcomers Land Among Friends. *Xtra: Canada's Gay and Lesbian News*. May 10, 2007.

Coutin Susan, Bibler. 2000. *Legalizing Moves: Salvadoran Immigrants' Struggle for U.S. Residency*. Ann Arbor: University of Michigan Press.

Cruz-Malave, Arnaldo and Martin F. Manalansan IV, eds. 2002. *Queer Globalizations: Citizenship and the Afterlife of Colonialism*. New York: New York University Press.

Cvetkovich, Anne. 2003. *An Archive of Feelings: Trauma, Sexuality and Lesbian Public Cultures*. Durham: Duke University Press.

Dave, Naisargi N. 2011. Indian, Lesbian and What Came Next: Affect, Commensuration and Queer Emergences. *American Ethnologist* 38(4): 650–65.

Davis, Erin Calhoun. 2008. Situating "Fluidity" (Trans) Gender Identification and the Regulation of Gender Diversity. *GLQ* 15(1): 97–130.

Decena, Carlos. 2011. *Tacit Subjects: Belonging and Same Sex Desire Amongst Dominican Immigrant Men*. Durham: Duke University Press.

Decena, Carlos, Michelle Shedlin, and Angela Martinez. 2006. Los hombres no mandan aqui: Narrating Immigrant Genders and Sexualities in New York. *Social Text* 88: 35–54.

Derlyn, Ilse, Charles Walters, Cindy Mels, and Eric Broekaert. 2012. 'We are all the same, cuz exist only one earth; why the border exist?': Messages of Migrants on Their Way. *Journal of Refugee Studies*. http://jrs.oxfordjournals.org/content/early/2012/12/19/jrs.fes042.short (accessed March 3, 2013).

Dua, Ena. 2007. Exclusion Through Inclusion: Female Asian Migration in the Making of Canada as a White Settler Nation. *Gender, Place and Culture* 14(4): 445–66.

Duggan, Lisa. 2003. *The Twilight of Equality? Neoliberalism, Cultural Politics and the Attack on Democracy*. Boston, MA: Beacon Press.

Dyck, Isabel and Parin Dossa. 2007. Place, Health and Home: Gender and Migration in the Constitution of Health Space. *Health & Place* 13: 691–701.

Eng, David. 2010. *The Feeling of Kinship: Queer Liberalism and the Racialization of Intimacy*. Durham, NC: Duke University Press.

Entrecote, Paul. 2012. Last Chance (film).

Epps, Brad, Keja Valens, and Bill Johnson-Gonzalez, eds. 2005. *Passing Lines: Sexuality and Immigration*. Cambridge, MA: Harvard University Press.

Espin, Oliva. 1999. *Women Crossing Boundaries: The Psychology of Immigration and the Transformations of Sexuality*. London, UK: Routledge.

Fassin, Didier. 2011. Policing Borders, Producing Boundaries: The Governmentality of Immigration in Dark Times. *Annual Review of Anthropology* 40: 213–26.

Fassin, Didier and Estelle D'Halluin. 2005. The Truth from the Body: Medical Certificates as Ultimate Evidence for Asylum Seekers. *American Anthropologist* 107(4): 597–608.

Fassin, Didier and Richard Rechtman. 2009. *The Empire of Trauma: An Inquiry into the Condition of Victimhood*. Princeton: Princeton University Press.

Feldman, Gregory. 2012. *The Migration Apparatus: Security, Labor, and Policymaking in the European Union*. Stanford: Stanford University Press.

Feldman, Ilana and Miriam Iris Ticktin. 2011. *In the Name of Humanity: The Government of Threat and Care*. Durham: Duke University Press.

Ferguson, Roderick. 2004. *Aberration in Black: Toward a Queer of Color Critique*. Minneapolis: University of Minnesota Press.

Freeman, Carla. 2000. *High Tech and High Heels in the Global Economy*. Durham: Duke University Press.

Glenwright, Danny. 2011. Holding on to Hard-won Rights. *Xtra*, September 22, 2011, p. 6.

————. 2012. Tory Embrace Just for Show. *Xtra*, October 4, 2012, p. 6.

Glick-Schiller, Nina, Linda Basch, and Cristina Szanton-Blanc. 1992. *Toward a Transnational Perspective on Migration: Race, Class, Ethnicity and Nationalism Reconsidered*. New York: New York Academy of Sciences.

The Globe and Mail. 2011. Editorial, December 30, 2011, p. A14.

Goldberg, David Theo. 2009. *The Threat of Race: Reflections on Racial Neoliberalism*. Hoboken: Wiley-Blackwell.

Good, Anthony. 2006. *Anthropology and Expertise in Asylum Courts*. London: Taylor and Francis.

Good, Anthony and Tobias Kelly. 2013. *Expert Country Evidence in Asylum and Immigration Cases in the United Kingdom: Best Practice Guide*. School of Social and Political Science, The University of Edinburgh.

Gopinath, Gayatri. 2005. Impossible Desires: Queer Diasporas and South Asian Public Cultures. Durham, NC: Duke University Press.

Graham, David. 2010. Escape from Iran. *Toronto Star*, November 13, 2010, p. 1.

Grewal, Inderpal. 2005. *Transnational America: Feminisms, Diasporas, Neoliberalisms*. Durham: Duke University Press.

Gupta, A. and J. Ferguson. 1992. Beyond 'Culture': Space, Identity and the Politics of Difference. *Cultural Anthropology* 7(1): 6–23.

Halberstam, Judith. 2011. *The Queer Art of Failure*. Durham: Duke University Press.

Hall, Alexandra. 2012. *Border Watch: Cultures of Immigration, Detention and Control*. London: Pluto.

Halperin, David. 2012. *How to Be Gay*. Cambridge: Harvard University Press. E-book.

Haritaworn, Jinthana. 2012. *The Biopolitics of Mixing: Thai Multiracialities and Haunted Ascendencies*. Abingdon: Ashgate.

Haritaworn, Jinthana, Adi Kuntsman and Silvia Posocco, eds. 2014. *Queer Necropolitics*. Abingdon: Routledge.

Hart, John. 2002. *Stories of Gay and Lesbian Immigration: Together Forever?* New York: Harrington Park.

Hasselriis, Kaj. 2013. *From Far & Wide*. Xtra, June 27–July 10, 2013, pp. 28–30.

Hetherington, Kregg. 2011. *Guerrilla Auditors: The Politics of Transparency in Neoliberal Paraguay*. Durham: Duke University Press.

Houston, Andrea. 2010. Mexican Asylum Seekers Allege Mistreatment. *Xtra*, November 18, 2010, p. 13.

————. 2012. Jason Kenny Defends Gay-Targeted Email. *Xtra*, October 4, 2012, p. 10.

Hull, Matthew. 2012. Documents and Bureaucracy. *Annual Review of Anthropology* 41: 251–67.

Hunter, Marcus. 2010. All the Gays are White and All the Blacks are Straight: Black Gay Males, Identity and Community. *Sexuality Research and Social Policy* 7(2): 81–92.

Iacovetta, Franca. 2000. The Sexual Politics of Moral Citizenship and Containing "Dangerous" Foreign Men in Cold War Canada, 1950s-1960s. *Social History* 33(66): 361–89.

Immigration and Refugee Protection Act. 2001. Statutes of Canada, c. 27.

Itaborahy, Lucas Paoli and Jingshu Zhu. 2013. *State Sponsored Homophobia A World Survey of Laws: Criminalisation, Protection and Recognition of Same-sex Love.* International Lesbian Gay Bisexual Trans and Intersex Association. www.ilga.org (accessed January 4, 2014).

Jenicek Ainsley, Alan D. Wong, and Edward Ou Jin Lee. 2009. Dangerous Shortcuts: Representations of Sexual Minority Refugees in the Post 9/11 Canadian Press. *Canadian Journal of Communications* 34(4): 635–58.

Jiminez, Marina. 2004. Gay Refugee Claimants Seeking Haven in Canada. *The Globe and Mail*, April 24, 2004.

Johnson, E. Patrick and Mae Henderson, eds. 2005. *Black Queer Studies: A Critical Anthology*. Durham, NC: Duke University Press.

Johnson, Toni A. M. 2011. On Silence, Sexuality and Skeletons: Reconceptualizing Narrative in Asylum Hearings. *Social and Legal Studies* 20(1): 57–78.

Jordan, Sharalynn. 2010. Un/Convention(al) Refugees: Contextualizing Accounts of Refugees Facing Homophobic or Transphobic Persecution. *Refuge* 26(2): 165–82.

Kaptani, Erene and Nira Yuval-Davis. 2008. Participatory Theatre as a Research Methodology: Identity, Performance and Social Action Among Refugees. *Sociological Research Online* 13(5). doi: 10.5153/sro.1789.

Kea, Pamela J. and Guy Roberts-Holmes. 2013. Producing Victim Identities: Female Genital Mutilation and the Politics of Asylum Claims in the UK. *Identities* 20(1): 96–113.

Kempadoo, Kamala. 2004. *Sexing the Caribbean: Gender, Race and Sexual Labor.* New York: Routledge.

Keung, Nicholas. 2010. 'Disneyland' for Gay Refugees. *Toronto Star*, December 1, 2010, p. 1.

Kinsman, Gary and Patricia Gentile. 2010. *The Canadian War on Queers: National Security as Sexual Regulation.* University of British Columbia Press.

Kuntsman, Adi. 2008. Between Gulags and Pride Parades: Sexuality, Nation and Haunted Speech Acts. *GLQ* 14(2–3): 263–88.

Larcher, Akim Ade. 2012. Canada's Gay Rights. *Xtra*, February 23, 2012, p. 14.

LaViolette, Nicole. 2004. *Sexual Orientation and The Refugee Determination Process: Questioning a Claimant About their Membership in the Particular Social Group.* Ottawa: Immigration and Refugee Board.

———. 2009. Independent Human Rights Documentation and Sexual Minorities: An Ongoing Challenge for the Canadian Refugee Determination Process. *The International Journal of Human Rights* 13(2–3): 437–76.

———. 2010. *Sexual Orientation, Gender Identity and the Refugee Determination Process*. Ottawa: Immigration and Refugee Board.

Leap, William and Tom Boellstorff, eds. 2004. *Speaking in Queer Tongues: Gay Language and Globalization.* Urbana: University of Illinois Press.

Levitt, Peggy and Nina Glick-Schiller. 2007. Conceptualizing Simultaneity: A Transnational Social Field Perspective on Society. In *Rethinking Migration: New Theoretical and Empirical Perspectives*, Alejandro Portes and Josh DeWind, eds. New York: Berghahn Books.

Lewin, Ellen and William L. Leap, eds. 2002. *Out in Theory: The Emergence of Lesbian and Gay Theory*. Urbana: University of Illinois Press.
———. 2009. *Out in Public: Reinventing Gay and Lesbian Anthropology*. Malden and Oxford: Wiley-Blackwell.
Lewis, Miranda. 2005. *Asylum: Understanding Public Attitudes*. Institute for Public Policy Research, London.
Lewis, Rachel. 2010. The Cultural Politics of Lesbian Asylum: Angelina Maccarone's 'Unveiled' and the Case of the Lesbian Asylum Seeker. *International Feminist Journal of Politics* 12(3–4): 424–43.
Ling, Justin. 2012. Playing with Refugees' Lives. *Xtra*, June 14, 2012, p. 13.
———. 2013. Mapping Progress. *Xtra*, June 27–July 10, 2013, pp. 36–7.
Loxley, James. 2006. *Performativity*. Abingdon, Oxon: Routledge.
Luibhéid, Eithne. 2002. *Entry Denied: Controlling Sexuality at the Border*. Minneapolis: University of Minnesota Press.
———. 2008. Queer/Migration: An Unruly Body of Scholarship. *GLQ* 14(2–3): 169–90.
Luibhéid, Eithne, ed. 2008. Queer/Migration. Special Issue of *GLQ* 14(2–3).
Luibhéid, Eithne and Lionel Cantú Jr., eds. 2005. *Queer Migrations: Sexuality, US Citizenship and Border Crossings*. Minneapolis: University of Minnesota Press.
Lutz, Catherine and White, Geoffrey. 1986. The Anthropology of Emotions. *Annual Review of Anthropology* 15: 405–36.
Macklin, Audrey. 2003. Dancing across Borders: 'Exotic dancers,' Trafficking, and Canadian Immigration Policy. International Migration Review 37(2): 464–501.
Malkki, Lisa. 1995. Refugees and Exile: From Refugee Studies to the National Order of Things. *Annual Review of Anthropology* 24: 495–523.
Manalansan, Martin F. 2003. *Global Divas: Filipino Gay Men in the Diaspora*. Durham: Duke University Press.
———. 2006. Queer Intersections: Sexuality and Gender in Migration Studies. *International Migration Review* 40(1): 224–49.
———. 2009. Homophobia at New York's Gay Central. In *Homophobias: Lust and Loathing Across Time and Space*, David A. B. Murray, ed., pp. 34–47. Durham: Duke University Press.
———. 2014. The 'Stuff' of Archives: Mess, Migration, and Queer Lives. *Radical History Review* 120: 94–107.
Mannik, Linda. 2013. *Photography, Memore and Refugee Identity: The Voyage of the SS Walnut, 1948*. Vancouver: UBC Press.
Marshall, Daniel, Kevin P. Murphy, and Zeb Tortorici. 2014. Editors' Introduction: Queering Archives: Historical Unravelings. *Radical History Review* 120: 1-1.
Maryns, Katrijn and Blommaert, Jan. 2002. Pretextuality and Pretextual Gaps: On De/Refining Linguistic Inequality. *Pragmatics* 12(1): 11–30.
Massumi, Brian. 2002. *Parables for the Virtual: Movement, Affect, Sensation*. Durham, NC: Duke University Press.
Mattingly, Cheryl. 2008. Reading Minds and Telling Tales in a Cultural Borderland. *Ethos* 36(1): 136–54.
McConnell-Ginet, Sally. 2006. Why Defining Is Seldom Just Semantics: Marriage and "Marriage". In *The Language and Sexuality Reader*, Don Kulick and Deborah Cameron, eds., pp. 227–40. Florence: Routledge.

McGranahan, Carole. 2012. Anthropology and the Truths of Political Asylum, Part II. *Anthropology News* 53(4): 20–1.

Millbank, Jenni. 2009a. 'The Ring of Truth': A Case Study of Credibility Assessment in Particular Social Group Refugee Determinations. *International Journal of Refugee Law* 21(1): 1–33.

———. 2009b. From Discretion to Disbelief: Recent Trends in Refugee Determinations on the Basis of Sexual Orientation in Australia and the United Kingdom. *The International Journal of Human Rights* 13(2–3): 391–414.

Miller, Alice. 2005. Gay Enough? Some Tensions in Seeking the Grant of Asylum and Protecting Global Sexual Diversity. In *Passing Lines: Sexuality and Immigration*, Brad Epps, Keja Valens, and Bill Johnson-Gonzalez, eds., pp. 137–87. Cambridge: Harvard University Press.

Moore, Mignon. 2011. *Invisible Families: Gay Identities, Relationships and Motherhood Among Black Women*. Berkeley: University of California Press.

Morris, Rosalind. 1995. All Made Up: Performance Theory and the New Anthropology of Sex and Gender. *Annual Review of Anthropology* 24: 567–92.

Mountz, Alison. 2010. *Seeking Asylum: Human Smuggling and Bureaucracy at the Border*. Minneapolis: University of Minnesota Press.

Munoz, Jose. 1999. *Disidentifications: Queers of Color and the Performance of Politics*. Minnesota: University of Minnesota Press.

Murray, David A. B. 2002. *Opacity: Gender, Sexuality, Race and the 'Problem' of Identity in Martinique*. New York: Peter Lang Press.

———. 2012. *Flaming Souls: Homosexuality, Homophobia and Social Change in Barbados*. Toronto: University of Toronto Press.

Murray, David A. B. ed. 2009. *Homophobias: Lust and Loathing Across Time and Space*. Durham: Duke University Press.

Nader, Laura. 1972. Up the Anthropologist: Perspectives Gained from Studying Up. In *Reinventing Anthropology*, Dell Hymes, ed., pp. 284–311. New York: Pantheon Books.

Newbold, Bruce and Pat DeLuca. 2007. Short-term Residential Changes to Toronto's Immigrant Communities: Evidence from Lsic Wave 1. *Urban Geography* 28(7): 635–56.

Offord, Baden. 2013. Queer Activist Intersections in Southeast Asia: Human Rights and Cultural Studies. *Asian Studies Review* 37(3): 335–49.

O'Leary, Barry. 2008. "We Cannot Claim Any Particular Knowledge of the Ways Homosexuals, Still Less of Iranian Homosexuals ...": The Particular Problems Facing Those Who Seek Asylum on the Basis of Their Sexual Identity. *Feminist Legal Studies* 16: 87–95.

Ong, Aihwa. 2003. *Buddha Is Hiding: Refugees, Citizenship, The New America*. Berkeley: University of California Press.

Ou Jin Lee, Edward and Shari Brotman. 2011. Identity, Refugeeness, Belonging: Experiences of Sexual Minority Refugees in Canada. *Canadian Review of Sociology* 48(3): 241–74.

Patton, Cindy and Benigno Sanchez-Eppler, eds. 2000. *Queer Diasporas*. Durham, NC: Duke University Press.

Personal Narratives Group. 1989. *Interpreting Women's Lives: Feminist Theory and Personal Narratives*. Bloomington: Indiana University Press.

Peutz, Nicholas and Nathalie De Genova. 2010. Introduction. In *The Deportation Regime: Sovereignty, Space and the Freedom of Movement*, Nicholas De Genova and Nathalie Peutz, eds., pp. 1–29. Durham: Duke University Press.

Povinelli, Elizabeth. 2001. Radical Worlds: The Anthropology of Incommensurability and Inconceivability. *Annual Review of Anthropology* 30: 319–34.

———. 2002. *The Cunning of Recognition: Indigenous Alterities and the Making of Australian Multiculturalism*. Durham: Duke University Press.

———. 2006. *The Empire of Love*. Durham: Duke University Press.

Povinelli, Elizabeth and George Chauncey, eds. 1999. Thinking Sexuality Transnationally. Special Issue of *GLQ* 5(4).

Protecting Canada's Immigration System Act. 2012. Statutes of Canada, c. 17.

Puar, Jasbir. 2007. Terrorist Assemblages: Homonationalism in Queer Times. Durham: Duke University Press.

Quan, Douglas. 2012. Homosexual Refugee Claimant Allowed to Remain. *The Montreal Gazette*, July 12, 2012, p. A11.

Randazzo, Timothy J. 2005. Social and Legal Barriers: Sexual Orientation and Asylum in the United States. In *Queer Migrations: Sexuality, U.S. Citizenship and Border Crossings*, Eithne Luibhéid and Lionel Cantú Jr., eds., pp. 30–60. Minneapolis: University of Minnesota Press.

Rapport, Nigel and Andrew Dawson. 1998. Home and Movement: A Polemic. In *Immigrants of Identity: Perceptions of Home in a World of Movement*, Nigel Rapport and Andrew Dawson, eds., pp. 19–38. Oxford: Berg.

Razack, Sherene. 1998. *Looking White People in the Eye: Gender, Race and Culture in Courtrooms and Classrooms*. Toronto: University of Toronto Press.

Rehaag, Sean. 2008. Patrolling the Borders of Sexual Orientation: Bisexual Refugee Claims in Canada. *McGill Law Journal* 53: 61–101.

Research Directorate, Immigration and Refugee Board. 2012. Treatment of Sexual Minorities, including Legislation, State Protection and Support Services. Immigration and Refugee Board. http://www.irb-cisr.gc.ca/Eng/ResRec/RirRdi/Pages/index.aspx?doc=454227 (accessed January 6, 2014).

Ricard, Nathalie. 2014. Testimonies of LGBTIQ Refugees as Cartographies of Political, Sexual and Emotional Borders. *Journal of Language and Sexuality* 3(1): 28–59.

Riles, Annelise. March 2006. Anthropology, Human Rights, and Legal Knowledge: Culture in the Iron Cage. *American Anthropologist* 108(1): 52–65.

Sajnani Rohan. 2014. *The Impact of Canada's New Immigration Regime*. Toronto: Envisioning Global LGBT Human Rights.

Salih, Sara. 2002. *Judith Butler*. New York: Routledge.

Scott, James C. 1998. *Seeing Like a State: How Certain Schemes to Improve the Human Condition Have Failed*. New Haven: Yale University Press.

Scott, Marian. 2015. Undocumented Mother Suffers: She Lives in Fear After Son was Deported in Fall. *Montreal Gazette*, May 9, 2015, p. A3.

Shieffelin, Edward L. 1998. Problematizing Performance. In *Ritual, Performance, Media*, F. Hughes-Freeland, ed., pp. 194–207, London: Routledge.

Showler, Peter. 2006. *Refugee Sandwich: Stories of Exile and Asylum*. Kingston, ON: McGill-Queen's University Press.

Simich, Laura, David Este, and Hayley Hamilton. 2010. Meanings of Home and Mental Well-Being Among Sudanese Refugees in Canada. *Ethnicity and Health* 15(2): 199–212.

Sinclair, Ed. 2005. Gloriously Free (film).

Sirriyeh, Ala. 2010. Home Journeys: Im/mobilities in Young Refugee and Asylum-seeking Women's Negotiations of Home. *Childhood* 17(2): 213–27.

Smith, Dale. 2012. Analysis: Unpacking the Latest Refugee Reform Bill. *Xtra* Online. http://www.xtra.ca/public/National/ANALYSIS_Unpacking_the_latest_refugee_reform_bill-11611.aspx, February 28, 2012 (accessed June 20, 2012).

Swink, Arwen. 2006. A Review of the Role of Country Condition Analysis in Asylum Adjudications for Members of Sexual Minorities. *Hastings International and Comparative Law Review* 29(2): 251–66.

Szczepanikova, Alice. 2010. Performing Refugeeness in the Czech Republic: Gendered Depoliticization Through NGO Assistance. *Gender, Place and Culture* 17(4): 461–77.

Tepper, Sean. 2014. The Voices of World Pride. *The Globe and Mail*, June 21, 2014, p. M4–5.

Thobani, Sunera. 2007. *Exalted Subjects: Studies in the Making of Race and Nation in Canada*. Toronto: University of Toronto Press.

Ticktin, Miriam. 2011. *Casualties of Care: Immigration and the Politics of Humanitarianism in France*. Berkeley: University of California Press.

Tomlinson, Maurice. 2013. *Progress in Barbados Despite Harsh Anti-gay Laws*. http://76crimes.com/2013/03/06/progress-in-barbados-despite-harsh-anti-gay-laws/ (accessed January 3, 2014).

Torpey, John. 2000. *The Invention of the Passport: Surveillance, Citizenship and the State*. Cambridge: Cambridge University Press.

United Nations High Commissioner for Refugees. 2009. *Handbook on Procedures and Criteria for Determining Refugee Status*. New York: UNHCR

Valverde, Mariana. 2008. Racial Purity, Sexual Purity, and Immigration Policy. In *The History of Immigration and Racism in Canada: Essential Reading*, Barrington Walker, ed., pp.175–88. Toronto: Canadian Scholars' Press.

Vertovec, Steven. 2011. The Cultural Politics of Nation and Migration. *Annual Review of Anthropology* 40: 241–56.

Weston, Kath. 1993. Lesbian/Gay Studies in the House of Anthropology. *Annual Review of Anthropology* 22: 339–67.

———. 1995. Get Thee to a Big City: Sexual Imaginary and the Great Gay Migration. *GLQ* 2(3): 253–77.

———. 1997. *Families We Choose: Families, Gays, Kinship*. New York: Columbia University Press.

———. 1998. *Long Slow Burn: Sexuality and Social Science*. Chicago: University of Chicago Press.

———. 2008. A Political Ecology of 'Unnatural Offences': State Security, Queer Embodiment and the Environmental Impacts of Prison Migration. *GLQ* 14(2–3): 217–37.

White, Melissa. Autumn 2010. *Intimate Archives, Migrant Negotiations: Affective Governance and the Recognition of "same-sex" Family Class Migration in*

Canada. Ph.D. dissertation, Graduate Program in Women's Studies, Canada: York University.

———. 2013. Ambivalent Homonationalisms. *Interventions: International Journal of Postcolonial Studies* 15(1): 37–54.

———. 2014. Archives of Intimacy and Trauma: Queer Migration Documents as Technologies of Affect. *Radical History Review* 120: 75–93.

Wilton, Katherine. 2011. Gay Couple Ordered to Leave Canada. *The Montreal Gazette*, October 18, 2011.

Yue, Audrey. 2008. Same-Sex Migration in Australia: From Interdependency to Intimacy. *GLQ* 14(2–3): 239–62.

Index

Note: "n" after a page number indicates an endnote; "nn" after a page number indicates two or more consecutive endnotes.

177

About the Author

David A. B. Murray is a Professor in the Department of Anthropology and Sexuality Studies Program at York University, Toronto, Canada. He is the author of *Opacity: Gender, Sexuality, Race and the 'Problem' of Identity in Martinique* (2002, Peter Lang Press) and *Flaming Souls: Homosexuality, Homophobia and Social Change in Barbados* (2012, University of Toronto Press) and editor of *Homophobias: Lust and Loathing Across Time and Space* (2009, Duke University Press).